POWER TOOLS & EQUIPMENT

Other Publications:

AMERICAN COUNTRY

VOYAGE THROUGH THE UNIVERSE

THE THIRD REICH

THE TIME-LIFE GARDENER'S GUIDE

MYSTERIES OF THE UNKNOWN

TIME FRAME

FIX IT YOURSELF

FITNESS, HEALTH & NUTRITION

SUCCESSFUL PARENTING

HEALTHY HOME COOKING

UNDERSTANDING COMPUTERS

LIBRARY OF NATIONS

THE ENCHANTED WORLD

THE KODAK LIBRARY OF CREATIVE PHOTOGRAPHY

GREAT MEALS IN MINUTES

THE CIVIL WAR

PLANET EARTH

COLLECTOR'S LIBRARY OF THE CIVIL WAR

THE EPIC OF FLIGHT

THE GOOD COOK

WORLD WAR II

HOME REPAIR AND IMPROVEMENT

THE OLD WEST

POWER TOOLS & EQUIPMENT

TIME-LIFE BOOKS
ALEXANDRIA, VIRGINIA

Fix It Yourself was produced by
ST. REMY PRESS

MANAGING EDITOR	Kenneth Winchester
MANAGING ART DIRECTOR	Pierre Léveillé

Staff for *Power Tools & Equipment*

Series Editor	Brian Parsons
Editor	Katherine Zmetana
Series Art Director	Diane Denoncourt
Art Director	Solange Pelland
Research Editor	Fiona Gilsenan
Designer	Julie Leger
Editorial Assistant	Naomi Fukuyama
Contributing Writers	Robert J. Eyre, Stewart Freed, Isabella Grigoroff, Grant Loewen, Michael R. MacDonald, Elizabeth Stewart, Myke Bryan Wilder
Electronic Designers	Benoît David, Maryse Doray
Contributing Illustrators	Gérard Mariscalchi, Jacques Proulx
Technical Illustrators	Nicolas Moumouris, Robert Paquet
Cover	Robert Monté
Index	Christine M. Jacobs
Administrator	Denise Rainville
Administrative Assistant	Natalie Watanabe
Coordinator	Michelle Turbide
Systems Manager	Shirley Grynspan
Systems Analyst	Simon Lapierre
Studio Director	Maryo Proulx

Time-Life Books Inc. is a wholly owned subsidiary of
TIME INCORPORATED

FOUNDER	Henry R. Luce 1898-1967
Editor-in-Chief	Jason McManus
Chairman and Chief Executive Officer	J. Richard Munro
President and Chief Operating Officer	N. J. Nicholas Jr.
Editorial Director	Richard B. Stolley
Executive Vice President, Books	Kelso F. Sutton
Vice President, Books	Paul V. McLaughlin

TIME-LIFE BOOKS INC.

EDITOR	George Constable
Executive Editor	Ellen Phillips
Director of Design	Louis Klein
Director of Editorial Resources	Phyllis K. Wise
Editorial Board	Russell B. Adams Jr., Dale M. Brown, Roberta Conlan, Thomas H. Flaherty, Lee Hassig, Donia Ann Steele, Rosalind Stubenberg
Director of Photography and Research	John Conrad Weiser
Asst. Director of Editorial Resources	Elise Ritter Gibson
PRESIDENT	Christopher T. Linen
Chief Operating Officer	John M. Fahey Jr.
Senior Vice Presidents	Robert M. DeSena, James L. Mercer, Paul R. Stewart
Vice Presidents	Stephen L. Bair, Ralph J. Cuomo, Neal Goff, Stephen L. Goldstein, Juanita T. James, Carol Kaplan, Susan J. Maruyama, Robert H. Smith, Joseph J. Ward
Director of Production Services	Robert J. Passantino
Supervisor of Quality Control	James King

Editorial Operations

Copy Chief	Diane Ullius
Production	Celia Beattie
Library	Louise D. Forstall
Correspondents	Elizabeth Kraemer-Singh (Bonn); Maria Vincenza Aloisi (Paris); Ann Natanson (Rome).

THE CONSULTANTS

Consulting editor **David L. Harrison** served as an editor for several Time-Life Books do-it-yourself series, including *Home Repair and Improvement*, *The Encyclopedia of Gardening* and *The Art of Sewing*.

Richard Day, a do-it-yourself writer for nearly a quarter of a century, is a founder of the National Association of Home and Workshop Writers and is the author of several home repair books.

Evan Powell is Director of Chestnut Mountain Research Inc. in Taylors, South Carolina, and Director of Product Testing for CNT ConsumerNet Television, which produces *First Look* and *Step-by-Step*. He is a contributing editor to several do-it-yourself magazines, and has written a number of books on power tools and equipment.

Jay Hedden, a former editor of Popular Mechanics and Workbench magazines, has written several books on home repair and maintains a workshop for power tool consulting.

Library of Congress Cataloging-in-Publication Data
Power tools & equipment.
    p. cm. – (Fix it yourself)
Includes index.
ISBN 0-8094-6268-0
ISBN 0-8094-6269-9(lib. bdg.)
1. Power tools—Maintenance and repair—Amateur's manuals.
I. Time-Life Books. II. Title:
Power tools and equipment. III. Series.
TJ1195.P68   1989
621.9—dc19   89-30742
                CIP

For information about any Time-Life book, please write:
Reader Information
Time-Life Customer Service
P.O. Box C-32068
Richmond, Virginia
23261-2068

CONTENTS

HOW TO USE THIS BOOK   6

EMERGENCY GUIDE   8

DRILLS   12

SANDERS   19

SABER SAWS   28

CIRCULAR SAWS   34

HEDGE TRIMMERS   41

STRING TRIMMERS   46

CHAIN SAWS   56

LAWN MOWERS   68

GARDEN TILLERS   84

SNOW THROWERS   96

TOOLS & TECHNIQUES   110

INDEX   126

ACKNOWLEDGMENTS   128

HOW TO USE THIS BOOK

Power Tools & Equipment is divided into three sections. The Emergency Guide on pages 8 to 11 provides information that can be indispensable, even lifesaving, in the event of a household emergency. Take the time to study this section *before* you need the important advice it contains.

The Repairs section — the heart of the book — is a comprehensive approach to troubleshooting and repairing power tools and equipment. Shown below are four sample pages from the chapter on chain saws with captions describing the various features of the book and how they work.

For example, if your chain saw does not start, the Troubleshooting Guide will suggest a number of possible causes. If the problem is a broken starter cord or rewind spring, you will be directed to page 66 for detailed instructions on servicing the starter assembly; for a clogged muffler, you will be referred to page 67 for steps on how to clean or replace the muffler.

Each job has been rated by degree of difficulty and by the average time it will take for a do-it-yourselfer to complete. Keep in mind that this rating is only a suggestion. Before

Introductory text
Describes the design and operation of the power tool or equipment, most common problems and basic safety precautions.

Troubleshooting Guide
To use this chart, locate the symptom that most closely resembles your power tool and equipment problem, review the possible causes in column 2, then follow the recommended procedures in column 3. Simple fixes may be explained on the chart; in most cases you will be directed to an illustrated, step-by-step repair sequence.

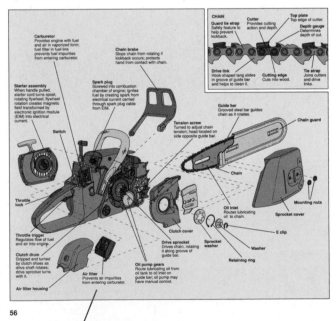

Exploded and cutaway diagrams
Locate and describe the various components of the power tool or equipment. Differences in models are described throughout the book, particularly if a repair procedure varies from one situation to another, or from older to newer units.

Degree of difficulty and time
Rate the complexity of each repair and how much time the job should take for a homeowner with average do-it-yourself skills.

Special tool required
Some repairs call for a specialized tool; for example, a multitester.

deciding whether you should attempt a repair, read all the instructions carefully. Then be guided by your own confidence, and the tools and time available to you. For more complex or time-consuming repairs, such as servicing a carburetor or motor, you may wish to seek professional help. You will still have saved time and money by diagnosing the problem yourself.

Most repairs in *Power Tools & Equipment* can be made with a basic set of screwdrivers, various wrenches and readily-available cleaning supplies. Any special tool required, such as

a multitester, is indicated in the Troubleshooting Guide. If you are a novice at repairing power tools and equipment, read the valuable advice on using tools and identifying components in the Tools & Techniques section starting on page 110. Before you undertake any repair, make sure that you turn off the power tool or equipment; unplug its power cord or disconnect its spark plug cable and, if instructed, empty its fuel tank. When disassembling your power tool or equipment, note the position of wires and linkages, drawing a diagram, if necessary, for reassembly.

Name of repair
You will be referred by the Trouble-shooting Guide to the first page of a specific repair job.

Lead-ins
Bold lead-ins summarize each step or highlight the key action shown in the illustration.

Tools and techniques
When a specific tool or method is required for a job, it is described within the step-by-step repair. General information on refueling and identifying components, for instance, is covered in the Tools & Techniques section (page 110).

Step-by-step procedures
Follow the numbered repair sequence carefully. Depending on the result of each step, you may be directed to a later step, or to another part of the book, to complete the repair.

Insets
Provide close-up views of specific steps and illustrate variations in techniques.

Cross-references
Direct you to important information elsewhere in the book, including alternative techniques and disassembly steps.

EMERGENCY GUIDE

Preventing problems with power tools and equipment.
Today's power tools and equipment are designed for years of safe and rugged operation. With proper use and care, your power tools and equipment can perform accident-free for many years beyond their warranties. A careful review of the operator's use and care manual, supplied with the tool or equipment, is important in avoiding breakdowns—and in preventing safety hazards. Some manufacturers offer toll-free lines for answering consumer questions; on request, you can often receive the operator's manual and the exploded diagram for your tool or equipment free of charge. Call the 800 operator for the telephone number of the manufacturer of your power tool or equipment.

The Troubleshooting Guide on page 9 puts emergency procedures for mishaps with power tools and equipment at your fingertips; it lists the quick-action steps to take and refers you to pages 9 to 11 for more detailed instructions. Read the instructions thoroughly before you need them to save valuable time in the event of an emergency. Post the telephone numbers for your local fire department, medical emergency services and utilities by the telephone; in most areas, dial 911 in the case of a life-threatening emergency.

Electrical shock and fire are life-threatening emergencies that can happen in the most safety-conscious of homes. If you must rescue someone from contact with a live current, do not touch the person; use a wooden implement of any kind to knock the victim free *(page 10)*. Deprive fire of its sneak attack by installing smoke alarms judiciously throughout your home—do not overlook your garage and workshop. Have the correct fire extinguisher on hand to snuff out a blaze before it gets the upper hand and learn how to use it before you need it *(page 10)*. Clean up any gas or oil spill immediately *(page 11)*.

The repair of power tools and equipment need not be any more dangerous than their daily use; indeed, the right repairs done properly can prevent hazardous conditions. The list of safety tips at right covers basic guidelines for the use and service of power tools and equipment. See the individual chapters in this book for more specific advice and review the information in Tools & Techniques *(page 110)*. Get professional technical help when you need it; if you are ever in doubt about the safety of any power tool or equipment, take it for professional service.

Always wear appropriate clothing when operating or servicing power tools and equipment. Unprotected skin can be severely burned by only a moment's contact with a hot muffler or housing. Wear long pants, a long-sleeved shirt and proper footgear; even the seemingly harmless nylon string of a string trimmer, for example, can cause serious cuts to bare feet, legs or arms. Whenever recommended in your operator's use and care manual or in this book, put on protective equipment such as work gloves and safety goggles.

SAFETY TIPS

1. Before attempting any repair in this book, read the entire procedure. Familiarize yourself with the specific safety information presented in each chapter.

2. Carefully review the use and care manual for the power tool or equipment. If you have misplaced the manual, order a new one from an authorized service center or the manufacturer.

3. Before each use of any power tool or equipment, check its safety features for damage. Do not use the power tool or equipment until any problem you find is corrected.

4. Only carry or transport power tools and equipment by their handles—never hold an electrical tool by its power cord. Unplug any electrical tool that is not use, even temporarily; disconnect it from the wall outlet by pulling on the plug, not the power cord or extension cord.

5. Before servicing any power tool or equipment, turn it off; also unplug it if it is electrical or disconnect the spark plug cable and, if instructed, drain the fuel if it is gas-powered. Allow the power tool or equipment to cool before servicing it.

6. Never use an electrical tool in wet or damp conditions. To guard against electrical shock, plug an electrical tool only into a GFCI-protected outlet. Never splice a power cord or remove the grounding prong from a 3-prong plug.

7. When working outdoors with an electrical tool, use only an extension cord that is rated for outdoor use and that is compatible with the tool *(page 115)*. Secure the connection between power cord and extension cord by knotting them loosely together before plugging in the electrical tool.

8. Never run any gas-powered tool or equipment indoors; do not fill its fuel tank while the engine is running or hot. Fill the fuel tank at least 10 feet away from the work area—and never indoors. Clean up any gas or oil spills immediately *(page 11)*.

9. Use only replacement parts that meet the same specifications as the originals. After repairing any electrical component, check the power tool or equipment for leaking voltage *(page 113)* before plugging it in.

10. Keep children away from power tools and equipment; never allow them to play with or operate any power tool or equipment. Store your power tools and equipment safely away in a clean, dry area, well beyond the reach of children.

11. Keep gas and oil only in containers designed specifically for fuel storage and clearly marked FUEL. Keep the containers away from sources of heat and flames. Place fuel-soaked rags in sealed metal containers and dispose of them according to municipal regulations.

12. When operating or servicing any power tool or equipment, tie back long hair and avoid wearing loose clothing, dangling scarves and any jewelry.

13. Always wear the proper protective gear: safety goggles when operating power tools and equipment, replacing tension springs or retaining rings, and cleaning with compressed air; work gloves when servicing saw chains or blades; insulated rubber gloves when servicing spark plugs; a dust mask when using a sander; hearing protection when operating noisy gas-powered tools or equipment.

TROUBLESHOOTING GUIDE

SYMPTOM	PROCEDURE
Fire in or near gas-powered tool or equipment or fuel container	Leave area and call fire department
Fire in or near electrical tool or equipment or electrical outlet	Call fire department, then use ABC-rated fire extinguisher *(p. 10)*; if fire spreads, leave area
Electrical shock	If victim is immobilized by live current, push him away from source with wooden implement *(p. 10)*; otherwise, unplug electrical tool from outlet or shut off power at service panel *(below)*
	Call for medical help and check whether victim is breathing and has pulse; if not, begin artificial resuscitation or cardiopulmonary resuscitation (CPR) only if you are qualified. Otherwise, place victim in recovery position *(p. 10)* until medical help arrives
Electrical tool sparks, shocks, hot to touch or trips GFCI	Unplug electrical tool from outlet or shut off power at service panel *(below)*; locate and repair cause before using electrical tool or outlet again
Power cord or extension cord sparks, shocks or hot to touch	Shut off power at service panel, then unplug electrical tool from outlet *(below)*. Service power cord and replace extension cord, if necessary *(p. 115)*; do not use electrical tool or extension cord until cause is located and repaired
Electrical tool falls into water while plugged in	Do not touch electrical tool or water; shut off power at service panel, then unplug electrical tool from outlet *(below)*. Take electrical tool for professional service before using again
Gas or oil spill	Soak up a small spill and clean spill area thoroughly *(p. 11)*; if spill is of more than 1 gallon, leave area and call fire department
Burn or scald	Soak burn or scald in cold water and apply dampened sterile gauze *(p. 11)*; if blistering occurs, cover with dry sterile gauze and seek medical attention. Never apply spray, ointment or butter
Cut or minor wound	Apply pressure with a clean cloth to stop bleeding *(p. 11)*; if bleeding persists or if wound is deep or gaping, seek medical attention
Faintness, dizziness, nausea or blurred vision around gas-powered tool or equipment	Leave area immediately to get fresh air *(p. 11)* and have helper close fuel containers; seek medical attention if necessary

CUTTING OFF ELECTRICAL POWER

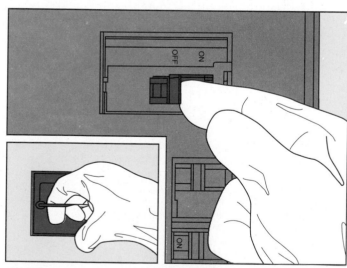

Shutting down power at the service panel. If the floor around the service panel is wet, stand on a dry board or a rubber mat or wear rubber boots. Wear heavy, dry rubber gloves and use only one hand; keep your other hand in your pocket or behind your back. At a circuit breaker panel, flip off the main breaker *(above)*. As an added precaution, use your knuckle; any shock will then jerk your hand away from the panel. At a fuse panel, grip the main fuse block by its handle and pull it out *(inset)*. If the fuse panel has a shutoff lever, shift it to the OFF position.

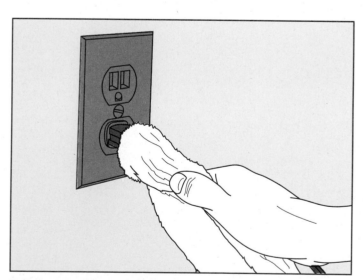

Pulling the power cord plug from the wall outlet. If the floor around the wall outlet is wet, or if the wall outlet itself is sparking or burning, do not touch the power cord or the electrical tool; instead, shut off power at the service panel *(step left)*. Otherwise, protect your hand with a thick, dry towel or a heavy work glove. Without touching the wall outlet or the electrical tool, grasp the power cord several inches from the plug and pull the plug out of the wall outlet *(above)*. Locate and repair the problem before using the wall outlet or the electrical tool again.

RESCUING A VICTIM OF ELECTRICAL SHOCK

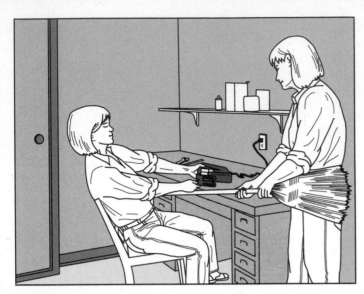

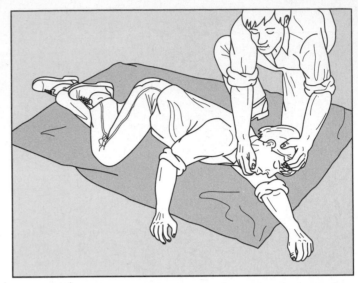

Freeing a victim from live current. Do not touch the victim or the electrical tool. Usually, a person who contacts live current is thrown back from the source, but sometimes muscles contract involuntarily around the source. Immediately pull the power cord plug from the wall outlet, if possible, or shut off power at the service panel *(page 9)*. If the power cannot be shut off immediately, use a wooden broom handle or a board to knock the victim free *(above)*. Then, place the victim in the recovery position *(step right)*.

Handling a victim of electrical shock. Call for medical help immediately. Check the victim's breathing and heartbeat. If there is no breathing or heartbeat, give artificial resuscitation or cardiopulmonary resuscitation (CPR) only if you are qualified. If the victim is breathing and has not sustained back or neck injuries, place him in the recovery position *(above)*. Tilt the head back with the face to one side and the tongue forward to maintain an open airway. Keep the victim calm until medical help arrives.

CONTROLLING A FIRE

Using a fire extinguisher. Call the fire department immediately; if there are flames or smoke near any gas-powered tool or fuel container, leave the house to call for help. To put out a small, accessible fire in an electrical tool or at a wall outlet, use a dry-chemical fire extinguisher rated ABC. Stand near a safe exit, 6 to 10 feet from the fire. Pull the lock pin out of the extinguisher handle and, holding the extinguisher upright, aim the nozzle at the base of the flames. Squeeze the two levers of the handle together, spraying in a quick side-to-side motion *(left)*. Keep spraying until the fire is completely extinguished. Watch carefully for flashback, or rekindling, and be prepared to spray again. You may also have to shut off power at the service panel *(page 9)* to remove the source of the fire. Find the cause of the fire and remedy it before using the electrical tool or the wall outlet again. Have the fire department examine the area even if the fire is extinguished.

CLEANING UP GAS OR OIL SPILLS

1 **Soaking up spilled gas or oil. Caution:** If more than 1 gallon of gas or oil is spilled, leave the area and call the fire department. If only a few drops of gas or oil is spilled, wipe up the area with a clean cloth. Otherwise, pour an absorbent material such as cat litter or vermiculite on the spill to soak it up *(above)*; avoid using sawdust, which is combustible. When the absorbent material has soaked up the spill, scoop it into a metal container using a shovel or a dust pan.

2 **Cleaning up the spill area.** Wash the spill area using a solution of household detergent and warm water, scrubbing with an old broom *(above)* or mop. Soak up the solution using an absorbent material and scoop it into a metal container; then, rinse the spill area. Repeat the procedure, if necessary. Place any soiled cloths into the metal container and seal it tightly. Dispose of the metal container and the broom or mop in accordance with local regulations. **Caution:** Storing gas- or oil-soaked absorbent material and cloths is a fire hazard; they can ignite spontaneously.

PROVIDING FIRST AID

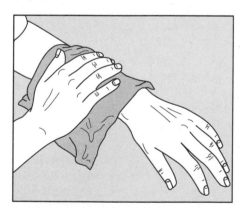

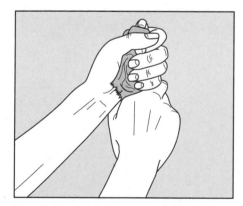

Treating a burn or a scald. If the injured area is red, soak it in cold water and apply a sterile gauze bandage dampened with water *(above)*. If the injured area blisters, keep it dry; protect it with a sterile gauze bandage, cover the bandage with plastic food wrap and seek medical attention. **Caution:** Do not apply any spray, ointment or butter.

Treating a cut. To stop a wound from bleeding, wrap it in a clean cloth and apply direct pressure with your hand, elevating the injured limb *(above)*. If the cloth becomes blood-soaked, wrap another cloth around it. Continue the procedure until the bleeding stops. If the wound is minor, wash it using soap and water, then bandage it with sterile gauze. Seek medical attention if the wound is deep or gaping or if the bleeding persists.

Treating exposure to toxic fumes. At the first sign of headache, dizziness, faintness, fatigue or nausea, leave the work area immediately and get fresh air. Loosen your clothing at the waist, chest and neck. If you feel faint, sit with your head lowered between your knees *(above)*. Have someone ventilate the work area, close all containers and call your local poison control center for medical advice.

DRILLS

Few home workshops are without an electric drill—of the plug-in or the cordless type. Versatile, the common drill can do more than bore or drill holes; with attachments, it can be used for driving screws, stripping paint, sharpening blades or buffing the car. Illustrated below is a typical 3/8-inch drill, rated by the largest-diameter bit its chuck can hold. The universal motor, usually activated by a variable-speed switch, turns the worm gear at the end of the armature shaft. Engaged by the worm gear, the pinion gear transfers rotating force to the drive gear which drives the spindle. The chuck, holding a bit or other attachment, is turned by the spindle. If the drill features a reverse control, the direction of rotation can be changed from clockwise to counterclockwise. The cordless drill works the same way, but runs on a direct current (DC) motor powered by a rechargeable battery pack.

Most problems with drills are due to misuse and can be avoided. Follow the operating instructions and maintenance procedures in the use and care manual supplied with your drill; recharge the battery pack of a cordless drill only when necessary (*page 18*). Always use the proper bit for the material you are drilling into and avoid forcing it into the workpiece. When your drill malfunctions, consult the Troubleshooting Guide (*page 13*) to help in diagnosing the problem. If your drill is a plug-in type, its internal components can be readily accessed, if necessary; if your drill is a cordless type, take it for professional service if you suspect an internal component is faulty. Refer to the Tools & Techniques chapter (*page 110*) for information on using a multitester, on servicing bearings, switches and brush assemblies that differ from the ones shown in this chapter, and on finding replacement parts.

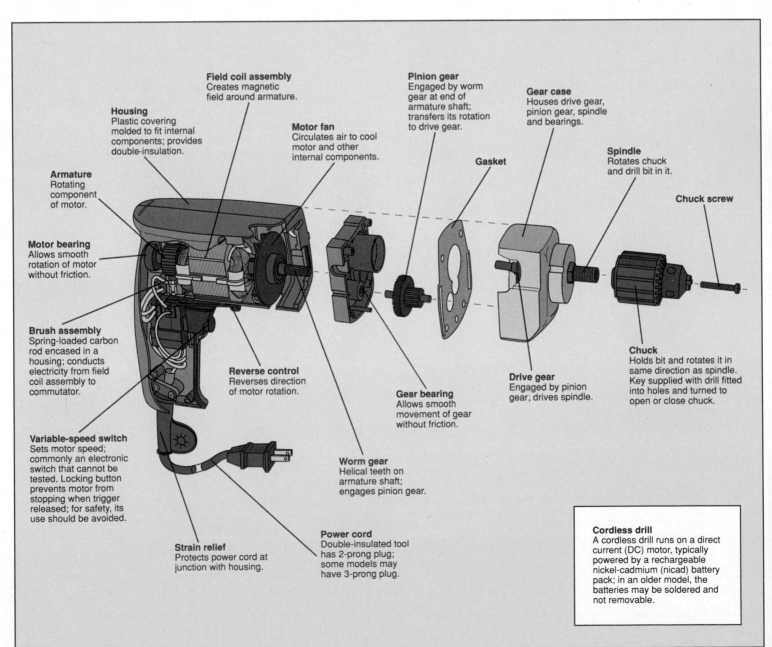

Field coil assembly
Creates magnetic field around armature.

Housing
Plastic covering molded to fit internal components; provides double-insulation.

Motor fan
Circulates air to cool motor and other internal components.

Pinion gear
Engaged by worm gear at end of armature shaft; transfers its rotation to drive gear.

Gear case
Houses drive gear, pinion gear, spindle and bearings.

Gasket

Spindle
Rotates chuck and drill bit in it.

Chuck screw

Armature
Rotating component of motor.

Motor bearing
Allows smooth rotation of motor without friction.

Brush assembly
Spring-loaded carbon rod encased in a housing; conducts electricity from field coil assembly to commutator.

Reverse control
Reverses direction of motor rotation.

Gear bearing
Allows smooth movement of gear without friction.

Drive gear
Engaged by pinion gear; drives spindle.

Chuck
Holds bit and rotates it in same direction as spindle. Key supplied with drill fitted into holes and turned to open or close chuck.

Variable-speed switch
Sets motor speed; commonly an electronic switch that cannot be tested. Locking button prevents motor from stopping when trigger released; for safety, its use should be avoided.

Worm gear
Helical teeth on armature shaft; engages pinion gear.

Strain relief
Protects power cord at junction with housing.

Power cord
Double-insulated tool has 2-prong plug; some models may have 3-prong plug.

Cordless drill
A cordless drill runs on a direct current (DC) motor, typically powered by a rechargeable nickel-cadmium (nicad) battery pack; in an older model, the batteries may be soldered and not removable.

TROUBLESHOOTING GUIDE

SYMPTOM	POSSIBLE CAUSE	PROCEDURE
PLUG-IN DRILLS		
Drill does not work at all	No power to outlet or outlet faulty	Reset breaker or replace fuse (p. 112) □○; have outlet serviced
	Power cord or extension cord faulty	Service power cord (p. 115) ▣○▲; replace extension cord (p. 115)
	Brush worn or dislodged	Service brush assemblies (p. 16) ▣○
	Variable-speed switch faulty	Replace switch (p. 17) ▣○
	Motor faulty	Inspect motor (p. 17) ▣○; service motor components (p. 118) ▣●▲
Motor hums, but drill does not work	Bit loose; jammed	Tighten chuck; set drill in reverse and withdraw bit from workpiece
	Bit incorrect or damaged	Replace bit (p. 14) □○
	Chuck damaged	Service chuck (p. 15) ▣○
	Gear or spindle damaged or bearing dry	Service gear assembly (p. 16) ▣○
	Motor faulty	Inspect motor (p. 17) ▣○; service motor components (p. 118) ▣●▲
Drill overheats or power diminished	Extension cord of incorrect size or rating	Replace extension cord (p. 115)
	Air vent blocked	Clear air vents with compressed air
	Bit incorrect or damaged	Replace bit (p. 14) □○
	Motor straining	Reduce strain on motor (p. 14) □○
	Brush worn or dislodged	Service brush assemblies (p. 16) ▣○
	Gear or spindle damaged or bearing dry	Service gear assembly (p. 16) ▣○
	Motor dirty or faulty	Inspect motor (p. 17) ▣○; service motor components (p. 118) ▣●▲
Drill rattles or vibrates excessively	Housing fastener loose	Tighten housing fasteners
	Bit loose; incorrect or damaged	Tighten chuck; replace bit (p. 14) □○
	Chuck damaged	Service chuck (p. 15) ▣○
	Gear or spindle damaged or bearing dry	Service gear assembly (p. 16) ▣○
	Motor fan damaged	Inspect motor (p. 17) ▣○; replace if necessary
Sparks fly from motor housing	Brush worn or dislodged	Service brush assemblies (p. 16) ▣○
	Motor dirty or faulty	Inspect motor (p. 17); service motor components (p. 118) ▣●▲
Drill runs only at one speed or in one direction	Variable-speed switch faulty	Replace switch (p. 17) ▣○
Bit sticks, overheats or jams	Bit loose; incorrect or damaged	Tighten chuck; replace bit (p. 14) □○
	Motor straining	Reduce strain on motor (p. 14) □○
	Chuck damaged	Service chuck (p. 15) ▣○
Bit wobbles	Bit loose; incorrect or damaged	Tighten chuck; replace bit (p. 14) □○
	Chuck damaged	Service chuck (p. 15) ▣○
	Gear or spindle damaged or bearing dry	Service gear assembly (p. 16) ▣○
CORDLESS DRILLS		
Drill does not work at all	Drill locked OFF	Turn on drill
	Battery pack discharged	Recharge battery pack (p. 18) □○
	Battery charger or battery pack faulty	Test battery charger and battery pack (p. 18) □○▲
Drill overheats or power diminished	Battery pack warm or motor straining	Allow drill to cool for 15 minutes; reduce strain on motor (p. 14) □○
	Battery pack resisting recharging	Discharge battery pack by running drill under no load; recharge battery pack (p. 18) □○
Bit sticks, overheats or jams	Bit loose; incorrect or damaged	Tighten chuck; replace bit (p. 14) □○
	Motor straining	Allow drill to cool for 15 minutes; reduce strain on motor (p. 14) □○
	Chuck damaged	Service chuck (p. 15) ▣○
Bit wobbles	Bit loose; incorrect or damaged	Tighten chuck; replace bit (p. 14) □○
	Chuck damaged	Service chuck (p. 15) ▣○

DEGREE OF DIFFICULTY: □ Easy ▣ Moderate ■ Complex
ESTIMATED TIME: ○ Less than 1 hour ◖ 1 to 3 hours ● Over 3 hours ▲ Special tool required

DRILL USE AND MAINTENANCE

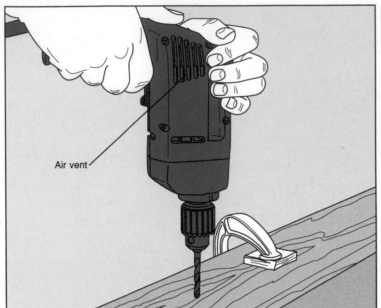

Air vent

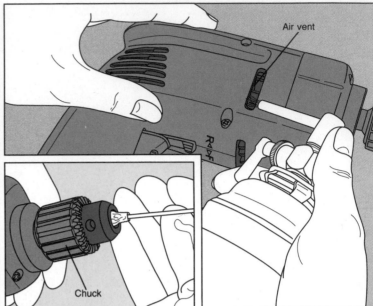

Air vent

Chuck

Operating a drill. If the workpiece is not steady, secure it with clamps or in a vise. Remove any obstructions such as fasteners from the area to be drilled; if drilling into a wall, check first for electrical wiring and other hidden hazards. Install a bit *(step below)* and set the drill speed, following the manufacturer's instructions. If you are using an extension cord, ensure it is of the correct size and rating *(page 115)*.

Wearing safety goggles, plug in the drill; with a cordless drill, ensure the battery pack is correctly charged and loaded *(page 18)*. Position the bit on the workpiece at a 90 degree angle and hold the drill with both hands, without blocking an air vent *(above, left)*. Keeping the power cord to one side and behind you, slowly depress the trigger switch, increasing pressure after the hole is started. Avoid straining the motor *(step below, right)* and withdraw the bit before releasing the trigger switch.

After each use of the drill, unplug it or lock it OFF and remove the bit *(step below, left)*. If the bit is sticky, wear rubber gloves and wipe it off using a clean cloth dipped in paint thinner. Clean the chuck with a cotton swab dipped in paint thinner *(inset)*. Blow compressed air through the air vents *(above, right)* to dislodge dust and debris.

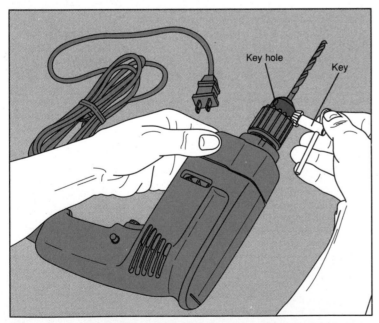

Key hole

Key

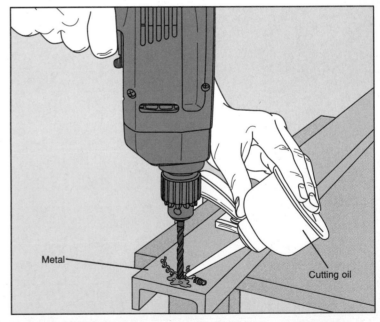

Metal

Cutting oil

Removing and installing a bit. Turn off and unplug or lock OFF the drill. Always use the correct bit for the type of material being drilled into; replace any damaged bit. To remove a bit, open the chuck wide enough using the key supplied with the drill. Before installing a bit, make sure the chuck is clean *(step above)* and open wide enough to fit it. Insert the bit as far as possible into the chuck, centering it. Close the chuck by hand and tighten it using the key supplied with the drill; fit the key in turn into each key hole and turn it *(above)*, making sure the bit is balanced and held tightly.

Reducing strain on the motor. When drilling into a hard material or for an extended period of time, the drill can overheat. With a plug-in drill, you can cool the motor by running the drill under no load; with a cordless drill, you must stop if the motor heats up. Make a starter hole before using a spade bit and when recommended by the manufacturer. When drilling into metal, squirt a few drops of cutting oil on the tip of the bit to reduce friction *(above)*. Before drilling into masonry, sprinkle water on the surface to keep the bit cool and minimize dust; do not, however, splash water on the drill or immerse it in water or any other liquid.

SERVICING THE CHUCK

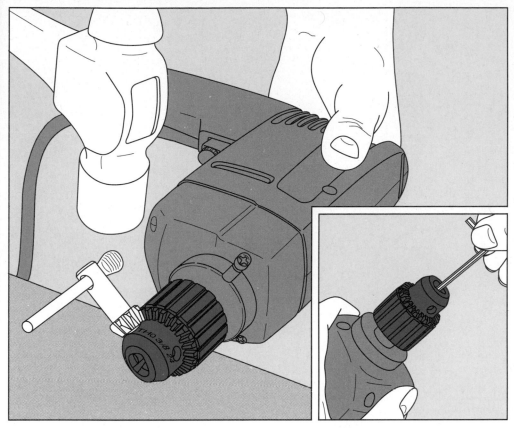

Removing and installing a threaded chuck.
Turn off and unplug or lock OFF the drill, then remove the bit *(page 14)*. To determine the type of chuck in your drill, consult your use and care manual; if the chuck is tapered, remove it *(step below)*. A new drill is likely to have a threaded chuck and may be stamped THD. To take off a threaded chuck, open it as far as possible using the key supplied with the drill. Then, remove the chuck screw with a hex wrench or a screwdriver, turning clockwise *(inset)*.

To take off the chuck, you must unscrew it counterclockwise. Set the chuck on the edge of a workbench or table with the key in a key hole at a 30 degree angle, as shown. Wearing safety goggles, hold the drill firmly and strike the key sharply with a ball-peen hammer *(left)* until the chuck loosens enough to be turned by hand. Unscrew the chuck and take it off the spindle; if it is damaged, replace it with an exact duplicate.

Wearing rubber gloves, clean off the spindle using a clean cloth dipped in paint thinner. If the spindle is damaged, screw the chuck back on loosely and service the drive gear, bearings and spindle *(page 16)*; take a cordless drill for professional service. Otherwise, screw back on the chuck and tighten it using the key and hammer. Put back the chuck screw, turning it counterclockwise, and reinstall the bit *(page 14)*.

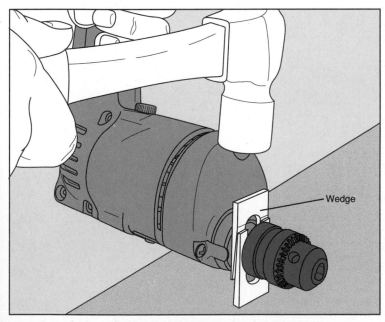
Wedge

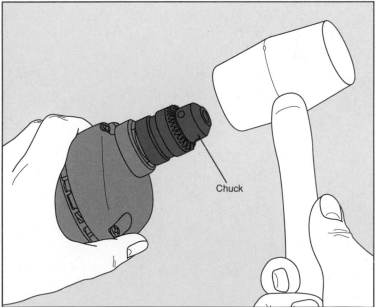
Chuck

Removing and replacing a tapered chuck. Turn off and unplug or lock OFF the drill, then remove the bit *(page 14)*. To determine the type of chuck in your drill, consult your use and care manual; if the chuck is threaded, remove it *(step above)*. An old drill is likely to have a tapered chuck and may be stamped TAPERED. To take off a tapered chuck, open it as far as possible using the key supplied with the drill. Then, remove the chuck screw with a hex wrench or a screwdriver, turning clockwise.

To take off the chuck, use special chuck-removal wedges. Fit the wedges opposite each other between the chuck and the gear case, as shown, and set the drill upside down with the chuck on the edge

of a workbench or table. Wearing safety goggles, hold the drill firmly and strike the top wedge sharply with a ball-peen hammer *(above, left)* until the chuck loosens enough to be pulled off by hand. Pull the chuck off the spindle; if it is damaged, replace it with an exact duplicate.

Wearing rubber gloves, clean off the spindle using a clean cloth dipped in paint thinner. If the spindle is damaged, push the chuck back on and service the drive gear, bearings and spindle *(page 16)*; take a cordless drill for professional service. Otherwise, push the chuck back onto the spindle and seat it using a mallet *(above, right)*. Put back the chuck screw, turning it counterclockwise, and reinstall the bit *(page 14)*.

SERVICING THE GEAR ASSEMBLY (Plug-in drill)

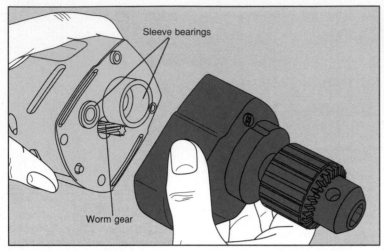

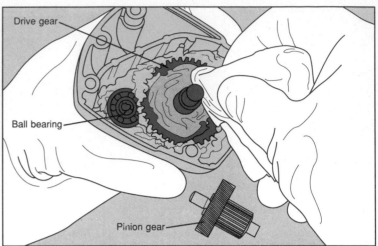

Lubricating the drive gear, bearings and spindle. Turn off and un-plug the drill, then remove the bit *(page 14)*. Unscrew the gear case and lift it off the motor housing *(above, left)*. Carefully set the gasket aside for reassembly; if it is damaged, replace it with an exact duplicate. Wearing rubber gloves, wipe off the old grease using a clean cloth. Lift out the drive gear and the pinion gear, noting their placement for reassembly, and clean them off with an old toothbrush dipped in paint thinner; if the drive gear is machine-pressed to the spindle and gear case, as in the model shown, clean it in place using the cloth *(above,*

right). If the drive gear, the pinion gear or the spindle is damaged, replace it or the entire gear case with an exact duplicate; to replace the entire gear case, screw it back on to remove the chuck *(page 15)*, then unscrew it again. Otherwise, reposition the drive gear, if you removed it, and the pinion gear. Refill the gear case halfway with clean white grease or the manufacturer's specified lubricant and apply a few drops of SAE 20 machine oil on each sleeve bearing in the motor housing. Reposition the gasket and screw back on the gear case. Put back the chuck, if you removed it *(page 15)*, and reinstall the bit *(page 14)*.

SERVICING THE BRUSH ASSEMBLIES (Plug-in drill)

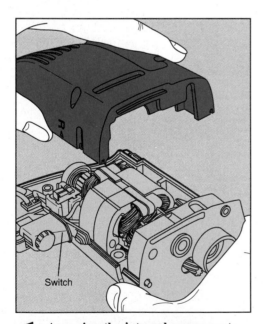

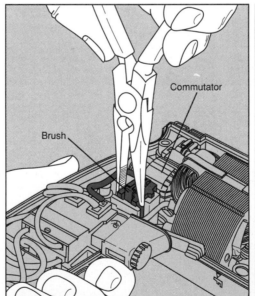

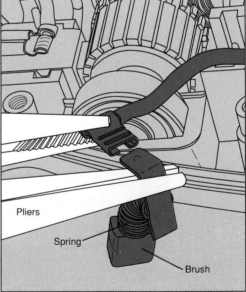

1 **Accessing the internal components.** Turn off and unplug the drill, then remove the bit *(page 14)*. Remove the gear case *(step above)* and set the drill on a flat surface. Unscrew the housing, gently separate it at the seam and lift off the half section *(above)*. Note the placement of wires, the power cord and other components, draw-ing a diagram, if necessary, for reassembly.

2 **Inspecting and replacing the brushes.** Locate the brush assembly on each side of the commutator. Using long-nose pliers, carefully lift out each brush assembly *(above, left)*— be prepared for a brush that may fly out. Push each brush once or twice to test its spring, then slide it out of its housing. If the spring is damaged, the housing is cracked, or the brush is pitted, uneven or worn shorter than its width, replace the component in each brush assembly or both entire brush assemblies with exact duplicates—even if only one is damaged. To disconnect each brush assembly, gently pull off the wire connector with long-nose pliers *(above, right)*. Re-place the damaged components and reconnect the brush assemblies. Fit each brush assembly into position, making sure the brush presses firmly against the commutator and matches its cur-vature. Screw the housing back together, put back the gear case and reinstall the bit *(page 14)*. Check the drill for leaking voltage *(page 113)*.

SERVICING THE MOTOR (Plug-in drill)

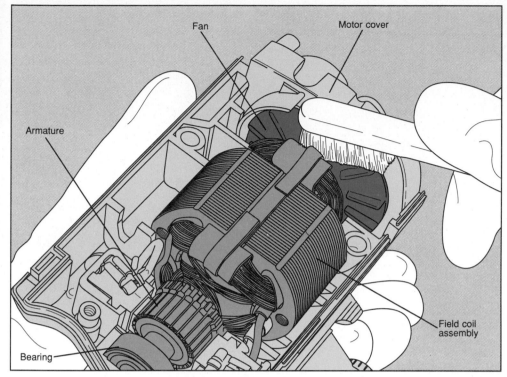

Fan

Motor cover

Armature

Field coil assembly

Bearing

Inspecting and cleaning the motor. Access the internal components *(page 16)*. Wearing safety goggles, blow compressed air around the motor to clean off dust. Use an old toothbrush to clean stubborn particles off the fan *(left)*. Turn the fan by hand; the armature should rotate freely inside the field coil assembly. If the armature binds, lubricate or replace the bearing at each end of the shaft, if possible *(page 120)*; if the bearings are machine-pressed to the shaft, as in the model shown, take the drill for professional service.

To inspect the motor, pull away the motor cover, and remove the brush assemblies. Lift up the motor and carefully slide the armature out of the field coil assembly. If the motor or windings are darkened, service the motor components *(page 118)*. Otherwise, slide the armature back into the field coil assembly, reposition the motor and the motor cover, and reinstall the brush assemblies *(page 16)*. Screw the housing back together, put back the gear case and reinstall the bit *(page 14)*. Check the drill for leaking voltage *(page 113)*.

REPLACING THE VARIABLE-SPEED SWITCH (Plug-in drill)

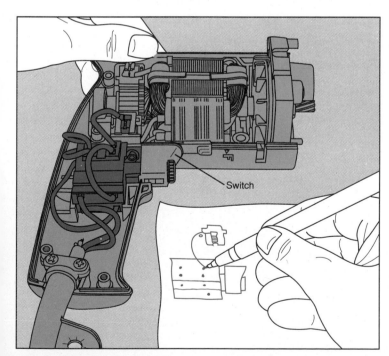

Switch

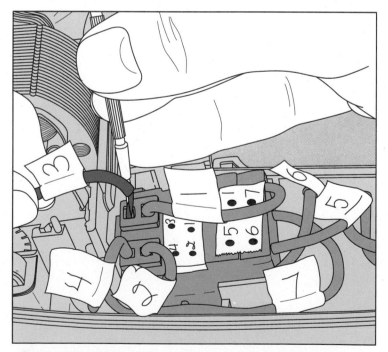

1 **Locating the switch.** Access the internal components *(page 16)* and find the switch. Identify the type of switch *(page 117)*. A variable-speed switch, as in the model shown, is common in most drills; although it cannot be tested, it can be replaced if you suspect it is faulty. Before removing the switch, note the position of its wires, drawing a diagram for reassembly *(above)*. Then, carefully lift the switch out of the housing and label its wires and their corresponding terminals.

2 **Replacing the switch.** To disconnect each wire from the switch, fit a small screwdriver into its push-in terminal to free it *(above)*. Replace the switch with an exact duplicate and reconnect the wires to it, fitting each wire in turn into its corresponding push-in terminal. Screw the housing back together, ensuring no wire is pinched. Put back the gear case and reinstall the bit *(page 14)*. Then, check the drill for leaking voltage *(page 113)*.

SERVICING THE BATTERY PACK AND CHARGER (Cordless drill)

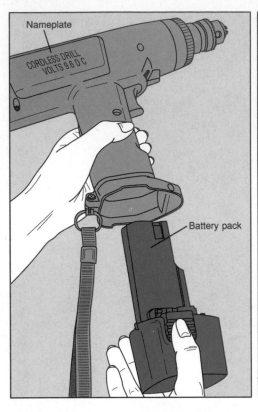

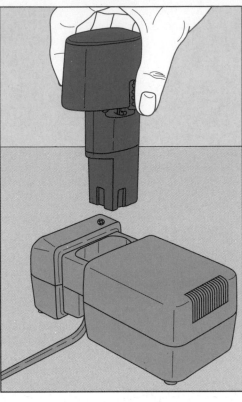

Recharging the battery pack. Turn off and lock OFF the drill, then remove the bit *(page 14)*. Holding the drill firmly in one hand, use the other hand to press on the tabs of the battery pack and pull it out *(far left)*; if it is warm, let it cool for at least 15 minutes. Set up a battery charger in a dry location away from any window; recharge the battery pack only at a temperature between 40 and 105 degrees fahrenheit. Use a clean, soft cloth to wipe dust off the battery charger and insert the battery pack into it *(near left)*, matching the negative and positive terminals. Plug the battery charger into a 120-volt outlet and turn it on; your model may not have an ON/OFF switch. Allow the battery pack to recharge for the time specified in the use and care manual supplied with the drill; undercharging the battery pack decreases its capacity to hold a charge. When the battery pack is recharged, turn off and unplug the battery charger. Remove the battery pack from the battery charger and allow it to cool for 15 minutes. Then, push the battery pack into the drill, making sure its tabs are locked in place. If the battery pack loses its charge rapidly, test the battery charger *(step below, left)*; if the problem persists, test the battery pack *(step below, right)*.

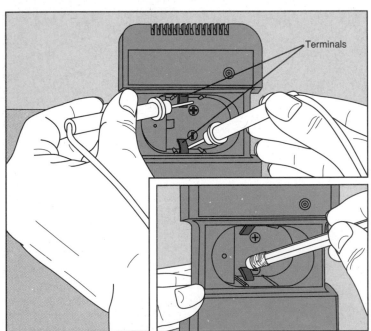

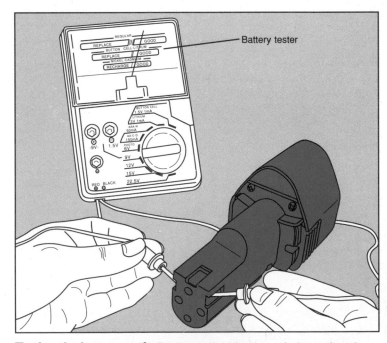

Testing the battery charger. Unplug the battery charger and wipe any dust off it using a clean, soft cloth; wearing safety goggles, blow compressed air through its air vents. If a terminal on the battery charger or the battery pack is darkened, rub it clean with a pencil eraser *(inset)*. To test the battery charger, plug it in and set a multitester to test for 50 volts (50 DCV) *(page 113)*. Touch the negative tester probe to the negative terminal of the battery charger and touch the positive tester probe to the positive terminal of the battery charger *(above)*. The multitester should register the voltage specified on the drill nameplate. If a deviation of more than 1 volt is registered, replace the battery charger with an exact duplicate; otherwise, test the battery pack *(step right)*.

Testing the battery pack. Recharge the battery pack *(step above)*, remove it from the battery charger and let it cool for 15 minutes. Set a battery tester to the setting on the DCV scale closest to the voltage specified on the drill nameplate; on the model shown, 9 volts (9 V). Touch the negative tester probe to the negative terminal of the battery pack and touch the positive tester probe to the positive terminal of the battery pack. The battery tester should register GOOD on the nickel-cadmium scale *(above)*. If RECHARGE is registered, discharge the battery pack by running the drill under no load. Then, recharge the battery pack and test it again. If RECHARGE is still registered, replace the battery pack with an exact duplicate.

SANDERS

A power sander can complete a sanding project five times faster than working by hand. Two common types of sanders are illustrated on page 20; the belt sander is heavy duty and designed for rough work, the orbital sander is lighter and best suited for finer work. Both types of sanders are powered by a universal motor, but they use different abrading actions. In the belt sander, sandpaper in the form of a belt rotates over two drums. The rear drum is driven by gears connected to a belt-and-pulley system; the front drum supports and rolls the sandpaper. In the orbital sander, an eccentric weight is connected to the motor shaft, moving the platen assembly with the sandpaper on it in a circular, reciprocating path as the motor spins. Proper use and regular maintenance will keep your sander running smoothly *(page 21)*.

To help diagnose the source of a problem, consult the Troubleshooting Guide *(below)*; a major cause is dust. Use the dust bag and empty it often, before dust builds up and blocks the fan. Clean off your sander after each use. To prevent dust from gumming up internal mechanisms, regularly clean any dust fan *(page 23)* and the motor fan *(page 27)*. For rough work, use a belt sander; using an orbital sander can overload its motor. Always turn off and unplug the sander before performing a repair—and before changing the sandpaper. Read your use and care manual and install the sandpaper as instructed. Refer to the Tools & Techniques chapter *(page 110)* for information on using a multitester, on servicing switches, bearings and brush assemblies that differ from the ones shown in this chapter, and on finding replacement parts.

TROUBLESHOOTING GUIDE

SYMPTOM	POSSIBLE CAUSE	PROCEDURE
Sander does not work at all	No power to outlet or outlet faulty	Reset breaker or replace fuse *(p. 112)* □○; have outlet serviced
	Power cord or extension cord faulty	Service power cord *(p. 115)* ▣○▲; replace extension cord *(p. 115)*
	Trigger switch faulty	Service switch *(p. 22)* ▣○▲
	Brush worn or dislodged	Service brush assemblies *(p. 27)* ▣○
	Motor faulty	Inspect motor *(p. 27)* ▣○; service motor components *(p. 118)* ▣◐▲
Motor hums, but sander does not work	Sander clogged with dust	Clean sander *(p. 21)* □○; clean dust fan (belt sander) *(p. 23)* □○
	Drive belt worn or broken (belt sander)	Service drive belt *(p. 23)* □○
	Gear or rear drum damaged (belt sander)	Service gears and rear drum *(p. 24)* ▣◐
	Platen assembly damaged (orbital sander)	Service platen assembly *(p. 26)* ▣◐
	Motor faulty or bearing seized	Inspect motor *(p. 27)* ▣○; service motor components *(p. 118)* ▣◐▲
Sander overheats or power diminished	Extension cord of incorrect size or rating	Replace extension cord *(p. 115)*
	Sander clogged with dust	Clean sander *(p. 21)* □○; clean dust fan (belt sander) *(p. 23)* □○
	Drive belt worn or broken (belt sander)	Service drive belt *(p. 23)* □○
	Gear or rear drum damaged (belt sander)	Service gears and rear drum *(p. 24)* ▣◐
	Platen assembly damaged (orbital sander)	Service platen assembly *(p. 26)* ▣◐
	Brush worn or dislodged	Service brush assemblies *(p. 27)* ▣○
	Motor dirty or faulty or bearing seized	Inspect motor *(p. 27)* ▣○; service motor components *(p. 118)* ▣◐▲
Sparks fly from motor housing	Brush worn or dislodged	Service brush assemblies *(p. 27)* ▣○
	Motor faulty	Inspect motor *(p. 27)* ▣○; service motor components *(p. 118)* ▣◐▲
Sparks fly from platen assembly (belt sander)	Sandpaper misaligned	Align sandpaper *(p. 21)* □○
	Front drum, platen or belt guide damaged	Service front drum and platen assembly *(p. 25)* ▣○
Sander works, but job uneven	Sandpaper worn or of incorrect grit	Follow use and care manual to change sandpaper
Sander veers to one side or sandpaper slides off	Sandpaper misaligned (belt sander)	Align sandpaper *(p. 21)* □○
	Rear drum damaged (belt sander)	Service gears and rear drum *(p. 24)* ▣○
	Front drum, platen, belt guide or belt lever damaged (belt sander)	Service front drum and platen assembly *(p. 25)* ▣○
	Platen assembly damaged (orbital sander)	Service platen assembly *(p. 26)* ▣◐
Dust bag does not collect dust	Dust vent clogged with dust	Clean sander *(p. 21)* □○; clean dust fan (belt sander) *(p. 23)* □○
	Motor fan clogged with dust	Inspect motor *(p. 27)* ▣○

DEGREE OF DIFFICULTY: □ Easy ▣ Moderate ■ Complex
ESTIMATED TIME: ○ Less than 1 hour ◐ 1 to 3 hours ● Over 3 hours   ▲ Special tool required

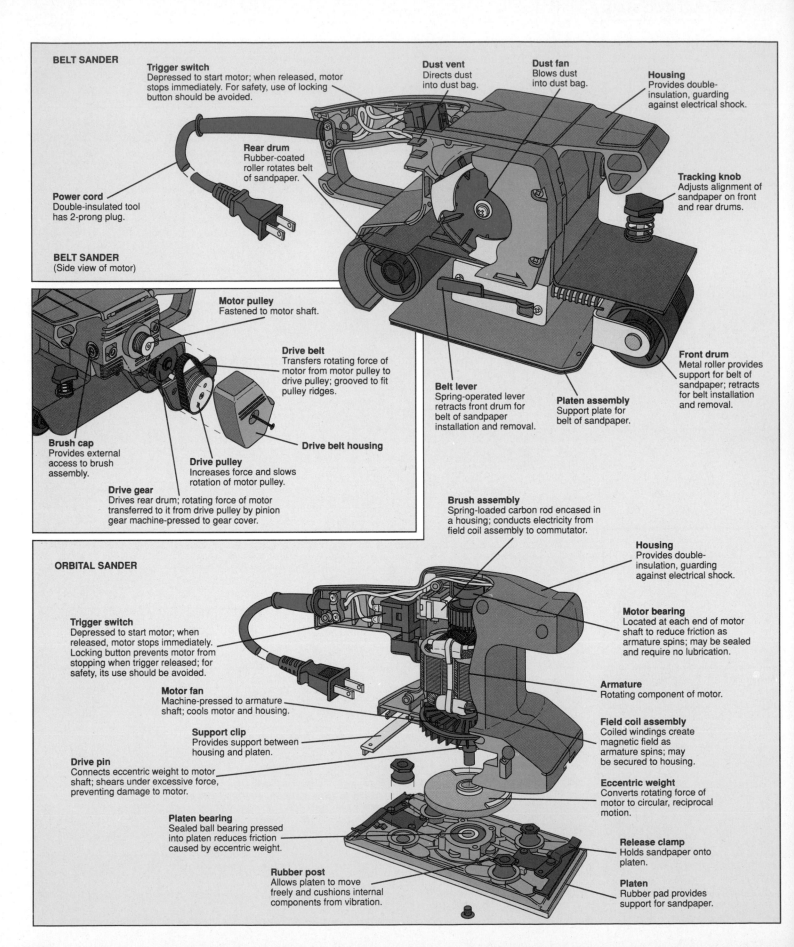

BELT SANDER

Trigger switch
Depressed to start motor; when released, motor stops immediately. For safety, use of locking button should be avoided.

Dust vent
Directs dust into dust bag.

Dust fan
Blows dust into dust bag.

Housing
Provides double-insulation, guarding against electrical shock.

Rear drum
Rubber-coated roller rotates belt of sandpaper.

Power cord
Double-insulated tool has 2-prong plug.

Tracking knob
Adjusts alignment of sandpaper on front and rear drums.

BELT SANDER
(Side view of motor)

Motor pulley
Fastened to motor shaft.

Drive belt
Transfers rotating force of motor from motor pulley to drive pulley; grooved to fit pulley ridges.

Belt lever
Spring-operated lever retracts front drum for belt of sandpaper installation and removal.

Platen assembly
Support plate for belt of sandpaper.

Front drum
Metal roller provides support for belt of sandpaper; retracts for belt installation and removal.

Brush cap
Provides external access to brush assembly.

Drive pulley
Increases force and slows rotation of motor pulley.

Drive belt housing

Drive gear
Drives rear drum; rotating force of motor transferred to it from drive pulley by pinion gear machine-pressed to gear cover.

Brush assembly
Spring-loaded carbon rod encased in a housing; conducts electricity from field coil assembly to commutator.

Housing
Provides double-insulation, guarding against electrical shock.

ORBITAL SANDER

Trigger switch
Depressed to start motor; when released, motor stops immediately. Locking button prevents motor from stopping when trigger released; for safety, its use should be avoided.

Motor bearing
Located at each end of motor shaft to reduce friction as armature spins; may be sealed and require no lubrication.

Motor fan
Machine-pressed to armature shaft; cools motor and housing.

Support clip
Provides support between housing and platen.

Armature
Rotating component of motor.

Field coil assembly
Coiled windings create magnetic field as armature spins; may be secured to housing.

Drive pin
Connects eccentric weight to motor shaft; shears under excessive force, preventing damage to motor.

Eccentric weight
Converts rotating force of motor to circular, reciprocal motion.

Platen bearing
Sealed ball bearing pressed into platen reduces friction caused by eccentric weight.

Release clamp
Holds sandpaper onto platen.

Rubber post
Allows platen to move freely and cushions internal components from vibration.

Platen
Rubber pad provides support for sandpaper.

SANDER USE AND MAINTENANCE

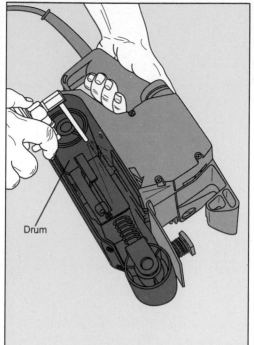

Drum

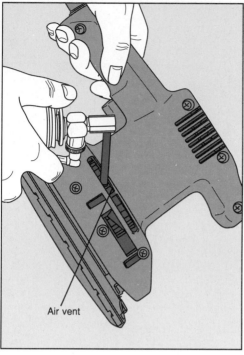

Air vent

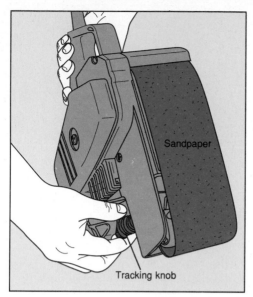

Sandpaper

Tracking knob

Aligning sandpaper on a belt sander.
Turn off and unplug the sander. Turn over
the sander and set it on a flat surface. Install
the sandpaper following the manufacturer's
instructions, aligning it with the outer edge of
the drums on the open side of the sander.
To center the sandpaper, adjust the position
of the front drum by turning the tracking knob
(above). Plug in and turn on the sander to
check its tracking; if necessary, turn it off,
unplug it and readjust it. If the sandpaper
misaligns repeatedly, service the front drum
and platen assembly *(page 25)*.

Cleaning with compressed air. Turn off and unplug the sander. Take off the dust bag and
empty it; to prevent the fan from clogging, the dust bag should be emptied before it is full. To
clean dust off the sander, remove the sandpaper and use compressed air; or, use a vacuum
cleaner with the hose connected to the exhaust port—never use suction. Wearing safety goggles,
blow off any accumulated dust, especially out of the vents and openings; be sure to clean around
each drum of a belt sander *(above, left)* and through the air vents of an orbital sander *(above,
right)*. Scrub gently with an old toothbrush to loosen clumps and sticky particles. With an orbital
sander, periodically remove the platen *(page 22)* and clean it thoroughly. A sander accumulates
dust rapidly; clean it after every use.

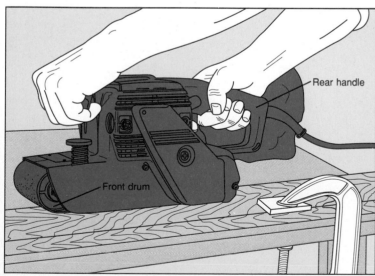

Rear handle

Front drum

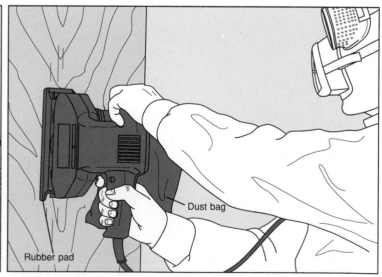

Rubber pad

Dust bag

Operating a sander. If the workpiece is not steady, secure it with
clamps or in a vise. Before sanding a surface, clear it of obstructions
and remove any protruding fasteners. Start with coarse sandpaper if
the surface is rough or heavily painted; start with medium sandpaper
if it is scratched or moderately painted. Use fine sandpaper for final
smoothing or if the surface is unfinished. Install the sandpaper following the manufacturer's instructions; align it if using a belt sander *(step
above, right)*. Wearing safety goggles and a dust mask, plug in the
sander. Keep the power cord to one side and behind you while sanding.

With a belt sander, depress the trigger switch and lower the sander
onto the surface, with the rear drum contacting it first. Gripping both
handles firmly, guide the sander along the wood grain using the rear
handle *(above, left)*; apply only gentle pressure, letting the sander do
the work. Lift the sander off the surface before releasing the trigger
switch. With an orbital sander, use the same procedure but lower it
evenly onto the surface *(above, right)*; guiding it along the wood grain is
not necessary. Turn off and unplug the sander when changing the sandpaper, emptying the dust bag or cleaning the sander *(step above, left)*.

ACCESS TO THE INTERNAL COMPONENTS (Orbital sander)

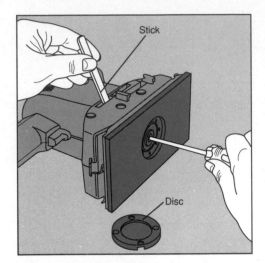

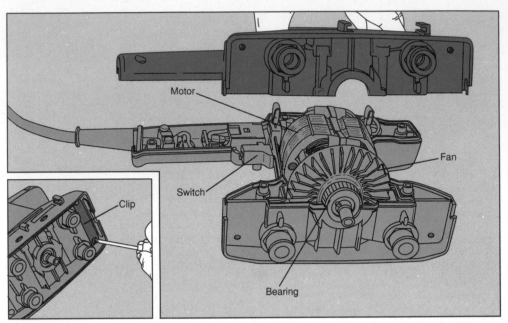

1 **Removing the platen.** Turn off and unplug the sander. Remove the dust bag and the sandpaper. To remove the platen, unscrew it from the housing. On the model shown, the screw is hidden under a disc in the rubber pad. Unscrew and remove the disc, then unscrew the platen, holding the fan steady with a small stick to prevent the motor from turning *(above)*. Slide the platen off the housing.

2 **Opening the housing.** To gain access to an internal component, you may have to open the entire housing or only the housing for the component. On the model shown, the entire housing must be opened. First unscrew each support clip *(inset)* and take it off the housing, and then remove all the housing screws. Gently separate the housing at the seam and lift off the half section *(above)*. Note the placement of wires, gears and other internal components, drawing a diagram, if necessary, for reassembly.

SERVICING THE SWITCH

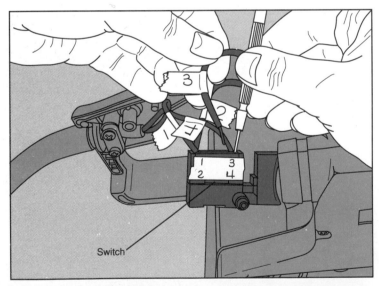

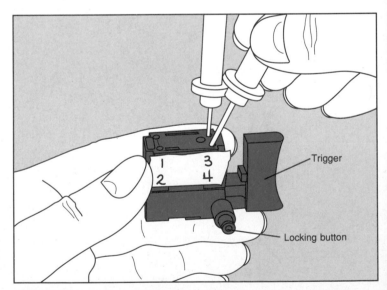

1 **Accessing the switch.** Turn off and unplug the sander. To reach the switch on most orbital sanders, access the internal components *(steps above)*. For other sanders, locate and remove the screws holding the handle housing together, then lift off the half section. Carefully lift the switch out of the housing. Label the switch wires and their corresponding terminals, then disconnect the wires from the switch; use the tip of a small screwdriver to release each wire from its push-in terminal *(above)*.

2 **Testing and replacing the switch.** Set a multitester to test for continuity *(page 113)*. Fit one tester probe into a line-terminal slot and the other tester probe in turn into each load-terminal slot *(page 117)*, first depressing and then releasing the trigger *(above)*. (On the switch shown, there is only one pair of line and load terminals, located next to the trigger.) The tester should show continuity once and only once with the trigger depressed. If the switch in your model has another line-terminal slot, fit one tester probe into it and repeat the test. If the switch tests faulty, replace it with an exact duplicate. Reconnect the switch wires and put the switch back into position. Screw the housing back together and check for leaking voltage *(page 113)*.

SERVICING THE DUST FAN (Belt sander)

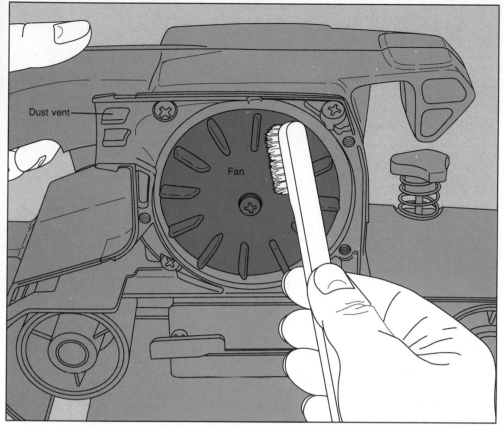

Cleaning the dust fan. Turn off and unplug the sander. Take off the dust bag to locate the dust fan housing on the side of the sander. On some models, the motor fan serves to blow dust into the dust bag; for these models, service the motor *(page 27)*. Otherwise, unscrew and remove the fan housing and lift off the fan cover. Using an old toothbrush, clean any debris off the fan blades *(above)*, the fan cover and the dust vents. Rotate the fan by hand to make sure it moves freely. If the fan does not move freely, unscrew it, slide it out and use a small stick to dislodge any clumps of dust behind it. Wearing safety goggles, blow compressed air around the fan and inside its housing to remove remaining particles. Put back the fan, if you removed it, reposition the fan cover and screw the housing back together.

SERVICING THE DRIVE BELT (Belt sander)

1 **Cleaning the drive belt.** Turn off and unplug the sander. To reach the drive belt, unscrew the drive belt housing on the side of the sander and lift it off. Rotate the drive belt by hand to check that it fits snugly and moves smoothly over the pulleys; if your model does not contain a drive belt, service the gears and rear drum *(page 24)*. If the pulleys do not rotate smoothly or the drive belt is sticky, loose, worn or broken, remove the drive belt *(step 2)*. Otherwise, use an old toothbrush to clean off the drive belt *(above)*. Then, screw on the drive belt housing.

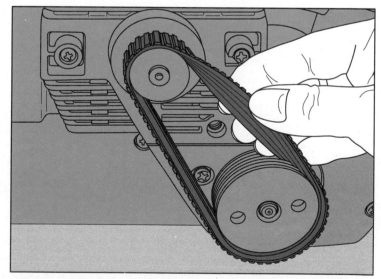

2 **Replacing the drive belt.** To remove the drive belt, rotate it and slip it off the pulleys one ridge at a time *(above)*. If the pulleys do not rotate smoothly, service the gears and rear drum *(page 24)*. If the drive belt is damaged, buy an exact duplicate. To install the drive belt, slip it onto the pulleys one ridge at a time, reversing the procedure used to remove the drive belt. Then, screw on the drive belt housing.

SERVICING THE GEARS AND REAR DRUM (Belt sander)

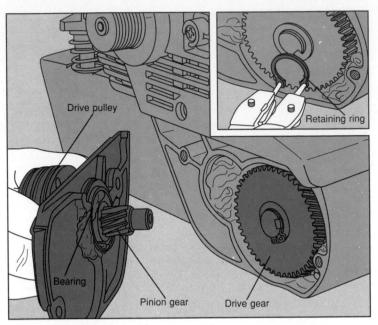

1 **Accessing the gears.** Turn off and unplug the sander, then remove the sandpaper. Remove the drive belt housing and the drive belt *(page 23)*. If the drive pulley does not rotate smoothly, suspect a dirty or broken gear. Unscrew the gear cover and lift it off the gear case *(above)*. (In the model shown, the drive pulley, the pinion gear and the pinion bearing are machine-pressed to the gear cover.) Wearing safety goggles, use external snap-ring pliers to take the retaining ring off the drive gear *(inset)*. Then, pull the washers and the drive gear off the drive shaft of the rear drum.

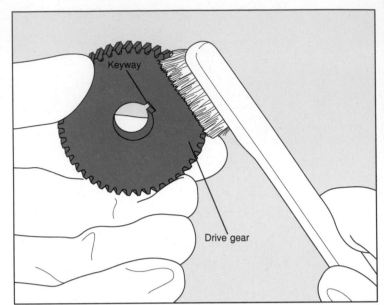

2 **Cleaning and replacing the gears.** Wearing rubber gloves, use a clean cloth to wipe off the grease; use an old toothbrush dipped in paint thinner to clean off the drive gear *(above)* and the pinion gear. Check that the pinion bearing rolls smoothly. If a component is damaged, replace it with an exact duplicate. (In the model shown, only the drive gear can be replaced independently.) Refill the gear case halfway with clean white grease or the manufacturer's specified lubricant. Reinstall the drive gear, the washers, the retaining ring and the gear cover. If the drive pulley does not turn smoothly, inspect the key *(step 3)*. Otherwise, reinstall the drive belt and its housing *(page 23)*.

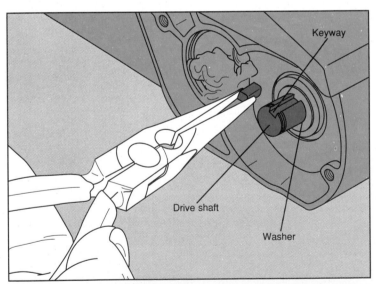

3 **Inspecting and replacing the key.** A loose or broken key can prevent the rear drum from turning smoothly. Unscrew the gear cover, take off the retaining ring, and pull off the washers and the drive gear. Using long-nose pliers, remove the key from its keyway in the rear drum shaft *(above)*. Examine the key for damage; insert it into the gear keyway, then back into the shaft keyway. If the key is not damaged, inspect the rear drum assembly *(step 4)*. Otherwise, replace the key with an exact duplicate. Put back the drive gear, the washers and the retaining ring. Ensuring the gear case is filled halfway with clean white grease or the manufacturer's specified lubricant, screw back on the gear cover. Reinstall the drive belt and its housing *(page 23)*.

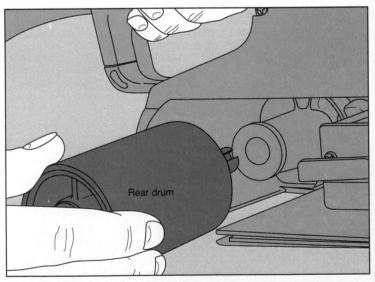

4 **Inspecting and replacing the rear drum assembly.** Remove the key from the keyway and take off the washer. From the opposite side of the sander, slide out the rear drum *(above)*; take the metal cap off its shaft. Examine the rear drum for nicks and other damage; also inspect all metal components. If a component is damaged, replace it with an exact duplicate. Put the metal cap back onto the shaft, reposition the rear drum and reinstall the washer. Reinstall the key in its keyway and put back the drive gear, the washers and the retaining ring. Ensuring the gear case is filled halfway with clean white grease or the manufacturer's specified lubricant, screw back on the gear cover. Reinstall the drive belt and its housing *(page 23)*.

SERVICING THE FRONT DRUM AND PLATEN ASSEMBLY (Belt sander)

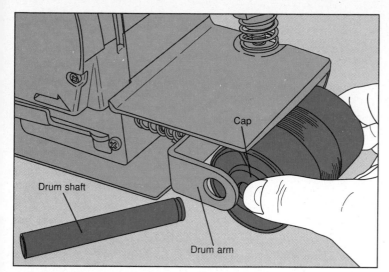

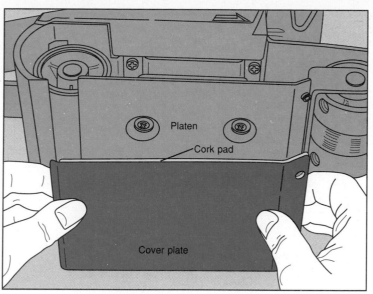

1 **Inspecting the front drum.** Turn off and unplug the sander, then remove the sandpaper. Wearing safety goggles, use external snap-ring pliers to take the retaining ring off the front drum shaft. From the opposite side of the sander, slide out the front drum shaft. Pull the front drum out from the drum arm *(above)* and remove the metal cap at each end of it. Inspect the front drum for worn or bent edges and deep grooves. If a component is damaged, replace it with an exact duplicate. Otherwise, put back the metal caps and reposition the front drum. Slide the front drum shaft back into place and reinstall the retaining ring. If the problem persists, remove the platen assembly *(step 2)*.

2 **Removing the platen assembly.** Turn off and unplug the sander, then remove the sandpaper. Unscrew the cover plate and cork pad and lift them off the platen *(above)*; inspect them for deep lines and rough cuts. Then, unscrew and lift off the platen; inspect it for cracks and bends. If the cover plate, cork pad and platen are not damaged, inspect the belt guide *(step 3)*. If the cover plate, cork pad or platen is damaged, replace it with an exact duplicate. Install the platen and screw the cork pad and cover plate onto it. If the problem persists, remove the platen assembly and inspect the belt guide.

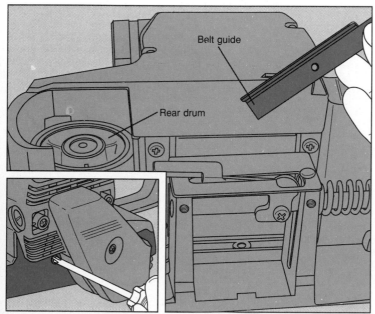

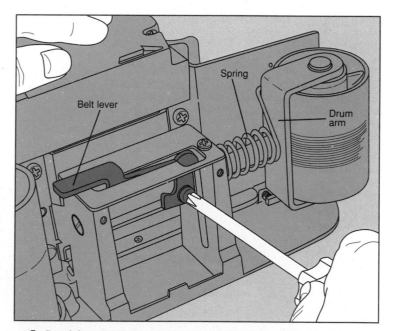

3 **Inspecting and replacing the belt guide.** Locate and remove the screw for the belt guide on the side of the sander next to the drive belt housing *(inset)*. Slide out the belt guide from the side of the sander opposite the screw and inspect it for grooves and broken edges. If the belt guide is not damaged, reposition it on the sander with its flanged edge at the top *(above)*; holding it in place, screw it back on from the other side of the sander. Then, service the belt-release assembly *(step 4)*. If the belt guide is damaged, replace it with an exact duplicate. Reinstall the platen and screw the cork pad and cover plate back onto it. If the problem persists, remove the platen assembly and service the belt-release assembly.

4 **Servicing the belt-release assembly.** Release the belt lever; then, wearing safety goggles and standing away from the front drum, unscrew it *(above)* and remove its spacer. If the belt lever is bent or broken, replace it with an exact duplicate. If the spring is broken or has lost its tension, pull out the front drum and drum arm to slide it off the shaft; replace it with an exact duplicate. To reinstall the belt-release assembly, have a helper wearing safety goggles and work gloves on hand. Slide the spring into place on the shaft and reposition the front drum and drum arm; having your helper press in the front drum and drum arm, position the spacer and screw on the belt lever. Reinstall the platen and screw the cork pad and cover plate back onto it.

SERVICING THE PLATEN ASSEMBLY (Orbital sander)

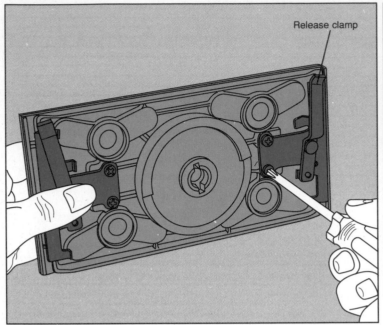

Release clamp

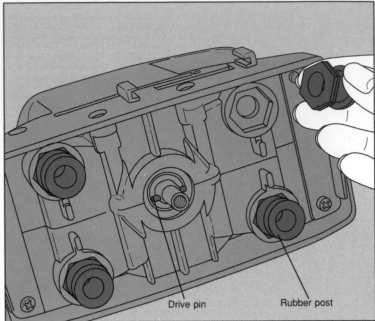

Drive pin   Rubber post

1 **Inspecting the platen assembly.** Remove the platen *(page 22)* and inspect the platen assembly for damage. If the rubber pad is worn or chipped, you may be able to peel it off and replace it independently; otherwise, replace the platen assembly. Rotate the platen bearing by hand; it should move smoothly. If the bearing is dry or seized, replace the platen assembly. Also check each release clamp; if the lever is stiff, place a few drops of light machine oil at the base of

it or at both ends of any spring. If the lever remains stiff or is bent or broken, unscrew the release clamp from the platen assembly *(above, left)* and replace it with an exact duplicate. Inspect the rubber posts on the bottom of the sander housing for broken or worn edges; if a post is damaged, replace all of them. To remove each post, grasp it firmly and pull it out *(above, right)*; on some models, you may have to unscrew it. Install exact duplicate posts.

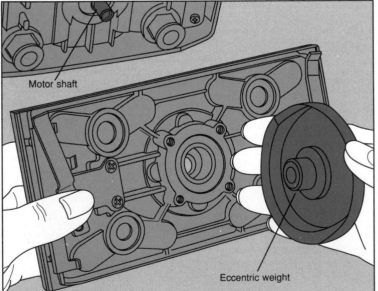

Motor shaft

Eccentric weight

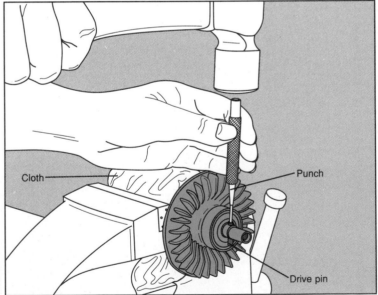

Cloth   Punch

Drive pin

2 **Servicing the eccentric mechanism.** Locate the eccentric weight on the motor shaft; or, remove the eccentric weight from the platen bearing *(above, left)* and slide it onto the motor shaft. Check that the eccentric weight fits snugly. If the eccentric weight is damaged, replace it with an exact duplicate. If the drive pin in the motor shaft is damaged, open the housing *(page 22)* and locate the motor; if there is no drive pin in the motor shaft of your model, open the housing and service the gears or belt driving the eccentric weight as you would the gears *(page 24)* or drive belt *(page 23)* in a belt sander. To remove the drive pin from the motor shaft, pull out the brush assemblies *(page*

27), lift out the motor and slide the armature out of the field coil assembly. Wrap the armature in a cloth and secure it in a vise. Using a pin punch and a ball-peen hammer, knock out the drive pin *(above, right)*. Buy an exact duplicate drive pin and knock it into place using the punch and hammer. Slide the armature back into the field coil assembly, reposition the motor and put back the brush assemblies, making sure that each brush presses firmly against the commutator and matches its curvature. Reposition the eccentric weight and reinstall the platen, reversing the procedure used to remove it.

SERVICING THE BRUSH ASSEMBLIES

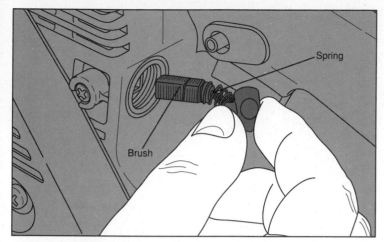

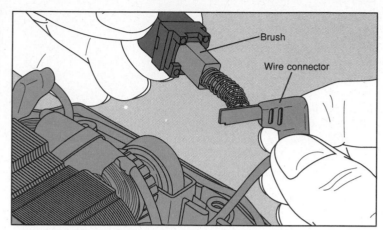

Replacing externally accessible brush assemblies. Turn off and unplug the sander. If there are no brush caps on the motor housing, replace the internal brush assemblies *(step right)*. Otherwise, slowly unscrew each brush cap—be prepared for a brush that may fly out when its spring is released. Pull out each brush assembly *(above)* and push each brush once or twice to test its spring. If the spring is damaged or the brush is pitted, uneven or worn shorter than its width, replace both entire brush assemblies with exact duplicates. Push each brush assembly carefully into position, making sure the brush matches the curvature of the commutator; then, screw on the brush cap. Check for leaking voltage *(page 113)*.

Replacing internal brush assemblies. Turn off and unplug the sander. If there are brush caps on the motor housing, replace the externally accessible brush assemblies *(step left)*. Otherwise, access the internal components *(page 22)* and carefully lift out each brush assembly—be prepared for a brush that may fly out. Push each brush to test its spring, then slide it out of its housing *(above)*. If the spring is damaged, the housing is cracked, or the brush is pitted, uneven or worn shorter than its width, replace the component in each brush assembly or both entire brush assemblies with exact duplicates. Disconnect each brush assembly, replace the components and then reconnect the brush assemblies. Fit each brush assembly into position, making sure the brush presses firmly against the commutator and matches its curvature. Screw the housing back together and reinstall the platen, reversing the procedure used to remove them. Check for leaking voltage *(page 113)*.

SERVICING THE MOTOR

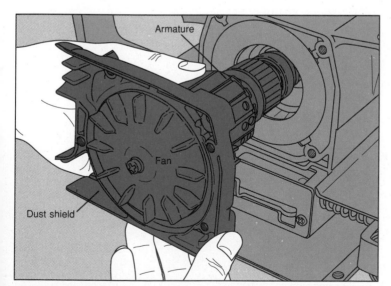

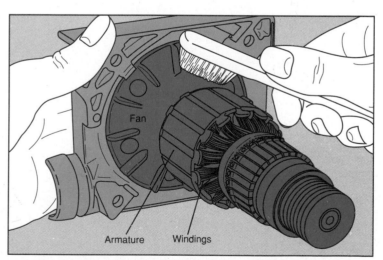

1 **Removing the motor.** With an orbital sander, access the internal components *(page 22)*. Gently pull out the brush assemblies *(step above)*, lift the motor out of the housing and slide the armature out of the field coil assembly. With a belt sander, remove the brush assemblies *(step above)*, take off the dust bag and unscrew the fan housing. Unscrew the dust shield and pull it out, keeping one hand ready to support the armature *(above)*. If the armature does not slide out easily, tap the motor pulley on the other side of the sander with a mallet; the drive pulley and bearings are machine-pressed to the armature.

2 **Inspecting and cleaning the motor.** Set the armature on a clean surface. Use an old toothbrush to clean dust off the fan *(above)* and the armature coils. Rotate the bearing on each end of the shaft. If a bearing does not turn smoothly, replace it with an exact duplicate; if it cannot be removed, as with the model shown, take the armature for professional service. Also inspect the field coil assembly; with a belt sander, remove the motor plate to locate it. If the motor or windings are darkened, service the motor components *(page 118)*. Put back the motor, reinstall the brush assemblies *(step above)* and screw the housing back together, reversing the procedure used to remove them. Check for leaking voltage *(page 113)*.

SABER SAWS

Best known for its ability to cut curves in wood and its maneuverability in tight corners, the saber saw—also known as the jig saw—is one of the most versatile tools in the home workshop. With the right blade, a typical saber saw *(below)* can be used to cut through a variety of materials other than wood: metal, drywall, asphalt, rubber or leather, for instance. The universal motor, commonly activated by a variable-speed switch, powers the drive gear and eccentric mechanism; its eccentric pin fits into the slide bracket on the shaft, converting the rotation of the drive gear into the reciprocal, up-and-down action of the shaft. The blade, usually 3 inches long, moves with the shaft, held securely onto it by the collar. Depending on the setting of the variable-speed switch, the blade makes 2000 to 4000 strokes per minute. The teeth of the blade face out from the saw and the cutting action is made only on the upstroke; ragged edges on the finished side of a workpiece can be minimized by cutting it upside down.

Most problems with saber saws are due to misuse—practices that allow the motor to overheat and can cause it to burn out. Always use the proper blade for the type of material you are cutting and avoid forcing it into the workpiece. Adjust the variable-speed switch to the setting appropriate for the job: a faster speed when cutting soft wood, a slower speed for hard wood and other dense materials. Run the blade slowly through

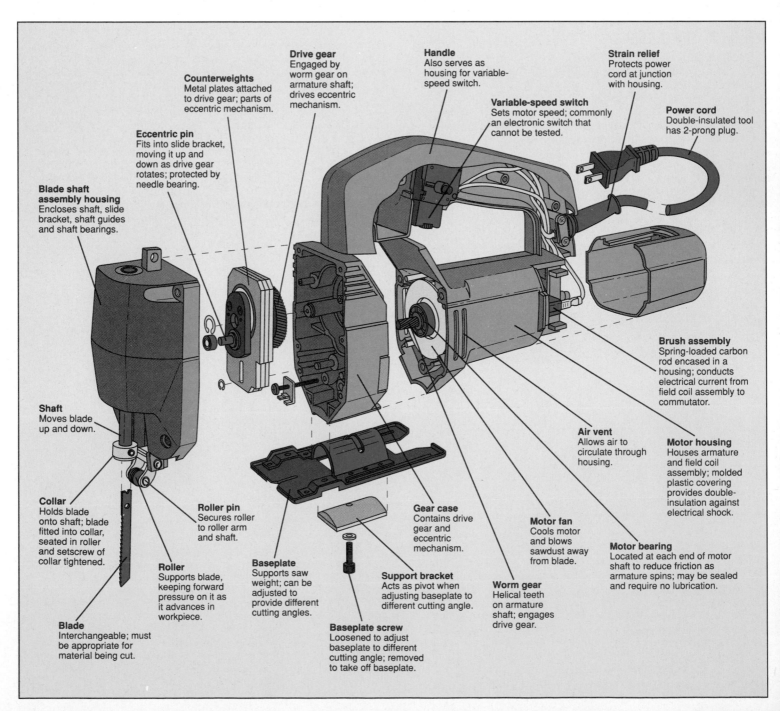

Counterweights
Metal plates attached to drive gear; parts of eccentric mechanism.

Drive gear
Engaged by worm gear on armature shaft; drives eccentric mechanism.

Handle
Also serves as housing for variable-speed switch.

Strain relief
Protects power cord at junction with housing.

Eccentric pin
Fits into slide bracket, moving it up and down as drive gear rotates; protected by needle bearing.

Variable-speed switch
Sets motor speed; commonly an electronic switch that cannot be tested.

Power cord
Double-insulated tool has 2-prong plug.

Blade shaft assembly housing
Encloses shaft, slide bracket, shaft guides and shaft bearings.

Brush assembly
Spring-loaded carbon rod encased in a housing; conducts electrical current from field coil assembly to commutator.

Shaft
Moves blade up and down.

Air vent
Allows air to circulate through housing.

Motor housing
Houses armature and field coil assembly; molded plastic covering provides double-insulation against electrical shock.

Collar
Holds blade onto shaft; blade fitted into collar, seated in roller and setscrew of collar tightened.

Roller pin
Secures roller to roller arm and shaft.

Gear case
Contains drive gear and eccentric mechanism.

Motor fan
Cools motor and blows sawdust away from blade.

Motor bearing
Located at each end of motor shaft to reduce friction as armature spins; may be sealed and require no lubrication.

Roller
Supports blade, keeping forward pressure on it as it advances in workpiece.

Baseplate
Supports saw weight; can be adjusted to provide different cutting angles.

Support bracket
Acts as pivot when adjusting baseplate to different cutting angle.

Worm gear
Helical teeth on armature shaft; engages drive gear.

Blade
Interchangeable; must be appropriate for material being cut.

Baseplate screw
Loosened to adjust baseplate to different cutting angle; removed to take off baseplate.

plastic or fiberglass; if it heats up, the material may melt and stick to it. Keep the air vents open: while using the saber saw, by avoiding blocking them with your hands; after using the saber saw, by clearing them with compressed air. The motor fan, which cools internal components as the saber saw operates, also serves to blow sawdust out of the path of the blade; to keep it from being obstructed, clean off the collar of the shaft and the opening at the bottom of the housing for the blade shaft assembly.

Always turn off and unplug the saber saw before changing the blade, cleaning off sawdust or performing a repair. Read the use and care manual supplied with your saber saw for guidance in choosing the correct blade and speed setting, as well as for information on lubricating and other routine maintenance procedures. When your saber saw malfunctions, consult the Troubleshooting Guide *(below)* to help you in diagnosing the problem. A specific repair may differ with a particular model of saber saw, depending on the variations in features it contains. Identify the type of switch *(page 117)* and the type of bearings *(page 120)* in your saber saw to determine whether they can be serviced or only replaced if you suspect they are faulty. Refer to Tools & Techniques *(page 110)* for instructions on using a multitester, tips on disassembly and reassembly, and information on finding replacement parts.

TROUBLESHOOTING GUIDE

SYMPTOM	POSSIBLE CAUSE	PROCEDURE
Saw does not work at all	No power to outlet or outlet faulty	Reset breaker or replace fuse *(p. 112)* □○; have outlet serviced
	Power cord or extension cord faulty	Service power cord *(p. 115)* ◾○▲; replace extension cord *(p. 115)*
	Brush worn or dislodged	Service brush assemblies *(p. 31)* ◾○
	Variable-speed switch faulty	Replace switch *(p. 31)* ◾○
	Motor faulty	Inspect motor *(p. 33)* ◾○; service motor components *(p. 118)* ◾◖▲
Motor hums, but saw does not work	Variable-speed switch set incorrectly or motor not reaching operating speed	Reset switch; allow motor to reach operating speed before engaging blade in workpiece
	Blade incorrect or dull	Replace blade *(p. 30)* □○
	Blade shaft assembly faulty	Service blade shaft assembly *(p. 32)* ◾○
	Drive gear or eccentric mechanism faulty	Service drive gear and eccentric mechanism *(p. 33)* ◾◖
	Motor faulty or bearing dry	Inspect motor and lubricate bearings *(p. 33)* ◾○; service motor components *(p. 118)* ◾◖▲
Saw overheats or power diminished	Extension cord of incorrect size or rating	Replace extension cord *(p. 115)*
	Air vent blocked	Clean saw *(p. 30)* □○
	Variable-speed switch set incorrectly or motor not reaching operating speed	Set switch at highest setting and allow motor to run under no load until cool; reset switch and allow motor to reach operating speed
	Blade incorrect or dull	Replace blade *(p. 30)* □○
	Brush worn or dislodged	Service brush assemblies *(p. 31)* ◾○
	Motor dirty or faulty or bearing dry	Inspect motor and lubricate bearings *(p. 33)* ◾○; service motor components *(p. 118)* ◾◖▲
Saw rattles or vibrates excessively	Housing fastener loose	Tighten housing fasteners
	Blade incorrect, dull or loose	Replace blade *(p. 30)* □○
	Blade shaft assembly faulty	Service blade shaft assembly *(p. 32)* ◾◖
	Drive gear or eccentric mechanism faulty	Service drive gear and eccentric mechanism *(p. 33)* ◾○
	Motor fan damaged	Inspect motor *(p. 33)* ◾○; replace if necessary
Sparks fly from motor housing	Brush worn or dislodged	Service brush assemblies *(p. 31)* ◾○
	Motor dirty or faulty	Inspect motor *(p. 33)* ◾○; service motor components *(p. 118)* ◾◖▲
Blade bends, breaks, overheats or jams	Blade incorrect or dull	Replace blade *(p. 30)* □○
	Baseplate damaged	Service baseplate *(p. 30)* □○
	Blade shaft assembly faulty	Service blade shaft assembly *(p. 32)* ◾○
Blade does not follow cutting lines	Blade bent	Replace blade *(p. 30)* □○
	Baseplate screw loose; baseplate damaged	Tighten baseplate screw; service baseplate *(p. 30)* □○

DEGREE OF DIFFICULTY: □ Easy ◾ Moderate ◼ Complex
ESTIMATED TIME: ○ Less than 1 hour ◖ 1 to 3 hours ● Over 3 hours   ▲ Special tool required

SABER SAW USE AND MAINTENANCE

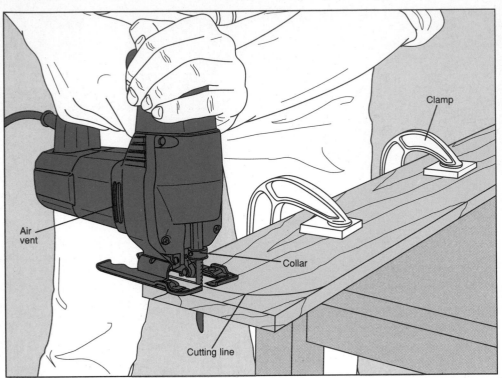

Clamp

Air vent

Collar

Cutting line

Operating a saber saw. If the workpiece is not steady, secure it with clamps or in a vise. Remove any obstructions such as fasteners from the area to be cut; if cutting into a wall, check first for electrical wiring and other hidden hazards. Install a blade in the saw *(step below, left)* according to the manufacturer's instructions. If you are using an extension cord, check that it is of the correct size and rating *(page 115)*.

Wearing safety goggles, plug in the saw and depress the trigger switch. Allow the saw to reach operating speed, then slowly advance the blade into the workpiece *(left)*. Grip the saw handle with one hand and use the other hand to help guide the saw, as shown; do not exert pressure or block an air vent. Keep the power cord to one side and behind you. Before withdrawing the saw from the workpiece, release the trigger switch and let the blade come to a full stop.

After each use of the saw, unplug it and clean off the base of the blade shaft assembly, the collar and the roller with an old toothbrush. Wearing safety goggles, blow compressed air through the air vents and into the opening at the base of the blade shaft assembly. Service the blade shaft assembly once a year *(page 32)*.

SERVICING THE BLADE AND THE BASEPLATE

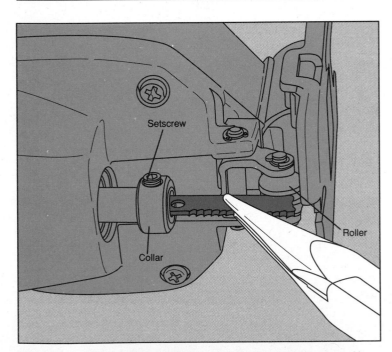

Setscrew

Roller

Collar

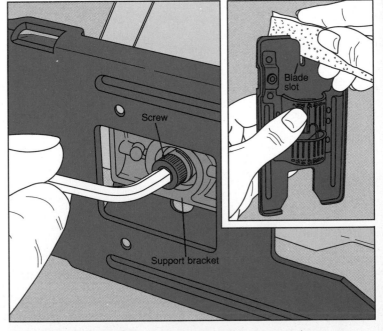

Screw

Blade slot

Support bracket

Removing and installing a blade. Turn off and unplug the saw. Always use the correct blade for the type of material being cut. Replace any bent or broken blade; if the blade sticks, cuts slowly or burns, also replace it. To remove the blade, loosen the setscrew on the collar of the blade shaft assembly with a hex wrench or the tool provided with the saw. Use long-nose pliers to pull any broken shard out of the collar *(above)*. To install a blade, insert it into the collar with its teeth facing away from the saw; make sure the edge of the blade opposite the teeth sits securely in the groove of the roller. Then, tighten the setscrew.

Inspecting the baseplate. Turn off and unplug the saw, then remove the blade *(step left)*. Remove the baseplate screw with a hex wrench *(above)* and take off any washers, noting their order for reassembly. Slide off the support bracket and the baseplate. Smooth any burrs or nicks along the blade slot of the baseplate using fine sandpaper *(inset)*. If the baseplate is bent or cracked, replace it with an exact duplicate. To reinstall the baseplate, fit it to the curve of the motor housing, position the support bracket and the washers, and put back the screw; tighten it with the hex wrench. Then, reinstall the blade *(step left)*.

SERVICING THE BRUSH ASSEMBLIES

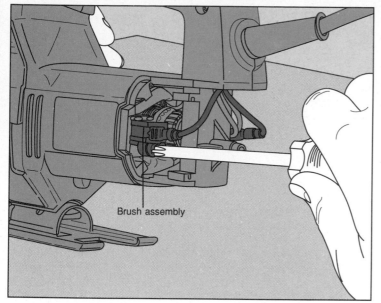

Brush assembly

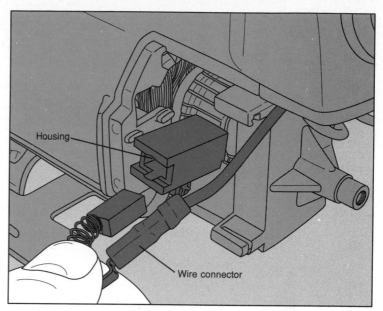

Housing

Wire connector

1 **Removing and inspecting the brush assemblies.** Turn off and unplug the saw, then remove the blade *(page 30)*. Unscrew and lift off the motor cover and locate the brush assembly on each side of the commutator. Unscrew *(above)* and carefully lift out each brush assembly—be prepared for a brush that may fly out. Push each brush once or twice to test its spring. If the spring is damaged, the housing is cracked, or the brush is pitted, uneven or worn shorter than its width, replace the component in each brush assembly or both entire brush assemblies.

2 **Replacing the brush assemblies.** Always replace the component in each brush assembly or both entire brush assemblies with exact duplicates—even if only one is damaged. On the model shown, the entire brush assemblies must be replaced. To disconnect each brush assembly, gently pull off its wire connector. Replace the damaged components and reconnect the brush assemblies. Fit each brush assembly into position *(above)* and screw it in place, making sure the brush presses firmly against the commutator and matches its curvature. Screw back on the motor cover, reinstall the blade *(page 30)* and check for leaking voltage *(page 113)*.

SERVICING THE VARIABLE-SPEED SWITCH

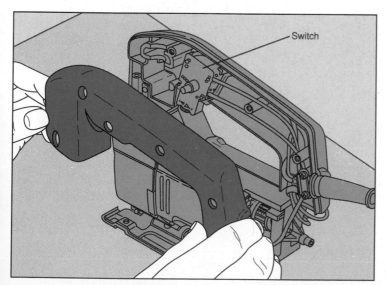

Switch

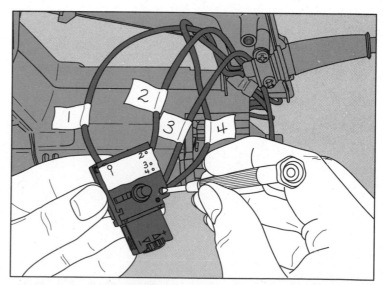

1 **Accessing the switch.** Turn off and unplug the saw, then remove the blade *(page 30)*. Unscrew the handle housing and gently separate it at the seam; it may be necessary to take off the motor cover first. Then, lift off the half section of the handle housing *(above)*. Note the placement of wires, the power cord and other components, drawing a diagram, if necessary, for reassembly. Identify the switch *(page 117)*; an electronic switch, as in the model shown, cannot be tested, but can be replaced if you suspect it is faulty.

2 **Replacing the switch.** Lift the switch out of the handle housing; label its wires and their corresponding terminals, then disconnect the wires from the switch. Use a small screwdriver to release each wire from its push-in terminal or to unscrew it *(above)*. Replace the switch with an exact duplicate and reconnect the wires to it. Position the switch and screw back on the half section of the handle housing; reinstall the motor cover if you removed it. Reinstall the blade *(page 30)* and check for leaking voltage *(page 113)*.

SERVICING THE BLADE SHAFT ASSEMBLY

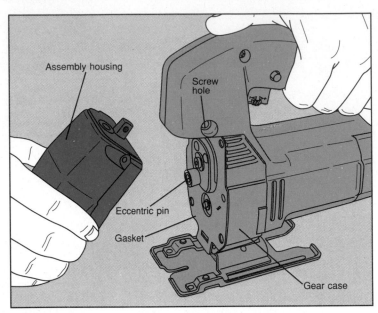

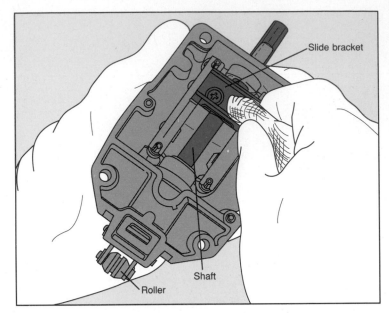

1 **Removing and installing the blade shaft assembly.** Turn off and unplug the saw, then remove the blade *(page 30)*. Pull the shaft to lower it as far as possible and unscrew the assembly housing; one screw is usually located in the handle. Holding the saw firmly with one hand, grasp the assembly housing and slide it off the gear case *(above)*. If the gasket between the assembly housing and the gear case is damaged, replace it with an exact duplicate. Clean and lubricate the blade shaft assembly *(step 2)*. To reinstall the assembly housing, lower the shaft fully and rotate the eccentric pin by hand to align it with the slide bracket. Position the gasket and push the assembly housing back into place, tilting it to fit the slide bracket onto the eccentric pin. Put back the screws and reinstall the blade *(page 30)*.

2 **Cleaning and lubricating the blade shaft assembly.** Wearing rubber gloves, use a clean cloth to wipe the old grease off the blade shaft assembly *(above)*; clean off each component with a small paintbrush dipped in paint thinner. Slide the shaft and the slide bracket by hand; each component should move smoothly. If the shaft wobbles in its bearings, replace the bearings; if they are machine-pressed to the assembly housing, as in the model shown, replace the entire blade shaft assembly. If the shaft, the slide bracket or the roller is damaged, remove the roller *(step 3)*. Otherwise, refill the assembly housing three-quarters full with white grease or the manufacturer's specified lubricant and apply a few drops of light machine oil on the felt pad of the roller. Then, reinstall the blade shaft assembly *(step 1)*.

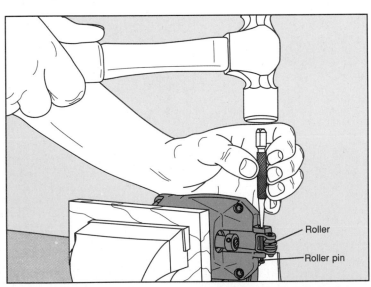

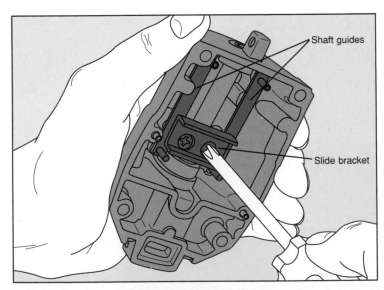

3 **Replacing the roller.** Secure the assembly housing in a vise, protecting it with wood blocks. Wearing safety goggles, pry the spring clip off the roller pin using a small screwdriver. Position a pin punch on top of the roller pin and tap it with a ball-peen hammer until the roller pin is free *(above)*. Take off the roller; the felt pad and cover should also lift off. If the shaft or the slide bracket is damaged, replace it *(step 4)*. If the roller is damaged, replace it with an exact duplicate; also replace the spring clip and the roller pin, if necessary. Reinstall the roller, reversing the procedure used to remove it, lubricate the blade shaft assembly *(step 2)* and reinstall the assembly housing *(step 1)*.

4 **Replacing the shaft and the slide bracket.** Unscrew the slide bracket *(above)* and take it off the shaft. If the shaft is damaged, slide it out through the bottom of the assembly housing. To replace the shaft or the slide bracket, buy an exact duplicate. Slide the shaft into place and position the slide bracket, making sure the shaft guides are aligned correctly; then, put back the screws. Reinstall the roller, reversing the procedure used to remove it *(step 3)*, lubricate the blade shaft assembly *(step 2)* and reinstall the assembly housing *(step 1)*. If the problem persists, service the drive gear and eccentric mechanism *(page 33)*.

SERVICING THE DRIVE GEAR AND ECCENTRIC MECHANISM

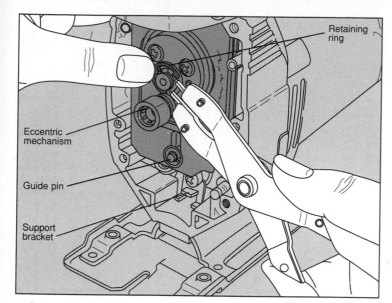

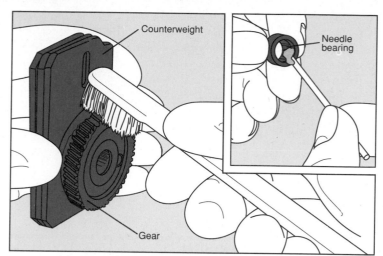

1 **Accessing the drive gear and eccentric mechanism.** Turn off and unplug the saw, then remove the blade *(page 30)*. Remove the blade shaft assembly *(page 32)*. Wearing safety goggles, use external snap-ring pliers to pull the retaining rings off the drive gear shaft *(above)* and the guide pin. Remove the washers, taking note of their placement and order for reassembly, and then lift off the eccentric mechanism. Remove the needle bearing from the eccentric pin, noting its location. Buy exact duplicate retaining rings for reassembly.

2 **Lubricating the drive gear and eccentric mechanism.** Wearing rubber gloves, use a clean cloth to wipe off the old grease. Use an old toothbrush dipped in paint thinner to clean the drive gear *(above)* and counterweights; for access, separate them, if possible. If a component is damaged, replace it or the entire drive gear and eccentric mechanism. Otherwise, reassemble the drive gear and eccentric mechanism. Apply a dab of white grease on the needle bearing *(inset)* and reposition it; if it does not turn smoothly, replace it. Refill the gear case halfway with white grease or the manufacturer's specified lubricant and put back the drive gear and eccentric mechanism, reversing the sequence used to remove it. Reinstall the blade shaft assembly *(page 32)*.

SERVICING THE MOTOR AND BEARINGS

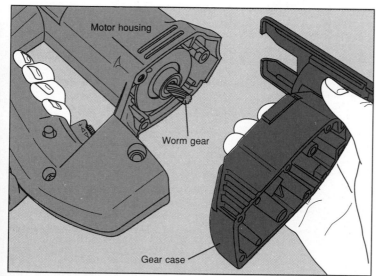

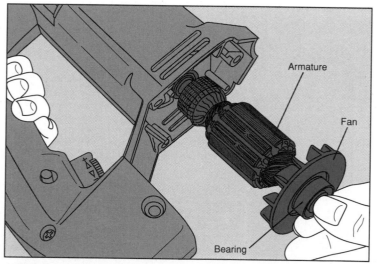

1 **Accessing the motor.** Turn off and unplug the saw, then remove the blade *(page 30)*. Remove the brush assemblies *(page 31)*, the blade shaft assembly *(page 32)*, and the drive gear and eccentric mechanism *(step 1, above)*. Unscrew the gear case and pull it off the motor housing *(above)*; you may first have to take off the roller support bracket. Wearing rubber gloves, clean off the worm gear using an old toothbrush dipped in paint thinner, taking care not to get any on the bearing or into the motor. Gently slide the armature out of the motor housing and set it on a clean surface. Brush any dust off the fan and the motor using an old toothbrush; if the fan is damaged, replace the entire armature.

2 **Inspecting the motor and lubricating the bearings.** Lubricate only the bearings that are not sealed *(page 120)*; on the model shown, only the bearing near the fan. To inspect the field coil assembly, take off the motor plate. If the motor or windings are darkened, service the motor components *(page 118)*. Otherwise, screw back on the motor plate and slide the armature in place *(above)*. Screw back on the gear case and any support bracket removed. Ensuring the gear case is filled halfway with clean white grease or the manufacturer's specified lubricant, put back the drive gear and eccentric mechanism, reversing the sequence used to remove it *(step 1, above)*. Reinstall the blade shaft assembly *(page 32)*, the brush assemblies *(page 31)* and the blade *(page 30)*. Check for leaking voltage *(page 113)*.

CIRCULAR SAWS

Long considered as a tool for only the professional, the circular saw is now as indispensable to the homeowner as the electric drill. Common in the home workshop is the 7 1/4-inch circular saw, rated by its blade diameter *(page 35)*. Powered by the universal motor that is activated by the trigger switch, the worm gear on the motor shaft rotates the drive gear. The spindle on the drive gear holds the blade and turns it counterclockwise, producing its upstroke cutting action. By adjusting the baseplate, the blade can cut through different thicknesses at different angles. As the blade advances into a cut, the lower guard retracts into the upper guard; at the end of a cut, it springs back over the blade—which spins for several seconds after the trigger switch is released.

Most problems with circular saws arise from misuse. Refer to your use and care manual for information on choosing the correct blade, installing it and setting its cutting depth and angle, as well as for guidance in routine maintenance procedures. Always use the proper blade for the type of material you are cutting; make sure it is clean and sharp *(page 36)*. Perform a safety check of the lower guard before each use of your circular saw *(page 38)*. When your circular saw malfunctions, consult the Troubleshooting Guide *(below)* to help in diagnosing the problem. Read Tools & Techniques *(page 110)* for information on using a multitester, on servicing switches, bearings and brush assemblies that differ from the ones shown in this chapter, and on finding replacement parts.

TROUBLESHOOTING GUIDE

SYMPTOM	POSSIBLE CAUSE	PROCEDURE
Saw does not work at all	No power to outlet or outlet faulty	Reset breaker or replace fuse *(p. 112)* □○; have outlet serviced
	Power cord or extension cord faulty	Service power cord *(p. 115)* ◨○▲; replace extension cord *(p. 115)*
	Trigger switch faulty	Service switch *(p. 37)* ◨○▲
	Brush worn or dislodged	Service brush assemblies *(p. 38)* □○
	Motor faulty	Inspect motor *(p. 40)* ◨○; service motor components *(p. 118)* ◨◕▲
Motor hums, but saw does not work	Blade too tight; incorrect, dirty or dull	Loosen blade bolt 1/8 turn; service blade *(p. 36)* ◨○
	Drive gear or spindle faulty	Service drive gear and spindle *(p. 40)* ◨◕
	Motor faulty or bearing dry	Inspect motor and lubricate bearings *(p. 40)* ◨○; service motor components *(p. 118)* ◨◕▲
Saw overheats or power diminished	Extension cord of incorrect size or rating	Replace extension cord *(p. 115)*
	Air vent or discharge chute blocked	Clean saw *(p. 35)* □○
	Blade incorrect, dirty or dull	Service blade *(p. 36)* ◨○
	Brush worn or dislodged	Service brush assemblies *(p. 38)* □○
	Motor dirty or faulty or bearing dry	Inspect motor and lubricate bearings *(p. 40)* ◨○; service motor components *(p. 118)* ◨◕▲
Saw rattles or vibrates excessively	Housing fastener loose	Tighten housing fasteners
	Blade loose; incorrect, dirty or dull	Tighten blade bolt 1/8 turn; service blade *(p. 36)* ◨○
	Lower guard or upper guard damaged	Service lower guard *(p. 38)* ◨◕ and upper guard *(p. 39)* ◨◕
	Drive gear or spindle faulty	Service drive gear and spindle *(p. 40)* ◨◕
	Motor fan damaged	Inspect motor *(p. 40)* ◨○; replace if necessary
Sparks fly from motor housing	Brush worn or dislodged	Service brush assemblies *(p. 38)* □○
	Motor dirty or faulty	Inspect motor *(p. 40)* ◨○; service motor components *(p. 118)* ◨◕▲
Blade sticks, jams, overheats or kicks back	Blade depth or baseplate angle incorrect	Reset blade depth and baseplate angle
	Blade loose; incorrect, dirty or dull	Tighten blade bolt 1/8 turn; service blade *(p. 36)* ◨○
	Baseplate damaged	Service baseplate *(p. 37)* □○
	Drive gear or spindle faulty	Service drive gear and spindle *(p. 40)* ◨◕
Blade does not follow cutting lines	Blade loose; dirty, dull or bent	Tighten blade bolt 1/8 turn; service blade *(p. 36)* ◨○
	Baseplate damaged	Service baseplate *(p. 37)* □○
Lower guard does not retract into upper guard	Guard or discharge chute clogged	Clean saw *(p. 35)* □○
	Lower guard or upper guard damaged	Service lower guard *(p. 38)* ◨◕ and upper guard *(p. 39)* ◨◕

DEGREE OF DIFFICULTY: □ Easy ◨ Moderate ◼ Complex

ESTIMATED TIME: ○ Less than 1 hour ◕ 1 to 3 hours ● Over 3 hours

▲ Special tool required

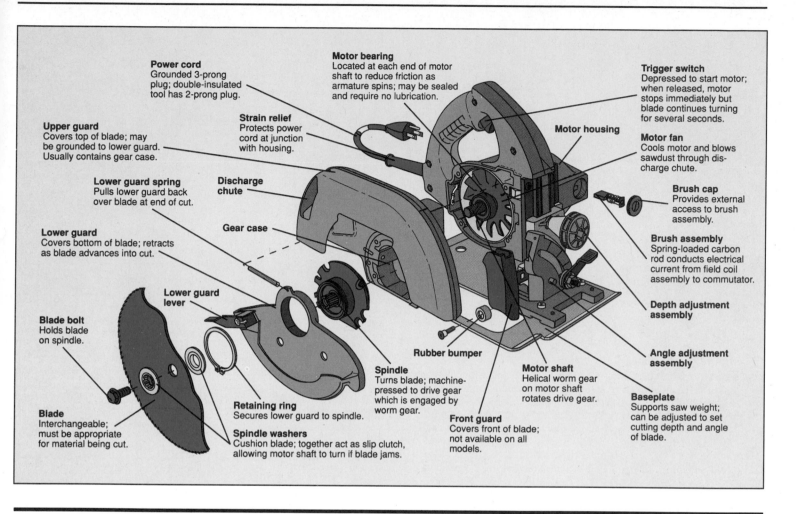

Power cord
Grounded 3-prong plug; double-insulated tool has 2-prong plug.

Motor bearing
Located at each end of motor shaft to reduce friction as armature spins; may be sealed and require no lubrication.

Trigger switch
Depressed to start motor; when released, motor stops immediately but blade continues turning for several seconds.

Upper guard
Covers top of blade; may be grounded to lower guard. Usually contains gear case.

Strain relief
Protects power cord at junction with housing.

Motor housing

Motor fan
Cools motor and blows sawdust through discharge chute.

Lower guard spring
Pulls lower guard back over blade at end of cut.

Discharge chute

Brush cap
Provides external access to brush assembly.

Lower guard
Covers bottom of blade; retracts as blade advances into cut.

Gear case

Brush assembly
Spring-loaded carbon rod conducts electrical current from field coil assembly to commutator.

Lower guard lever

Depth adjustment assembly

Blade bolt
Holds blade on spindle.

Angle adjustment assembly

Rubber bumper

Blade
Interchangeable; must be appropriate for material being cut.

Spindle
Turns blade; machine-pressed to drive gear which is engaged by worm gear.

Motor shaft
Helical worm gear on motor shaft rotates drive gear.

Baseplate
Supports saw weight; can be adjusted to set cutting depth and angle of blade.

Retaining ring
Secures lower guard to spindle.

Spindle washers
Cushion blade; together act as slip clutch, allowing motor shaft to turn if blade jams.

Front guard
Covers front of blade; not available on all models.

CIRCULAR SAW USE AND MAINTENANCE

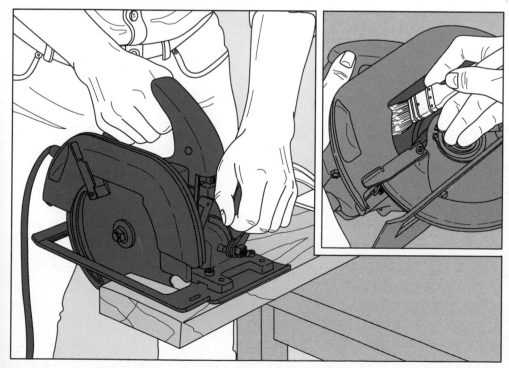

Operating a circular saw. If the workpiece is not steady, secure it with clamps or in a vise. Remove any obstructions such as fasteners from the area to be cut. Service the blade *(page 36)*, following the manufacturer's instructions; set it to a depth of 1/8 to 1/4 inch more than the workpiece thickness. Check the lower guard *(page 38)*. If using an extension cord, ensure it is of the correct size and rating *(page 115)*.

Wearing safety goggles, plug in the saw and depress the trigger switch. Allow the saw to reach operating speed, then slowly advance the blade into the workpiece *(left)*; stay opposite the blade. Grip the handles firmly, using the front handle to help guide the saw, as shown; keep the baseplate flat and do not apply pressure. Keep the power cord to one side and behind you. Release the trigger switch and let the blade come to a full stop before withdrawing the saw from the workpiece; if the saw kicks or jerks, stop and remedy the cause before proceeding.

After each use of the saw, unplug it and use a stiff paintbrush to clean off each guard and the discharge chute *(inset)*. Blow compressed air through the air vents. Once a year, service the drive gear and spindle *(page 40)*.

SERVICING THE BLADE

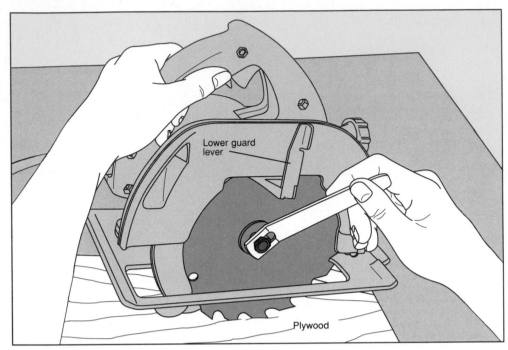

Plywood

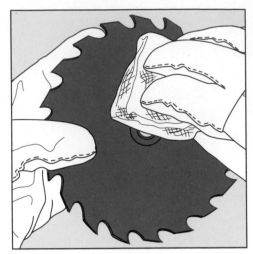

2 **Cleaning and inspecting the blade.** Wearing work gloves, use a clean cloth to wipe off the blade *(above)* and the blade bolt; use a small paintbrush to clean off the spindle. If the blade is sticky, clean it with a paintbrush dipped in paint thinner. If the blade teeth are dull, sharpen the blade *(step 3)*; if the blade is carbide tipped or its teeth are worn or damaged, install a replacement instead *(step 1)*.

1 **Removing and installing a blade.** Turn off and unplug the saw. Always use the correct blade for the type of material being cut. To remove a blade, retract the lower guard enough to press the teeth into a scrap of plywood. Holding the saw, remove the blade bolt using the wrench supplied with the saw *(above)*. Wearing work gloves, take off the washer, retract the lower guard fully and lift off the blade; remove the inner washer. Clean and inspect the blade *(step 2)*.

To install a blade, first slide the inner washer back onto the spindle. Wearing work gloves, position the blade on the spindle with its teeth pointing counterclockwise. Then, slide the other washer back onto the spindle and reinstall the blade bolt; turn it by hand until it is as tight as possible, then tighten it one-half turn using the wrench supplied the saw.

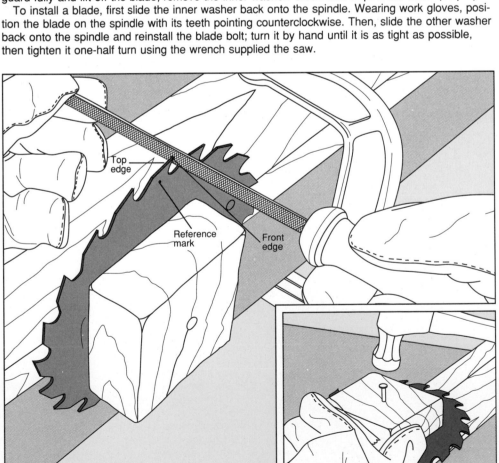

Top edge

Reference mark

Front edge

3 **Sharpening the blade.** Wearing work gloves, prepare the blade for sharpening by sandwiching it between a 2-by-4 long enough to be clamped and a small wood block. Drive a nail through the wood block and the hole in the center of the blade into the 2-by-4 *(inset)*. Then, clamp the 2-by-4 to the edge of a table or workbench. Stand facing the blade and use a felt-tipped pen to mark a tooth curving away from you as a reference.

Place a smooth triangular file on the front edge of the reference tooth *(left)*, laying it flat against the original bevel—usually about 30 degrees. Using light pressure, push the file forward across the tooth 3 or 4 times, lifting it away from the tooth on the return stroke. Repeat the procedure on each tooth curving away from you, turning the blade as necessary, until you return to the reference tooth. Then, file the top edge of each tooth facing away from you the same way.

To complete the job, unclamp the 2-by-4, pull out the nail and turn over the blade; drive a nail through the wood block and the hole in the center of the blade into the 2-by-4, then reclamp the 2-by-4. Use the same procedure to file the front edge and the top edge of each tooth facing away from you. After sharpening the blade, wipe it off with a clean cloth and reinstall it *(step 1)*.

SERVICING THE BASEPLATE

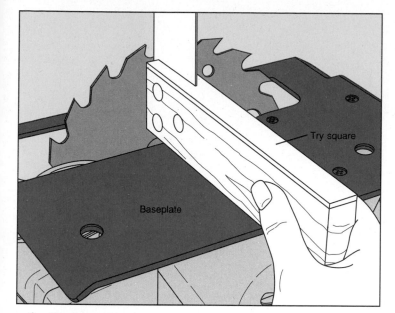

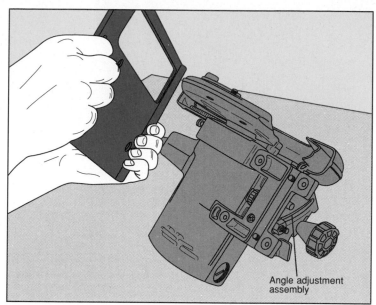

1 **Checking the baseplate.** Turn off and unplug the saw. To ensure the blade is not the problem, replace it *(page 36)*. Tighten the baseplate screws, set the blade to its maximum cutting depth and adjust the baseplate to a 90 degree angle. Turn the saw upside down and set it on a flat surface. Position a try square on the baseplate and against the blade *(above)*. If the blade is not at a 90 degree angle to the baseplate, service the drive gear and spindle *(page 40)*. Otherwise, try using the saw; if the problem persists, replace the baseplate *(step 2)*.

2 **Replacing the baseplate.** Turn off and unplug the saw, then remove the blade *(page 36)*. Turn the saw onto its side and set it on a flat surface. Unscrew the baseplate and lift it off the motor housing and angle adjustment assembly *(above)*; if it is riveted in place, take the saw for professional service. Otherwise, buy an exact duplicate baseplate, position it on the motor housing and angle adjustment assembly, and put back the screws. Reinstall the blade *(page 36)* and try using the saw; if the problem persists, take it for professional service.

SERVICING THE SWITCH

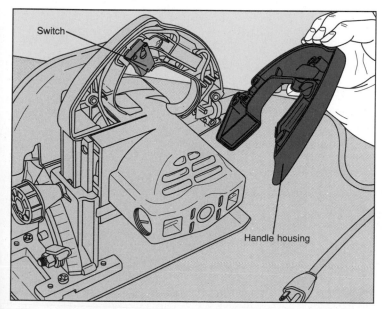

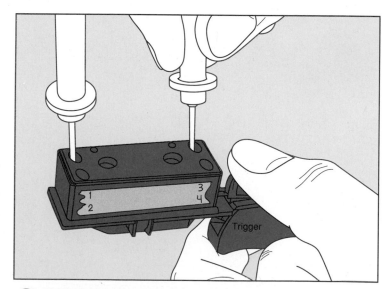

1 **Accessing the switch.** Turn off and unplug the saw, then remove the blade *(page 36)*. Place the saw on its side and unscrew the handle housing. Turn the saw upright, gently separate the handle housing at the seam and lift off the half section *(above)*. Note the placement of wires, gears and other components, drawing a diagram, if necessary, for reassembly. Carefully lift the switch out of the handle housing; label its wires and their corresponding terminals, then disconnect the wires from the switch.

2 **Testing and replacing the switch.** Set a multitester to test for continuity *(page 113)*. Fit one tester probe into a line-terminal slot and the other tester probe in turn into each load-terminal slot *(page 117)*, first depressing and then releasing the trigger *(above)*. The tester should show continuity once and only once with the trigger depressed. Push one tester probe into the other line-terminal slot and repeat the test. If the switch tests faulty, replace it with an exact duplicate. Reconnect the switch wires and reposition the switch. Screw the handle housing back together, reinstall the blade *(page 36)* and check the saw for leaking voltage *(page 113)*.

SERVICING THE BRUSH ASSEMBLIES

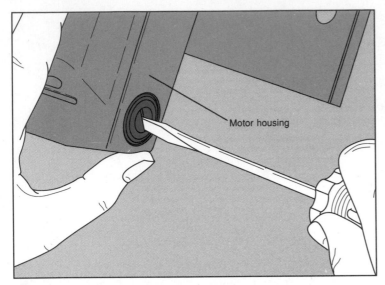

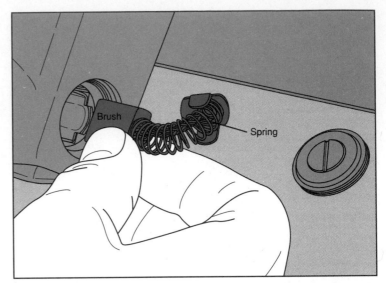

1 **Removing and inspecting the brush assemblies.** Turn off and unplug the saw, then remove the blade *(page 36)*. Locate the brush cap on each side of the motor housing. Slowly unscrew each brush cap *(above)* and carefully lift out each brush assembly—be prepared for a brush that may fly out when its spring is released. Push each brush once or twice to test its spring. If the spring is damaged, the housing is cracked, or the brush is pitted, uneven or worn shorter than its width, replace the component in each brush assembly or both entire brush assemblies.

2 **Replacing the brush assemblies.** Always replace the component in each brush assembly or both entire brush assemblies with exact duplicates—even if only one is damaged. On the model shown, the entire brush assemblies must be replaced. Push each brush assembly carefully into position *(above)*, making sure the brush matches the curvature of the commutator; then, screw back on its brush cap. Reinstall the blade *(page 36)* and check for leaking voltage *(page 113)*.

SERVICING THE LOWER GUARD

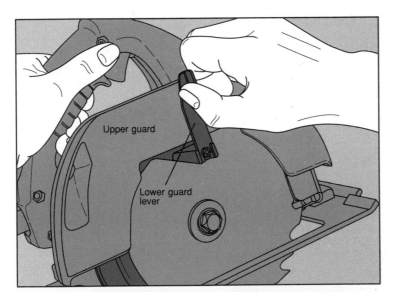

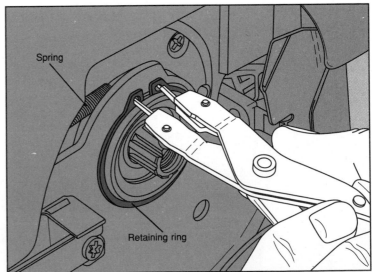

1 **Checking the lower guard.** As a safety check before each use of the saw, inspect the lower guard and its rubber bumper for damage; keep the saw unplugged. To test the action of the lower guard, pull its lever forward *(above)* and release it; the lower guard should retract, then spring back and cover the blade. If the lower guard rubs the upper guard, has lost its spring action or is otherwise damaged, remove the blade *(page 36)* and the lower guard *(step 2)*; if its rubber bumper is damaged, replace it with an exact duplicate.

2 **Removing the lower guard.** Wearing safety goggles, use external snap-ring pliers to take the retaining ring off the spindle *(above)*; for easiest access, first set the saw to its minimum cutting depth. Grasp the lower guard firmly and slide it off the spindle. Carefully unhook the spring from the lower guard and the upper guard; in some models, the spring is a flat-coiled type. Check the spring for loss of tension and inspect the rim and center hole (sometimes fitted with a shim) of the lower guard for nicks and cracks. If any component is damaged, buy an exact duplicate.

SERVICING THE LOWER GUARD (continued)

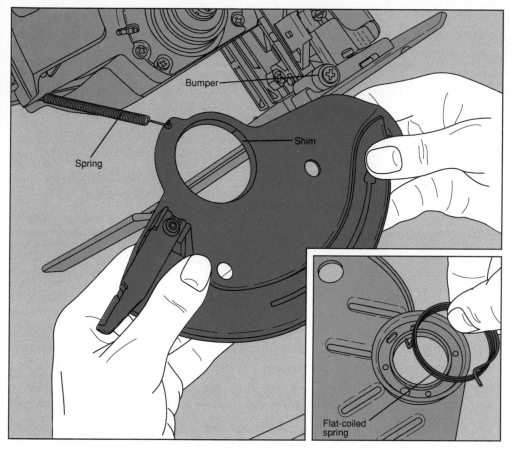

3 **Reinstalling the lower guard.** If the lower guard is not equipped with a flat-coiled spring, first hook the spring back into its slot in the upper guard and the lower guard *(left)*. If the center hole of the lower guard is fitted with a shim, make sure the shim is coiled inside it. Then, reposition the lower guard on the spindle and slide it into place under the upper guard, taking care not to disconnect the spring or dislodge the shim. Put back the retaining ring, reinstall the blade *(page 36)* and check the lower guard *(step 1)*.

If the lower guard is equipped with a flat-coiled spring, first hook the spring inside the lower guard *(inset)*. Holding the spring in place with one hand, guide the lower guard onto the spindle with the other hand; in some models, you may need to remove the rubber bumper for access. With the lower guard in position, press it and turn it counterclockwise into the upper guard until the hook of the spring clicks into the slot in the upper guard. Then, put back the retaining ring, reinstall the blade *(page 36)* and check the lower guard *(step 1)*.

SERVICING THE UPPER GUARD

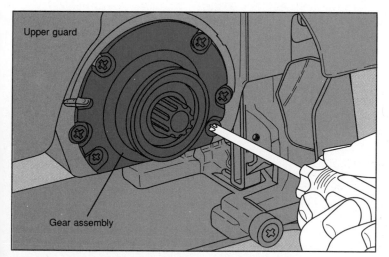

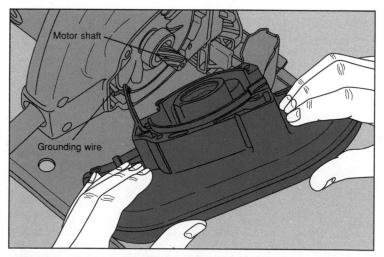

1 **Removing the upper guard.** Turn off and unplug the saw, then remove the blade *(page 36)* and the lower guard *(page 38)*. To access the screws for the upper guard in most models, first unscrew the gear assembly *(above)* and take it off the upper guard. Then, unscrew the upper guard and carefully pull it off the motor housing; if necessary, fit a finger behind it and onto the motor shaft to hold the motor inside its housing. Disconnect any grounding wire from the upper guard, noting its position for reassembly.

2 **Reinstalling the upper guard.** If the upper guard is cracked, bent or broken, replace it with an exact duplicate. Reconnect the grounding wire, then carefully slide the upper guard onto the motor shaft *(above)*. Screw the upper guard into place on the motor housing. Position the gear assembly and rotate the spindle by hand; if it does not turn smoothly, service the drive gear and spindle *(page 40)*. Otherwise, screw the gear assembly back into place, put back the lower guard *(step 3, above)* and reinstall the blade *(page 36)*. Check the saw for leaking voltage *(page 113)*.

SERVICING THE DRIVE GEAR AND SPINDLE

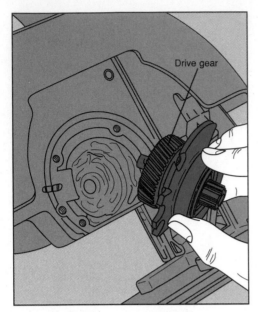

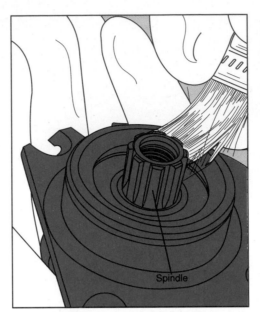

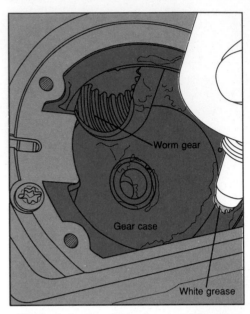

1 **Removing the gear assembly.** Turn off and unplug the saw. Remove the blade *(page 36)* and the lower guard *(page 38)*. Unscrew the gear assembly, gently pull out the spindle and then lift the gear assembly off the upper guard *(above)*.

2 **Cleaning the gear assembly.** Wearing rubber gloves, use a clean cloth to wipe the old grease off the gear assembly and the gear case; clean each component using a small paintbrush dipped in paint thinner *(above)*, being careful not to get any inside the motor housing. If the drive gear or the spindle is damaged, replace the entire gear assembly with an exact duplicate.

3 **Lubricating the gear assembly.** Fill the gear case halfway with clean white grease *(above)* or the manufacturer's specified lubricant. Fit the gear assembly back into the gear case and rotate the spindle to ensure the drive gear is engaged with the worm gear. Screw the gear assembly into place, put back the lower guard *(page 39)* and reinstall the blade *(page 36)*.

SERVICING THE MOTOR AND BEARINGS

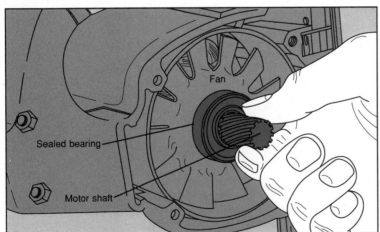

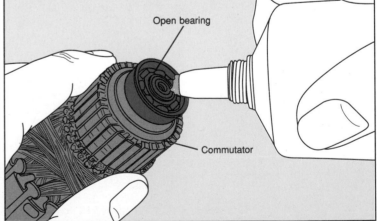

Inspecting the motor and lubricating the bearings. Turn off and unplug the saw, then remove the blade *(page 36)*. Take off the lower guard *(page 38)* and the upper guard *(page 39)*; if the gear case on your model does not come off with the upper guard, also remove it. Carefully remove the brush assemblies *(page 38)*. Pull out the motor shaft *(above, left)*, keeping one hand ready to support the armature. Use an old toothbrush to clean dust off the motor fan and the armature coils. Apply a dab of white grease or the manufacturer's specified lubricant on any open bearing at each end of the motor shaft *(above,* *right)*; on the model shown, only the bearing near the commutator is open and can be lubricated. Then, rotate the bearing at each end of the motor shaft. If a bearing does not turn smoothly, replace it with an exact duplicate; if it cannot be removed, take the armature for professional service. Also inspect the field coil assembly, fastened inside the motor housing. If the motor or windings are darkened, service the motor components *(page 118)*. Put back the motor, the upper and lower guards *(page 39)*, and the brush assemblies *(page 38)*. Reinstall the blade *(page 36)* and check the saw for leaking voltage *(page 113)*.

HEDGE TRIMMERS

With its multi-toothed cutting blade and light motor, a hedge trimmer makes fast work of grooming shrubbery. A typical hedge trimmer *(below)* can cut twigs and branches up to 3/8 inch in diameter. The trigger switch activates the universal motor, turning the drive gear at the base of the blade assembly. The eccentric pin on the drive gear converts the rotating motion to a reciprocal action, pushing the cutting blade back and forth over the stationary blade from 3000 to 4000 times a minute. Twigs and small branches are caught between the two blades and sliced off by the teeth of the cutting blade. Most hedge trimmer malfunctions are caused by misuse. Cutting with a hedge trimmer that is too small for the job or that has a dull cutting blade strains the drive gear and bearings—causing the motor to overheat and eventually burn out.

Proper use and regular maintenance of your hedge trimmer will keep it running smoothly *(page 42)*. Never operate the hedge trimmer in wet or damp conditions. Before each use of your hedge trimmer and when storing it for the season, wipe off the blades with a clean cloth dampened with light machine oil. Keep the cutting blade sharp and file any nicks off the stationary blade *(page 43)*. Inspect the brush assemblies and replace worn brushes *(page 44)*. Periodically inspect the motor and lubricate the bearings *(page 44)*. For the solution to a specific problem, consult the Troubleshooting Guide on page 44. Read Tools & Techniques *(page 110)* for information on using a multitester, on servicing switches, bearings and brush assemblies that differ from the ones shown in this chapter, and on finding replacement parts.

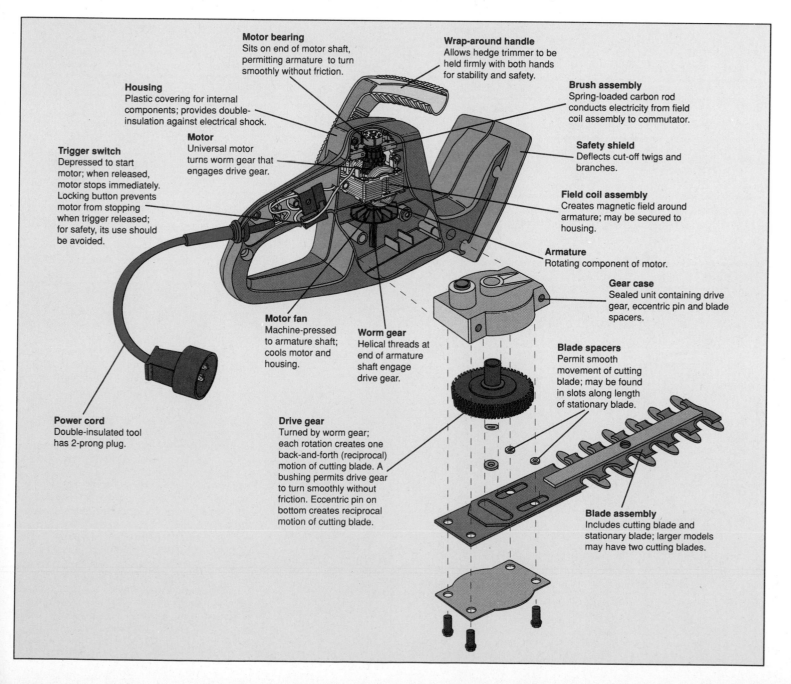

Motor bearing
Sits on end of motor shaft, permitting armature to turn smoothly without friction.

Wrap-around handle
Allows hedge trimmer to be held firmly with both hands for stability and safety.

Brush assembly
Spring-loaded carbon rod conducts electricity from field coil assembly to commutator.

Housing
Plastic covering for internal components; provides double-insulation against electrical shock.

Motor
Universal motor turns worm gear that engages drive gear.

Safety shield
Deflects cut-off twigs and branches.

Trigger switch
Depressed to start motor; when released, motor stops immediately. Locking button prevents motor from stopping when trigger released; for safety, its use should be avoided.

Field coil assembly
Creates magnetic field around armature; may be secured to housing.

Armature
Rotating component of motor.

Gear case
Sealed unit containing drive gear, eccentric pin and blade spacers.

Motor fan
Machine-pressed to armature shaft; cools motor and housing.

Worm gear
Helical threads at end of armature shaft engage drive gear.

Blade spacers
Permit smooth movement of cutting blade; may be found in slots along length of stationary blade.

Power cord
Double-insulated tool has 2-prong plug.

Drive gear
Turned by worm gear; each rotation creates one back-and-forth (reciprocal) motion of cutting blade. A bushing permits drive gear to turn smoothly without friction. Eccentric pin on bottom creates reciprocal motion of cutting blade.

Blade assembly
Includes cutting blade and stationary blade; larger models may have two cutting blades.

TROUBLESHOOTING GUIDE

SYMPTOM	POSSIBLE CAUSE	PROCEDURE
Hedge trimmer does not work at all	No power to outlet or outlet faulty	Reset breaker or replace fuse *(p. 112)* □○; have outlet serviced
	Power cord or extension cord faulty	Service power cord *(p. 115)* ▬○▲; replace extension cord *(p. 115)*
	Plug connection loose at extension cord	Use retainer clip or knot extension and power cords *(below)*
	Trigger switch faulty	Service switch *(p. 43)* ▬○▲
	Brush worn or dislodged	Service brush assemblies *(p. 44)* ▬○
	Motor faulty	Inspect motor *(p. 44)* □○; service motor components *(p. 118)* ▬○▲
Motor hums, but hedge trimmer does not work	Blade jammed by debris or nicks	Unjam blade and file nicks *(p. 43)* □○
	Blade bent or broken; spacer damaged	Service blade assembly *(p. 45)* ▬◑
	Drive gear stripped or gear bushing worn	Service gear assembly *(p. 45)* ▬◑
	Motor faulty or bearing dry	Inspect motor and lubricate bearings *(p. 44)* ▬○; service motor components *(p. 118)* ▬◑▲
Hedge trimmer overheats or power diminished	Extension cord of incorrect size or rating	Replace extension cord *(p. 115)*
	Blade jammed by debris or nicks	Unjam blade and file nicks *(p. 43)* □○
	Brush worn or dislodged	Service brush assemblies *(p. 44)* ▬○
	Motor dirty or faulty or bearing dry	Inspect motor and lubricate bearings *(p. 44)* ▬○; service motor components *(p. 118)* ▬◑▲
Hedge trimmer rattles or vibrates excessively	Housing or blade assembly fastener loose	Tighten housing and blade assembly fasteners
	Drive gear stripped or gear bushing worn	Service gear assembly *(p. 45)* ▬◑
	Motor fan damaged	Inspect motor *(p. 44)* □○; replace if necessary
Blades do not cut cleanly through twigs or branches	Hedge trimmer not powerful enough	Use hedge trimmer with higher rating or hedge shears
	Blade dirty, dull or nicked	Clean and lubricate blades *(below)* □○; service blades *(p. 43)* ▬◑
	Blade bent or broken; spacer damaged	Service blade assembly *(p. 45)* ▬◑

DEGREE OF DIFFICULTY: □ Easy ▬ Moderate ■ Complex
ESTIMATED TIME: ○ Less than 1 hour ◑ 1 to 3 hours ● Over 3 hours
▲ Special tool required

HEDGE TRIMMER USE AND MAINTENANCE

Extension cord

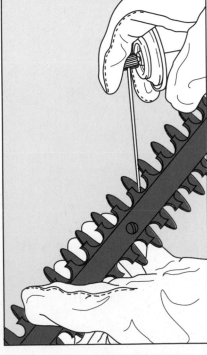

Operating a hedge trimmer. Connect the hedge trimmer power cord to an extension cord rated for outdoor use *(page 115)*; to prevent the cords from pulling apart, knot them loosely together, as shown, or secure them with the manufacturer's retainer clip. Put on safety goggles and work gloves before plugging in the hedge trimmer. To prevent the cord from tangling in hedge branches or wrapping around your legs, keep it to one side of you, away from the cutting action *(far left)*. Grip the hedge trimmer with both hands at all times, keeping your balance and footing. Never overreach.

After each use, or if the blades stick during use, turn off and unplug the hedge trimmer, and place it on a flat surface. Clean off the blades with a damp cloth, then wipe them dry. Apply a small amount of petroleum-based spray lubricant or the manufacturer's specified lubricant on both sides of each blade *(near left)*. Work the lubricant into the blades by plugging in and turning on the hedge trimmer for a few seconds. Store the hedge trimmer in a warm, dry place, away from fertilizers and other chemicals, making sure the trigger switch is not locked on.

SERVICING THE BLADES

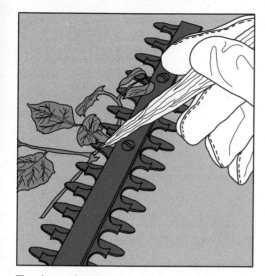

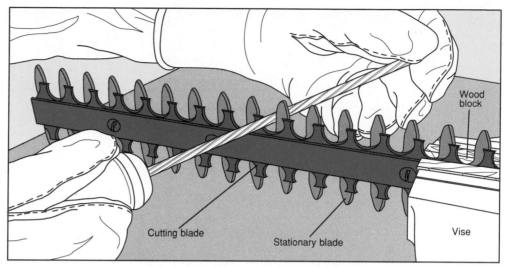

Wood block

Cutting blade

Stationary blade

Vise

Freeing a jammed blade. Turn off and unplug and the hedge trimmer; set it on a flat surface. Wearing work gloves, inspect the blades for jammed twigs or leaves and interfering nicks. Grip the handle with one hand while you use a wedge-shaped piece of wood in the other hand to gently push out any debris *(above)*. Clean and lubricate the blades *(page 42)*. File down any nicks that interfere with the movement of the cutting blade and sharpen the cutting blade *(step right)*, if necessary. If the cutting blade continues to jam, service the gear assembly *(page 45)*.

Sharpening the cutting blade. If the blade is jammed, free it *(step left)*. If a tooth is damaged, service the blade assembly *(page 45)*. To sharpen the cutting blade, use a smooth metal file; a round file works best on curved teeth. Wearing work gloves, start, then stop the hedge trimmer to position the cutting blade with one side of its beveled teeth exposed. Unplug the hedge trimmer and secure it in a vise, using wood blocks to protect the blades. Lay the file against the cutting edge of the first tooth at the original angle of the bevel, usually about 30 degrees. Push the file with strong, even pressure for 4 or 5 strokes across the tooth, without exerting pressure on the return stroke. Knock the file to clean off shavings. Work to the other end of the blade, filing each tooth with the same angle and pressure *(above)*; do not file the teeth of the stationary blade except to remove protrusions caused by nicks. Unclamp, turn over and reclamp the hedge trimmer to file the bottom teeth. Then, unclamp the hedge trimmer, start it, then stop it to position the cutting blade with the other side of its beveled teeth exposed. File each tooth using the same procedure. Then, clean and lubricate the blades *(page 42)*.

SERVICING THE SWITCH

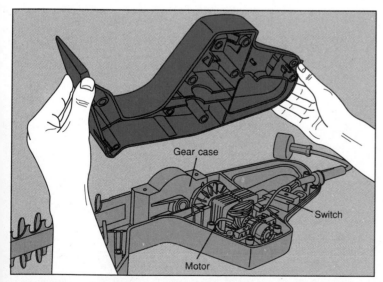

Gear case

Switch

Motor

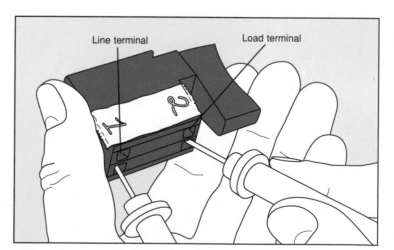

Line terminal

Load terminal

1 **Gaining access to the internal components.** Turn off and unplug the hedge trimmer. Place the hedge trimmer on its side on a flat surface. To gain access to an internal component, you may have to open the entire housing or only the housing for the component. To reach the switch on the model shown, remove all the housing screws, gently separate the housing at the seam, and then lift off the half section *(above)*. Note the placement of wires, gears and other internal components, drawing a diagram, if necessary, for reassembly.

2 **Testing and replacing the switch.** Carefully lift the switch out of the housing; label its wires and their corresponding terminals, then disconnect the wires from the switch. Set a multitester to test for continuity *(page 113)*. Push one tester probe into a line-terminal slot and the other tester probe in turn into each load-terminal slot *(page 117)*, first depressing and then releasing the trigger *(above)*. The tester should show continuity once and only once with the trigger depressed. Push one tester probe into the other line-terminal slot and repeat the test. If the switch tests faulty, replace it with an exact duplicate. Reconnect the switch wires and reposition the switch. Screw the housing back together and check for leaking voltage *(page 113)*.

SERVICING THE BRUSH ASSEMBLIES

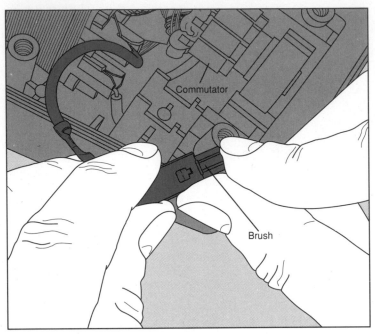

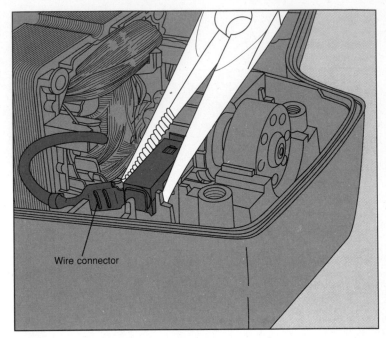

1 **Removing and inspecting the brush assemblies.** Access the internal components *(page 43)* and locate the brush assembly on each side of the commutator. Using long-nosed pliers, carefully lift out each brush assembly—be prepared for a brush that may fly out of its housing. Push each brush once or twice to test its spring *(above).* If the spring is damaged, the housing is cracked, or the brush is pitted, uneven or worn shorter than its width, replace the component in each brush assembly or both entire brush assemblies.

2 **Replacing the brush assemblies.** Always replace the component in each brush assembly or both entire brush assemblies with exact duplicates—even if only one is damaged. On the model shown, the entire brush assemblies must be replaced. To disconnect each brush assembly from its wires, gently pull off the wire connector. Replace the damaged components and reconnect the brush assemblies. Using long-nose pliers, fit each brush assembly into position *(above),* making sure the brush presses firmly against the commutator and matches its curvature. Screw the hedge trimmer housing back together and check for leaking voltage *(page 113).*

SERVICING THE MOTOR

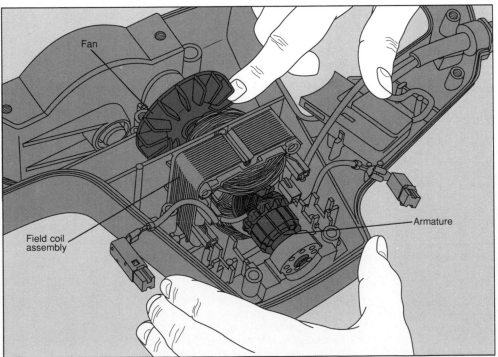

Inspecting the motor and lubricating the bearings. Access the internal components *(page 43)* and remove each brush assembly *(step 1, above).* Replace any damaged wire connection *(page 116).* Gently brush any dust off the motor and its fan with a toothbrush. Keeping clear of the blade assembly, hold the hedge trimmer steady with one hand and turn the fan with the other hand *(left).* The armature should rotate freely inside the field coil assembly, allowing the cutting blade to move smoothly back and forth. If the armature binds, lubricate the bearing at each end of its shaft with 2 or 3 drops of SAE 20 non-detergent machine oil and turn the fan again. If the armature wobbles as it rotates or the blades seize, service the gear and blade assembly *(page 45).* If the motor or windings are darkened, service the motor components *(page 118).* Reinstall each brush assembly *(step 2, above),* screw the hedge trimmer housing back together and check for leaking voltage *(page 113).*

SERVICING THE GEAR AND BLADE ASSEMBLY

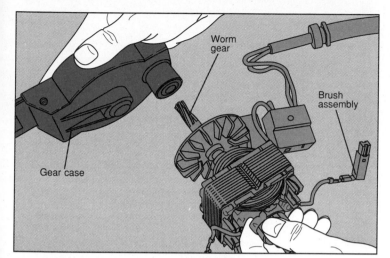

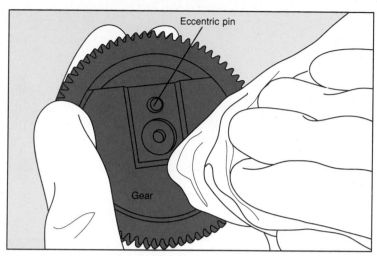

1 **Disassembling the gear case and blade assembly.** Unscrew the gear case from the housing, then turn over the hedge trimmer and access the internal components *(page 43)*. Remove the strap holding the armature in place; then, take out the brush assemblies *(page 44)* and lift out the motor and the blade assembly. Slide the motor out of the gear case *(above)*; place the bearings and washers aside, taking note of their placement and order for reassembly. To access the drive gear, turn over the gear case and the blade assembly and remove the screws holding the bottom plate. Turn the gear case and the blade assembly back over and lift off the gear case; note the position of any gasket or sealant between it and the bottom plate.

2 **Cleaning and lubricating the drive gear.** Lift the drive gear off the blade assembly. Note the location of the washers for reassembly and remove any from the eccentric pin. Wearing rubber gloves, use a clean cloth dipped in paint thinner to wipe off the drive gear *(above)* and the worm gear. If the drive gear is damaged, buy an exact duplicate. Remove the old lubricant from the gear case and wipe it off with the cloth; replace any worn bushing *(step 3)*. Refill the gear case halfway with clean white grease or the manufacturer's specified lubricant, taking care not to put it inside any bushing. Then, check the blade assembly and blade spacers *(step 4)*.

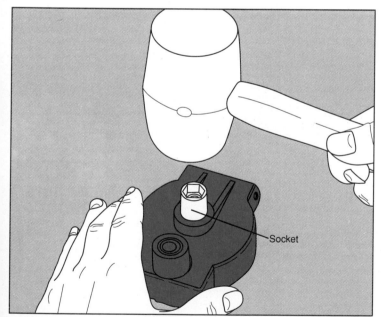

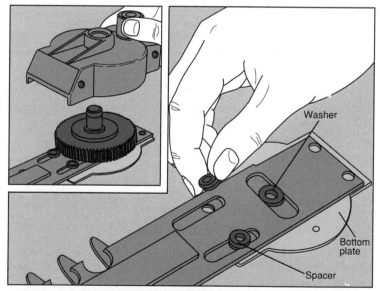

3 **Replacing a bushing.** A worn bushing can prevent a gear from turning properly. If the bushing is not visible from both sides of the gear case, have it removed at a service center. Otherwise, set the gear case on a firm surface. Place an old socket slightly smaller than the bushing outside diameter on top of the bushing. Using a mallet, tap the socket sharply 4 or 5 times to knock out the bushing. Buy a replacement bushing of the same metal and exact diameter to fit the opening. Turn over the gear case and tap the new bushing into place using the socket and mallet. Lubricate the bushing with a few drops of SAE 20 non-detergent machine oil. Refill the gear case halfway with clean white grease or the manufacturer's specified lubricant, taking care not to put it inside any bushing.

4 **Replacing the blade assembly and blade spacers.** Examine the blade spacers and make sure they fit snugly in their slots. (In some models, you must separate the two blades to locate the spacers along the length of the stationary blade.) If the blade assembly or any spacer is damaged, buy an exact duplicate component. Position the blade assembly on the bottom plate; reinstall any gasket or reapply sealant, if necessary. Place each spacer in its slot over its screw hole *(above)*. Put back any washer removed from the eccentric pin and reposition the drive gear on the blade assembly, fitting the eccentric pin into the washer in the slot. Position the gear case on the drive gear and the spacers *(inset)*. Turn over the gear case and blade assembly and screw on the bottom plate. Put back the motor, the brush assemblies *(page 44)* and the strap. Screw the hedge trimmer housing back together, screw the gear case onto it and check for leaking voltage *(page 113)*.

STRING TRIMMERS

A string trimmer is a basic tool to many homeowners for whom well-groomed garden borders are a hallmark. Two string trimmers are shown below: one with a two-cycle engine run on gasoline; one with a universal motor run on electricity. While a gasoline and an electrical string trimmer differ in the way rotating force is produced, each drives a cutting head assembly that holds a spool of string. However innocuous the string, a nylon filament, may seem when stationary, the speed at which it whirls yields a powerful cutting action.

Observe the guidelines for operating a string trimmer in your owner's manual and on page 48. When a problem occurs, consult the Troubleshooting Guide *(below)*. Check the cutting head assembly *(page 49)* before each use of the string trimmer. Before undertaking any repair, turn off the string trimmer and disconnect its spark plug cable or unplug it. Refer to Tools & Techniques *(page 110)* for information on refueling or extension cords, using a multitester and finding replacement parts, as well as for tips on seasonal storage.

TROUBLESHOOTING GUIDE

SYMPTOM	POSSIBLE CAUSE	PROCEDURE
GASOLINE STRING TRIMMERS		
String trimmer does not start	Control set incorrectly	Consult manual to start string trimmer
	Starter cord or rewind spring broken	Service starter assembly *(p. 51)* ▣●
	Fuel contaminated or fuel tank empty	Drain fuel tank *(p. 48)* □○; refuel string trimmer *(p. 121)* □○
	Spark plug faulty or cable disconnected	Connect cable *(p. 48)* □○; service spark plug *(p. 123)* □○
	Fuel line or fuel filter dirty or damaged	Service fuel line and fuel filter *(p. 53)* □○
	Switch faulty	Service switch *(p. 50)* □○▲
	Carburetor adjusted incorrectly or faulty	Consult manual to adjust carburetor; take string trimmer for service
	Muffler clogged	Service muffler *(p. 55)* □○
	EIM gapped incorrectly or faulty	Service EIM *(p. 54)* ▣○▲
	Engine faulty	Take string trimmer for service
String trimmer starts, but power diminished; or, runs erratically or stalls	Fuel tank cap vents blocked	Clear vents with toothpick
	Air filter dirty	Service air filter *(p. 52)* □○
	Fuel contaminated	Drain fuel tank *(p. 48)* □○ and refuel string trimmer *(p. 121)* □○
	Fuel line or fuel filter dirty or damaged	Service fuel line and fuel filter *(p. 53)* □○
	Carburetor adjusted incorrectly or faulty	Consult manual to adjust carburetor; take string trimmer for service
	Throttle assembly faulty	Service throttle assembly *(p. 53)* ▣●
	Muffler clogged	Service muffler *(p. 55)* □○
	Engine faulty	Take string trimmer for service
String trimmer overheats	Engine cooling fins dirty or muffler clogged	Service engine cooling fins and muffler *(p. 55)* □○
	Air filter dirty	Service air filter *(p. 52)* □○
	Fuel contaminated	Drain fuel tank *(p. 48)* □○ and refuel string trimmer *(p. 121)* □○
	Gear assembly dry	Service gear assembly *(p. 52)* □○▲
	Engine faulty	Take string trimmer for service
String trimmer does not cut	Cutting head assembly empty or damaged	Service cutting head assembly *(p. 49)* □○
ELECTRICAL STRING TRIMMERS		
String trimmer does not work at all	No power to outlet or outlet faulty	Reset breaker or replace fuse *(p. 112)*; have outlet serviced
	Power cord or extension cord faulty	Service power cord *(p. 115)* ▣○▲; replace extension cord *(p. 115)*
	Trigger switch faulty	Service switch *(p. 50)* □○▲
	Brush worn or motor faulty	Inspect brushes and motor *(p. 50)* □○
String trimmer overheats or power diminished	Extension cord of incorrect size or rating	Replace extension cord *(p. 115)*
	Brush worn or motor faulty	Inspect brushes and motor *(p. 50)* □○
String trimmer does not cut	Cutting head assembly empty or damaged	Service cutting head assembly *(p. 49)* □○

DEGREE OF DIFFICULTY: □ Easy ▣ Moderate ■ Complex
ESTIMATED TIME: ○ Less than 1 hour ● 1 to 3 hours ● Over 3 hours
▲ Special tool required

ELECTRICAL STRING TRIMMER

Trigger switch
Depressed to start motor; when released, motor stops immediately.

Handle
Adjusted to height of operator.

Extension tube
Hollow tube carries wires from plug and trigger switch to motor.

Motor
Universal motor turns worm gear that engages drive gear; on model shown, motor riveted in place and enveloped in rubber sleeve.

Power cord
Double-insulated tool has 2-prong cord.

Upper housing

Cutting head assembly
Rotating drum contains spool, cone and driver; string emerges from eyelet in drum. Spool whirls string wound around it; typically, more string released when spool hub tapped on ground.

GASOLINE STRING TRIMMER

Gear case
Gear assembly transfers rotating force from drive shaft to cutting head assembly.

Shield

Deflector
Protects operator from contact with string and blocks flying grass and debris.

Deflector
Protects operator from contact with string and blocks flying grass.

Drum
Rotating drum of cutting head assembly contains spool, cone and driver; string emerges from eyelet in drum.

Handle
Adjusted to height of operator.

Throttle assembly
Meters fuel into carburetor; linked to throttle trigger by throttle cable.

Spark plug
Screwed into combustion chamber of engine; ignites fuel by creating spark from electrical current carried through spark plug cable.

Engine housing

Control unit housing

Cooling fin
Increases engine surface area, helping to cool it.

Spool
Whirls string wound around it; typically, more string released when spool hub tapped on ground.

Extension tube
Hollow tube protects drive shaft.

Spark plug cable
Carries electrical current from EIM to spark plug.

Switch

Grip

Muffler
Reduces noise and directs fumes out of engine cylinder.

Throttle trigger
Regulates flow of fuel and air to carburetor.

Flywheel
Rotation creates magnetic field transformed by electronic ignition module (EIM) into electrical current; on model shown, EIM next to flywheel and trigger module in bracket on fuel tank.

Carburetor
Provides engine with fuel and air in vaporized form; diaphragm type shown. Fuel filter on fuel line inside fuel tank prevents fuel impurities from entering carburetor.

Primer bulb

Fuel tank

Air filter
Prevents air impurities from entering carburetor.

Air filter housing

Fuel drain tube
Overflow tube connected to carburetor drains off excess fuel.

Starter assembly housing
When handle pulled, starter cord turns flywheel; rewind spring retracts starter cord when handle released.

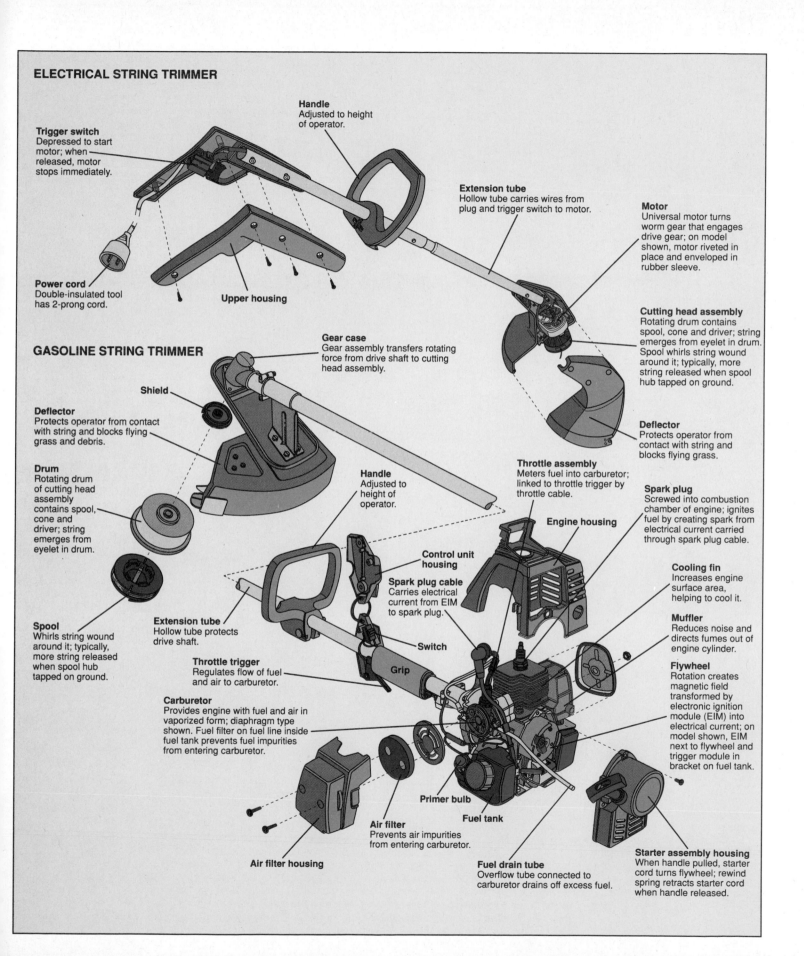

STRING TRIMMER USE AND MAINTENANCE

Harness

Extension
cord

Operating a string trimmer. When using a string trimmer, wear work gloves, safety goggles, close-fitting clothes and sturdy boots, and tie back any long hair; with a gasoline string trimmer, also wear head and ear protection. Before starting the string trimmer, remove obstructions from the work area. Clean clippings and dirt off the deflector with a stiff brush or a stick. Service the cutting head assembly *(page 49)*.

With a gasoline string trimmer, add fuel to the fuel tank at least 10 feet away from the lawn *(page 121)*. Connect the spark plug cable *(step below, left)* and start the string trimmer according to the manufacturer's instructions. While using the string trimmer, keep it clipped to any harness provided with it *(far left)*. With an electrical string trimmer *(near left)*, use only an extension cord rated for outdoor use *(page 115)*; knot it loosely to the power cord, as shown, or fit it into the retaining clip before plugging it in. Always hold the string trimmer firmly by the handles. Never overreach or turn the string trimmer sideways. Use a broad, sweeping motion, moving from a trimmed area into an untrimmed area; if the untrimmed area is thick and high, trim it in stages to the desired height.

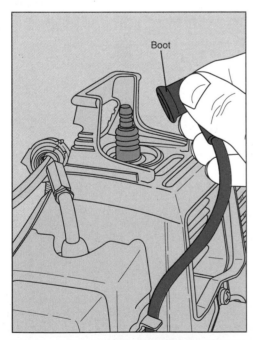

Boot

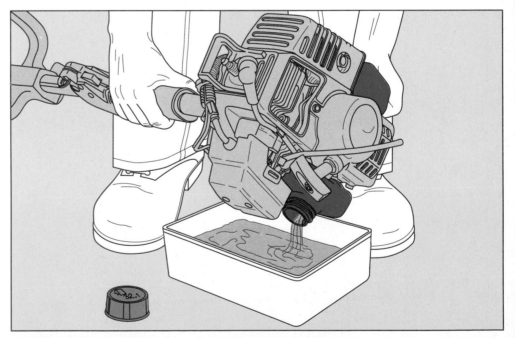

Disconnecting and reconnecting the spark plug cable. After using and before servicing a gasoline string trimmer, turn it off and move it to a level surface. Grasp the spark plug cable by the boot and pull it off the spark plug *(above)*; set the boot well away from the spark plug. If necessary, service the spark plug *(page 123)*. To reconnect the spark plug cable, fit the boot back onto the spark plug.

Emptying the fuel tank. For safety, drain the fuel from the string trimmer before repairing it or storing it for the season. Turn off the string trimmer and disconnect the spark plug cable *(step left)*. Allow the string trimmer to cool for at least 15 minutes. Move the string trimmer outdoors at least 10 feet away from the work area. Position a metal container on a flat surface. Unscrew the fuel tank cap and set it to one side. Holding the string trimmer engine firmly with both hands, tilt it slowly onto its side to pour the fuel into the container *(above)*. Then, screw the cap back onto the fuel tank, wipe up any spill and dispose of the fuel safely *(page 11)*; do not reuse drained fuel. Staying outdoors, move the string trimmer at least 10 feet away from the draining site. Reconnect the spark plug cable *(step left)* and start the string trimmer. Allow the string trimmer to run until it uses up any remaining fuel; then, turn it off and disconnect the spark plug cable again.

SERVICING THE CUTTING HEAD ASSEMBLY

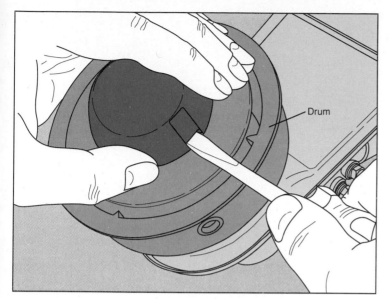

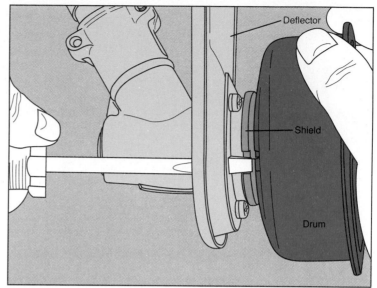

1 **Removing the spool.** Turn off the string trimmer and disconnect its spark plug cable *(page 48)* or unplug it. To remove the spool, fit an old screwdriver into the slot and twist gently *(above)*; on some models, there may be tabs or a screw. Lift the spool and any remaining string out of the drum. If the spool is damaged, buy an exact duplicate with string wound onto it. If the spool is empty or contains only a little string, buy replacement string specified by the manufacturer. If the head assembly is cracked, nicked or otherwise damaged, remove the drum and disassemble it *(step 2)*. Otherwise, install the string and the spool *(step 4)*.

2 **Removing and disassembling the drum.** On a gasoline string trimmer, fit an old screwdriver through the opening in the deflector and into the notch in the shield, as shown, to lock the shaft. To remove the drum, turn it by hand *(above)*; on the model shown, clockwise. To disassemble the drum, wear work gloves and safety goggles to turn the cone by hand and remove it along with the driver from the drum; on the model shown, also clockwise. Be prepared for the spring to fly out of the drum. On an electrical string trimmer, use the same procedure in the reverse sequence, first disassembling the drum, then removing it by pulling it off.

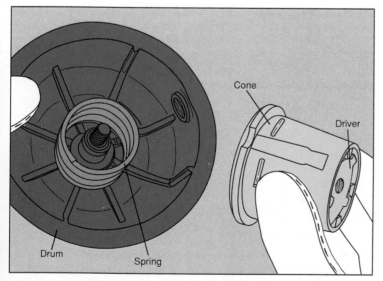

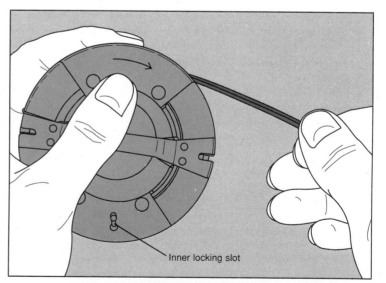

3 **Reassembling and installing the drum.** If the drum, the spring, the cone or the driver is damaged, replace it with an exact duplicate. Wearing work gloves and safety goggles, reassemble the drum, reversing the disassembly sequence used. On a gasoline string trimmer, install the spring in the drum and fit the driver into the cone. Position the cone along with the driver on the drum *(above)* and turn in the opposite direction used to remove them. Then, install the drum, turning in the opposite direction used to remove it. On an electrical string trimmer, use the same procedure in the reverse sequence, first installing the drum, then reassembling it.

4 **Installing the string and the spool.** To wind new string onto the spool, remove any old string. Fit one end of the new string into the inner locking slot on the spool, ensuring it protrudes no more than 1/8 inch; on a model with two strings, fit each string into the inner locking slot on the spool, as shown. Wind the string onto the spool in the direction of the arrow stamped on it *(above)*; if there are two strings, avoid crossing them. To install the spool, thread each string through its eyelet in the drum, then position the spool in the drum and turn it until it snaps into place. Reconnect the spark plug cable *(page 48)* or plug in the string trimmer.

SERVICING THE SWITCH

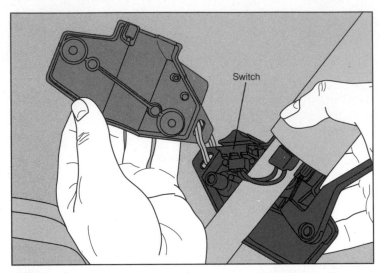

1 **Removing the switch.** Turn off the string trimmer, then disconnect its spark plug cable and drain its fuel tank *(page 48)* or unplug it. To reach the switch, remove the screws from its housing, gently separate the housing at the seam, and then lift off the half section *(above)*; on a gasoline string trimmer, as shown, the switch is in the control unit housing. Note the placement of the switch and other internal components, drawing a diagram, if necessary, for reassembly. Carefully lift the switch out of the housing; label its wires and their corresponding terminals, then disconnect the wires from the switch.

2 **Testing the switch.** Set a multitester to test for continuity *(page 113)*. Push one tester probe into a line-terminal slot *(page 117)* and the other tester probe in turn into each load-terminal slot *(above)*, setting the switch first in one position, then in the other position; if necessary, clip a sewing needle to each probe, as shown. The tester should show continuity once and only once. If there is another line-terminal slot, push the tester probe into it and repeat the test. If the switch tests faulty, replace it with an exact duplicate. Reconnect the wires, install the switch and screw the housing back together. Refuel the string trimmer *(page 121)* and reconnect the spark plug cable *(page 48)* or check for leaking voltage *(page 113)* and plug in the string trimmer.

SERVICING THE INTERNAL COMPONENTS (Electrical string trimmer)

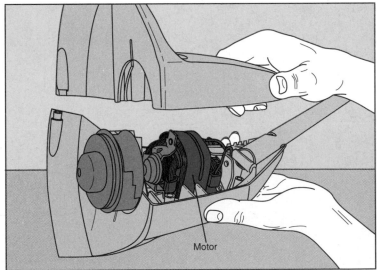

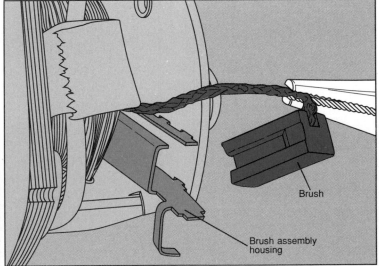

Inspecting the brushes and the motor. Turn off the string trimmer and unplug it. To reach the internal components, remove the screws from the motor housing, gently separate the housing at the seam, and then lift off the half section *(above, left)*. Note the placement of wires and other internal components, drawing a diagram, if necessary, for reassembly. Locate the brush assembly on each side of the commutator and inspect it. Using long-nose pliers, pry up the tabs on the brush assembly housing and lift out the brush *(above, right)*—be prepared for the spring to fly out. If the brush is pitted, uneven or worn shorter than

its width, replace both brushes; if the brushes cannot be removed, as in the model shown, take the string trimmer for professional service. Otherwise, press each brush into place, ensuring it matches the curvature of the commutator, and push back its tabs. Gently brush any dust off the motor and its fan with a toothbrush. If the motor or windings are darkened, service the motor components *(page 118)*; if the motor cannot be removed, as in the model shown, take the string trimmer for professional service. Screw the motor housing back together, check for leaking voltage *(page 113)* and plug in the string trimmer.

SERVICING THE STARTER ASSEMBLY (Gasoline string trimmer)

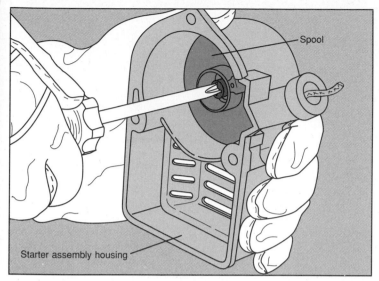

Spool

Starter assembly housing

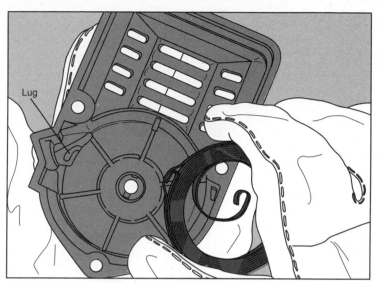

Lug

1 Removing the starter assembly. Turn off the string trimmer, disconnect the spark plug cable and drain the fuel tank *(page 48)*. Unscrew the starter assembly housing and lift it off the engine; the starter assembly is secured inside it. Pull the starter cord out of the handle, untie or cut off its knot and allow it to rewind slowly, releasing tension on the rewind spring. Wearing work gloves and safety goggles, unscrew the spool *(above)*, take off the washer and carefully lift the spool out of the starter assembly housing—be prepared for the rewind spring to uncoil and pop out. If the rewind spring is not damaged, leave it in place and replace the starter cord *(step 3)*.

2 Replacing the rewind spring. Replace any rewind spring that is damaged or uncoils and pops out of the starter assembly housing. Wearing work gloves and safety goggles, unhook the rewind spring from the lug with long-nose pliers and lift it out of the starter assembly housing. Buy an exact duplicate rewind spring; a new rewind spring usually comes coiled and bound with a wire or string. Position the rewind spring in the starter assembly housing *(above)* and hook its outside end to the lug. Lubricate the rewind spring with a few drops of light machine oil or the manufacturer's specified lubricant. Then, holding the rewind spring in place, cut the wire or string binding it.

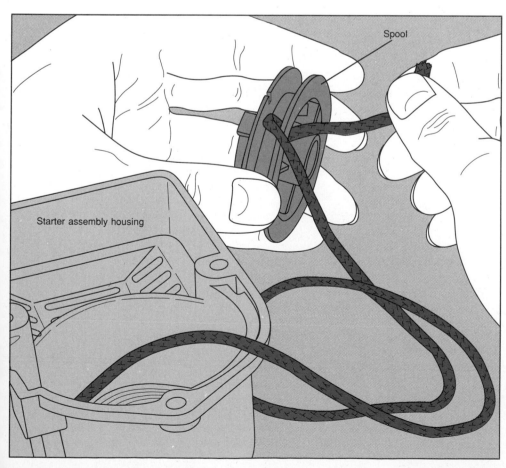

Spool

Starter assembly housing

3 Replacing the starter cord. If the starter cord is damaged, unwind it from the spool, cutting off or freeing the knot at the end of it; replace the starter cord with an exact duplicate. Thread one end of the starter cord through the opening in the starter assembly housing and the opening in the handle, then knot it. Cauterize the knot by holding a flame under it without touching it. Thread the other end of the starter cord through the opening in the spool *(left)*, knot it and cauterize the knot. Fit the knot into the spool and wind all but the last 6 inches of the starter cord clockwise around the spool.

Position the spool in the starter assembly housing, fitting the starter cord into the slot on the spool to hold it. Turn the spool back and forth until it is seated, then reinstall the washer and screw in the spool. Holding the end of the wound starter cord against the spool, rotate the spool counterclockwise 1 or 2 turns. Hold the spool and pull the handle to straighten the unwound starter cord. Then, holding the handle, release the spool and let the unwound starter cord wind slowly onto it. If the handle droops, repeat the procedure, rotating the spool 1 extra turn. If the spool cannot be rotated counterclockwise at least 2 full turns when the starter cord is extended, repeat the procedure, rotating the spool 1 less turn. Otherwise, reinstall the starter assembly housing. Refuel the string trimmer *(page 121)* and reconnect the spark plug cable *(page 48)*.

SERVICING THE GEAR ASSEMBLY (Gasoline string trimmer)

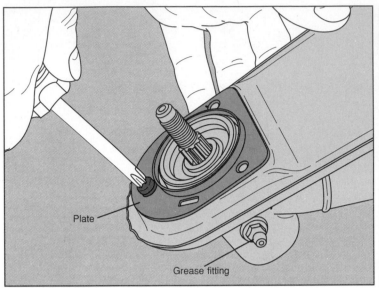

Plate

Grease fitting

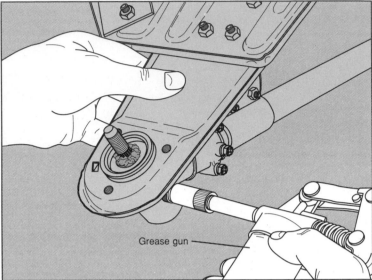

Grease gun

Cleaning and lubricating the gear assembly. Clean and lubricate the gear assembly after each 40 hours of use and when recommended in the owner's manual. Turn off the string trimmer and disconnect the spark plug cable *(page 48)*. Remove the drum of the cutting head assembly *(page 49)*. Lift off the shield and any spacer, then unscrew the plate *(above, left)*, take off its washers and lift it off the deflector. Wearing rubber gloves, clean off the shield, the plate and the deflector around the shaft with a cloth dipped in paint thinner.

To lubricate the gears, use a special grease gun. Load a cylinder of the grease specified by the manufacturer into the gun. Press the gun nozzle firmly onto the grease fitting of the gear case and squeeze the gun trigger *(above, right)*, injecting grease into the gear case. Continue injecting grease until it emerges around the shaft. Then, position the plate on the deflector, put back its washers and screw it in place. Reinstall any spacer removed, the shield and then the drum of the cutting head assembly. Reconnect the spark plug cable *(page 48)*.

SERVICING THE AIR FILTER (Gasoline string trimmer)

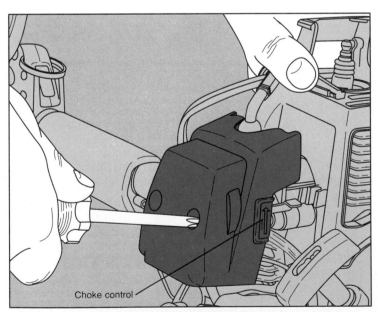

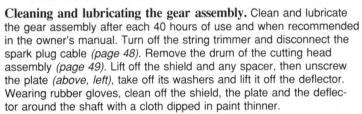

Choke control

Air filter

Grid

1 **Removing the air filter.** Turn off the string trimmer and disconnect the spark plug cable *(page 48)*. Set the choke control to its fully closed position; on the model shown, in the direction of the arrow. Unscrew the air filter housing *(above)* and lift it off the carburetor. Take any screen, the grid and the air filter out of the air filter housing, noting their placement and order for reassembly. If the air filter, the grid or any screen is damaged, replace it with an exact duplicate.

2 **Cleaning the air filter.** Wearing rubber gloves, wash the air filter and the grid in a solution of mild household detergent and water; clean any screen using paint thinner. Rinse off the air filter and the grid, then let them dry thoroughly; if the air filter is of felt, wear safety goggles and blow compressed air through it. If the air filter is of sponge, wrap a clean cloth around it and squeeze out excess moisture, then apply 1 teaspoon of SAE 30 oil *(above)* and squeeze it to distribute the oil. Install the air filter, the grid and any screen, then screw on the air filter housing. Reconnect the spark plug cable *(page 48)*.

SERVICING THE FUEL LINE AND FUEL FILTER (Gasoline string trimmer)

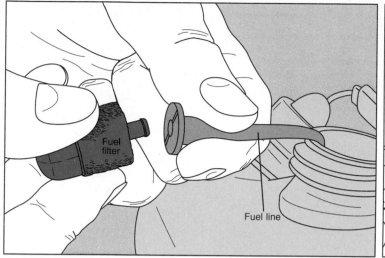

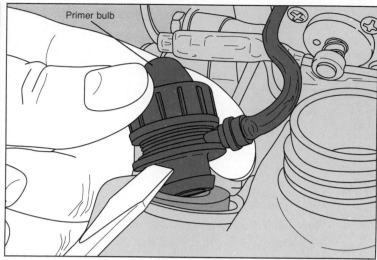

Cleaning and replacing the fuel line and fuel filter. Turn off the string trimmer, disconnect the spark plug cable and drain the fuel tank *(page 48)*. Shape a stiff wire into a hook. take the cap off the fuel tank and fish out the fuel filter. Pull the fuel filter off the fuel line *(above, left)*; to avoid dropping the fuel line, bend the wire around it and across the opening of the fuel tank, if necessary. Pull the fuel line off the carburetor. If there is a primer bulb, as in the model shown, use an old screwdriver to pry it off the fuel tank *(above, right)*; pull the portion of the fuel line off it. To clean the fuel filter and fuel line, wear safety goggles and use compressed air.

If the fuel filter, the fuel line or the primer bulb is damaged, replace it with an exact duplicate; use a flashlight to check the portion of the fuel line inside the fuel tank, if necessary. To replace the portion of the fuel line inside the fuel tank, pry it out of its opening; push the new fuel line into place and fish out the end of it using the wire. Install the fuel filter, drop it into the fuel tank and screw on the cap; then, connect the fuel line to the carburetor. If there is a primer bulb, connect the fuel line to it and install it. Refuel the string trimmer *(page 121)* and reconnect the spark plug cable *(page 48)*.

SERVICING THE THROTTLE ASSEMBLY (Gasoline string trimmer)

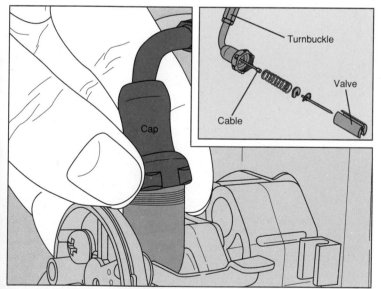

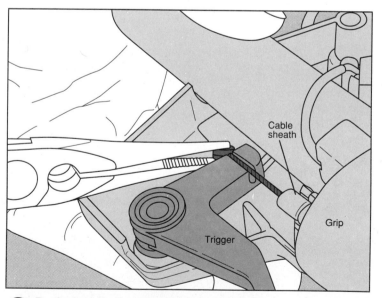

1 **Removing the throttle cable.** Turn off the string trimmer, disconnect the spark plug cable and drain the fuel tank *(page 48)*. Remove the air filter housing, then unscrew the cap *(above)* and lift the throttle assembly off the carburetor. Push the valve toward the cap to free the cable; note the placement and order of each part *(inset)*, drawing a diagram. If the throttle assembly is clogged with dirt, suspect a faulty carburetor and take the string trimmer for professional service; if a part is damaged, buy an exact duplicate. To reach the other end of the cable, unscrew the control unit housing, separate it and lift off the half section. Using long-nose pliers, free the cable from the trigger and pull it out by its sheath, noting its route.

2 **Replacing the throttle cable.** Buy an exact duplicate cable and work from the trigger to feed it through the grip and the casing to the carburetor. Use long-nose pliers to hook the cable onto the trigger *(above)*, then screw the control unit housing back together. Feed the cable through the turnbuckle and use your diagram to put the throttle assembly together, pushing the valve toward the cap to hook the cable onto it. Position the throttle assembly on the carburetor and screw on the cap. Refuel the string trimmer *(page 121)* and reconnect the spark plug cable *(page 48)*. Adjust the carburetor as instructed in the owner's manual, then reinstall the air filter housing.

SERVICING THE ELECTRONIC IGNITION MODULE (EIM) (Gasoline string trimmer)

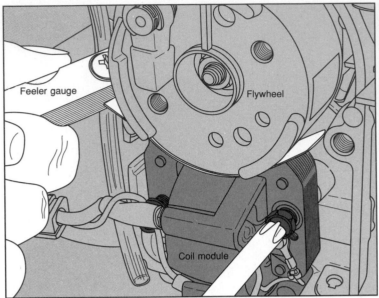

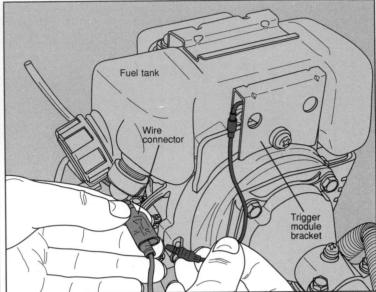

1 **Gapping the coil module.** Turn off the string trimmer, disconnect the spark plug cable and drain the fuel tank *(page 48)*. Remove the starter assembly housing, locate the EIM and identify it *(page 121)*. To gap the coil module, use a brass or plastic feeler gauge that matches the gap specified by the manufacturer. Rotate the flywheel until its magnets are as far as possible from the coil module. Loosen the coil module screws and slide the coil module enough to fit the feeler gauge horizontally between it and the flywheel. Rotate the flywheel until its magnets are aligned with the coil module. Then, tighten the coil module

screws *(above, left)* and pull out the feeler gauge. Reinstall the starter assembly housing, refuel the string trimmer *(page 121)* and reconnect the spark plug cable *(page 48)*.

If the problem persists, access the EIM again to replace the trigger module and the coil module. Trace the wire connected to the trigger module to its other end and disconnect it *(above, right)*, noting its terminal; then, unscrew the trigger module and remove it from its bracket. Use the same procedure to disconnect the wire connected to the coil module, then remove the coil module.

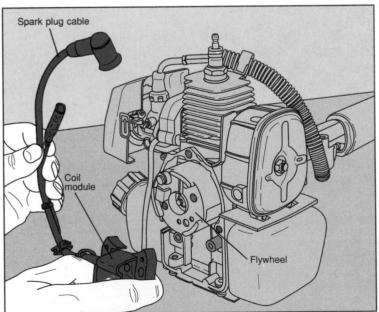

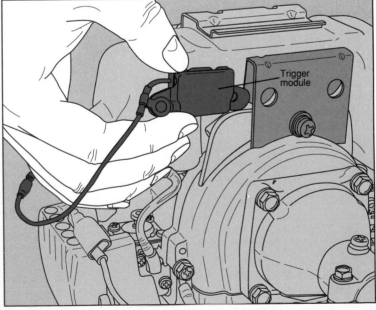

2 **Replacing the coil assembly and the trigger module.** Buy an exact duplicate coil module and trigger module. Position the coil module next to the flywheel *(above, left)* and screw it loosely in place. Route the wire connected to the coil module and connect the end of it. Then, position the trigger module in the bracket on the fuel tank *(above, right)* and screw it in place. Route the wire connected to the trigger module and connect the end of it. Gap the coil module *(step 1)*. Then, reinstall the starter assembly housing, refuel the string trimmer *(page 121)* and reconnect the spark plug cable *(page 48)*.

SERVICING THE ENGINE COOLING FINS (Gasoline string trimmer)

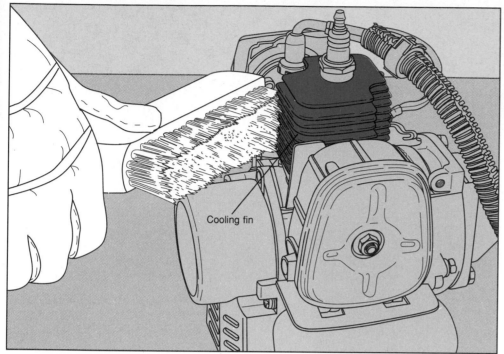

Cooling fin

Cleaning the engine cooling fins. Turn off the string trimmer and disconnect the spark plug cable *(page 48)*. Allow the engine to cool for at least 15 minutes, then wear work gloves to unscrew and take off the engine housing. Use a wire brush to clean dirt, clumps of grass clippings and carbon deposits off the engine cooling fins *(left)*. To clean off any stubborn carbon deposits, first apply a small amount of decarbonizing spray and then scrub with the brush. Reposition the engine housing and screw it back in place, then reconnect the spark plug cable *(page 48)*.

SERVICING THE MUFFLER

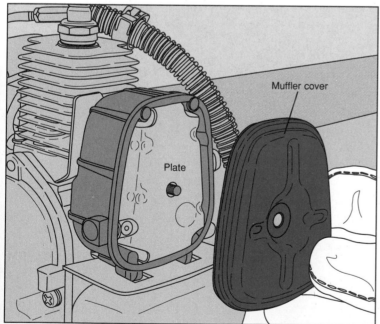

Muffler cover

Plate

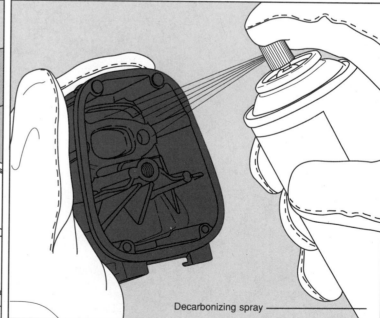

Decarbonizing spray

Cleaning and replacing the muffler. Turn off the string trimmer, disconnect the spark plug cable and drain the fuel tank *(page 48)*. Wearing work gloves, unscrew and take off the engine housing. Remove the nut from the muffler cover, take off any washer and pull off the muffler cover *(above, left)*; remove any gasket between it and the muffler. Lift the plate along with any spark arrester out of the muffler. Then, remove each nut holding the muffler to the engine, take off any washers and pull off the muffler; remove the gasket between it and the engine. For reassembly, buy an exact duplicate gasket to replace each gasket you removed; never reinstall a used gasket.

Clean dirt, clumps of grass clippings and carbon deposits off the muffler, the plate, any spark arrester and the muffler cover using a wire brush; to clean off any stubborn carbon deposits, first apply a small amount of decarbonizing spray *(above, right)*. If any part of the muffler is damaged, replace it with an exact duplicate. Position the gasket and the muffler, put back any washers and reinstall the nuts. Install any spark arrester along with the plate, position any gasket and the muffler cover, then put back any washer and the nut. Reinstall the engine housing, refuel the string trimmer *(page 121)* and reconnect the spark plug cable *(page 48)*.

CHAIN SAWS

The powerful chain saw can save hours of strenuous log chopping and tree felling; a typical one is shown below. Driven by a two-cycle engine on a fuel mixture of gasoline and oil, the chain saw can be operated at any angle without the engine flooding—thanks to its carburetor. When the engine is started, the rotation of the drive shaft forces the clutch shoes against the clutch drum, turning it and the drive sprocket. The drive sprocket engages the chain, which moves along the guide bar, and turns the gears of the oil pump, which routes lubricating oil to the chain. The chain cutters provide the cutting action and depth; its drive links support it in the guide bar and help to clean the groove.

A hazard of chain saws is kickback, the sudden forcing of the guide bar back toward the operator—which can occur if its nose touches an object or the chain is pinched while cutting. Read your owner's manual to familiarize yourself with the use and maintenance needs of your chain saw; if any safety feature is not functioning, take it for professional service. To help you in solving a chain saw problem, consult the Troubleshooting Guide (*page 57*). Before beginning any repair, disconnect the spark plug cable (*page 58*) and, whenever instructed, drain the fuel tank (*page 60*). Refer to Tools & Techniques (*page 110*) for information on refueling and the diagnosis of spark plugs, as well as for tips on seasonal storage.

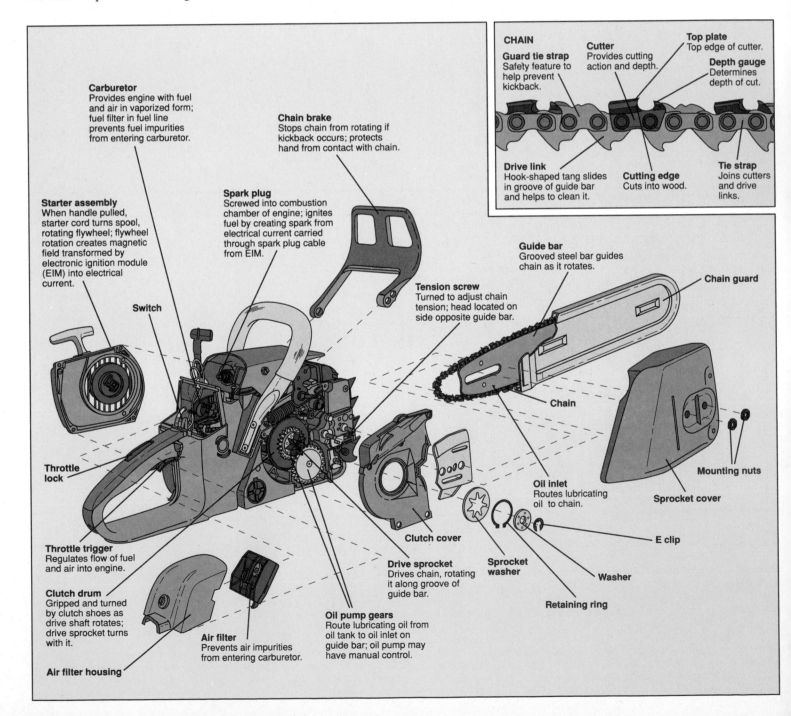

CHAIN

Guard tie strap
Safety feature to help prevent kickback.

Cutter
Provides cutting action and depth.

Top plate
Top edge of cutter.

Depth gauge
Determines depth of cut.

Drive link
Hook-shaped tang slides in groove of guide bar and helps to clean it.

Cutting edge
Cuts into wood.

Tie strap
Joins cutters and drive links.

Carburetor
Provides engine with fuel and air in vaporized form; fuel filter in fuel line prevents fuel impurities from entering carburetor.

Chain brake
Stops chain from rotating if kickback occurs; protects hand from contact with chain.

Starter assembly
When handle pulled, starter cord turns spool, rotating flywheel; flywheel rotation creates magnetic field transformed by electronic ignition module (EIM) into electrical current.

Spark plug
Screwed into combustion chamber of engine; ignites fuel by creating spark from electrical current carried through spark plug cable from EIM.

Guide bar
Grooved steel bar guides chain as it rotates.

Chain guard

Tension screw
Turned to adjust chain tension; head located on side opposite guide bar.

Switch

Chain

Throttle lock

Oil inlet
Routes lubricating oil to chain.

Mounting nuts

Sprocket cover

Throttle trigger
Regulates flow of fuel and air into engine.

Clutch cover

E clip

Drive sprocket
Drives chain, rotating it along groove of guide bar.

Sprocket washer

Washer

Clutch drum
Gripped and turned by clutch shoes as drive shaft rotates; drive sprocket turns with it.

Air filter
Prevents air impurities from entering carburetor.

Oil pump gears
Route lubricating oil from oil tank to oil inlet on guide bar; oil pump may have manual control.

Retaining ring

Air filter housing

TROUBLESHOOTING GUIDE

SYMPTOM	POSSIBLE CAUSE	PROCEDURE
Chain saw does not start	Switch control or chain brake set incorrectly	Consult manual to start chain saw
	Starter cord or rewind spring broken	Service starter assembly (p. 66) ▪●
	Fuel contaminated or fuel tank empty	Drain fuel tank (p. 60) □○; refuel chain saw (p. 121) □○
	Spark plug faulty or cable disconnected	Service spark plug (p. 58) □○
	Fuel line or fuel filter dirty or damaged	Service fuel line and fuel filter (p. 64) ▪●
	Switch faulty	Service switch (p. 65) □○▲
	Carburetor adjusted incorrectly or faulty	Consult manual to adjust carburetor; service carburetor (p. 63) ▪●
	Muffler clogged	Service muffler (p. 67) □○
	EIM gapped incorrectly or faulty	Service EIM (p. 67) ▪○▲
	Engine faulty	Take chain saw for professional service
Chain saw starts, but power diminished	Fuel tank cap vents blocked	Clear vents with toothpick
	Air filter dirty	Service air filter (p. 59) □○
	Fuel contaminated or mixed incorrectly	Drain fuel tank (p. 60) □○ and refuel chain saw (p. 121) □○
	Fuel line or fuel filter dirty or damaged	Service fuel line and fuel filter (p. 64) ▪●
	Carburetor adjusted incorrectly or faulty	Consult manual to adjust carburetor; service carburetor (p. 63) ▪●
	Muffler clogged	Service muffler (p. 67) □○
	EIM gapped incorrectly or faulty	Service EIM (p. 67) ▪○▲
	Engine faulty	Take chain saw for professional service
Chain saw runs erratically or stalls	Fuel tank cap vents blocked	Clear vents with toothpick
	Air filter dirty	Service air filter (p. 59) □○
	Fuel contaminated or mixed incorrectly	Drain fuel tank (p. 60) □○ and refuel chain saw (p. 121) □○
	Chain tension adjusted incorrectly	Adjust chain tension (p. 59) □○
	Fuel line or fuel filter dirty or damaged	Service fuel line and fuel filter (p. 64) ▪●
	Carburetor adjusted incorrectly or faulty	Consult manual to adjust carburetor; service carburetor (p. 63) ▪●
	Muffler clogged	Service muffler (p. 67) □○
	Engine faulty	Take chain saw for professional service
Chain saw overheats	Engine cooling fins dirty	Remove engine cover and clean engine cooling fins with wire brush
	Air filter dirty	Clean or replace air filter (p. 59) □○
	Fuel contaminated or mixed incorrectly	Drain fuel tank (p. 60) □○ and refuel chain saw (p. 121) □○
	Muffler clogged	Service muffler (p. 67) □○
	Oil pump faulty	Take chain saw for professional service
Chain saw rattles or vibrates excessively	Housing fastener loose	Tighten housing fasteners
	Chain tension adjusted incorrectly	Adjust chain tension (p. 59) □○
	Drive sprocket or clutch assembly faulty	Service drive sprocket and clutch assembly (p. 62) ▪●
	Muffler clogged	Service muffler (p. 67) □○
	Engine faulty	Take chain saw for professional service
Chain cuts slowly or unevenly	Chain tension adjusted incorrectly	Adjust chain tension (p. 59) □○
	Chain dull; guide bar or chain dirty or faulty	Sharpen chain (p. 60) ▪●▲; service guide bar and chain (p. 61) ▪○
	Drive sprocket or clutch assembly faulty	Service drive sprocket and clutch assembly (p. 62) ▪●
	Oil pump faulty	Take chain saw for professional service
Chain turns when engine idles	Carburetor adjusted incorrectly	Consult manual to adjust carburetor
	Drive sprocket or clutch assembly faulty	Service drive sprocket and clutch assembly (p. 62) ▪●
Chain saw runs when turned off	Switch faulty	Service switch (p. 65) ▪○

DEGREE OF DIFFICULTY: □ Easy ▪ Moderate ■ Complex

ESTIMATED TIME: ○ Less than 1 hour ● 1 to 3 hours ● Over 3 hours

▲ Special tool required

CHAIN SAW USE AND MAINTENANCE

Guide bar

Operating a chain saw. Professional training is necessary to use a chain saw safely; also ensure you study the owner's manual. When using the chain saw, wear work gloves, safety goggles, work boots, a hard hat, and hearing protection. Make sure your clothes are close-fitting and any long hair is tied back. Operate the chain saw only outdoors on a dry, clear day.

Mix fuel and add it to the fuel tank at least 10 feet away from the work area *(page 121)*; also make sure the oil tank is filled. Service the air filter and adjust the chain tension *(page 59)*. To start the chain saw, carry it to the work area and place it on the ground; make sure the chain is not contacting anything. Following the manufacturer's instructions, connect the spark plug cable *(step 1, below)* and set the switch control. Brace the chain saw with your foot and one hand, as shown, and use your other hand to pull the starter cord *(left)*.

While operating the chain saw, hold it firmly with both hands and keep the arm supporting the front handle straight. Before starting to cut, check the chain brake to ensure it engages and look for oil flowing off the guide bar, indicating the chain is being lubricated. If the chain brake does not engage or the chain is not being lubricated, take the chain saw for professional service. Otherwise, begin cutting, making sure the guide bar does not contact anything.

SERVICING THE SPARK PLUG

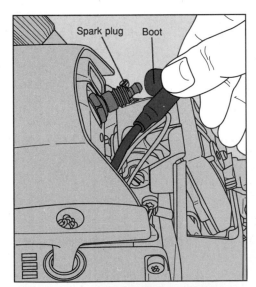

Spark plug   Boot

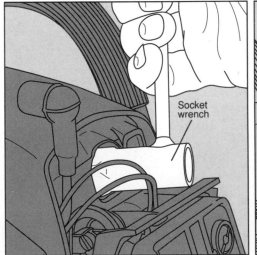

Socket wrench

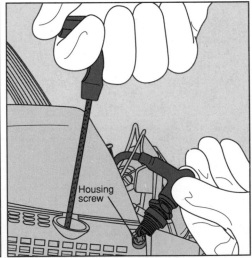

Housing screw

1 Disconnecting and reconnecting the spark plug cable. Turn off the chain saw and set it on a flat surface. To reach the spark plug on the model shown, unscrew the air filter cover. Grasp the cable by the boot and pull it off the spark plug *(above)*. If necessary, test and replace the spark plug *(step 2)*. To reconnect the cable, fit the boot back onto the spark plug. Put back the air filter cover or any other housing removed.

2 Testing and replacing the spark plug. Loosen the spark plug using the socket wrench supplied with the chain saw *(above, left)*, then unscrew it by hand. Clean and gap the spark plug *(page 123)*. To test the spark plug and other parts of the ignition system, drain the fuel tank *(page 60)*. Push the spark plug into the boot and set the switch control to the start position. Wearing heavy rubber gloves, hold only the boot and touch the spark plug threads to an exposed metal part of the engine block as far as possible from the spark plug opening; on the model shown, a housing screw. Pull the starter cord 2 or 3 times *(above, right)*. If there is a bright, snapping spark, the spark plug and other parts of the ignition system are not faulty. Otherwise, repeat the test with a new spark plug. If there is still no spark, service the switch *(page 65)*, then, if necessary, the EIM *(page 67)*. Pull the boot off the spark plug, screw in the spark plug and tighten it. Refuel the chain saw *(page 121)* and reconnect the spark plug cable *(step 1)*.

SERVICING THE AIR FILTER

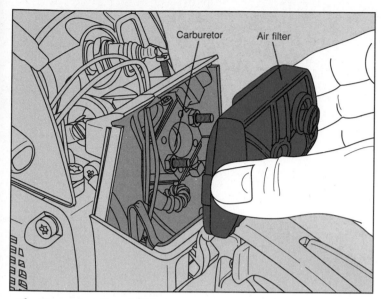

Carburetor   Air filter

1 **Removing the air filter.** Check the air filter before each use of the chain saw and if it loses power while in operation. Turn off the chain saw and disconnect the spark plug cable *(page 58)*. Use a small paintbrush to clean off debris around the air filter, then unscrew it and pull it off the carburetor *(above)*. If the air filter is clogged with embedded dirt, clean it *(step 2)*. If the air filter is damaged, replace it with an exact duplicate. Otherwise, screw the air filter onto the carburetor, then reconnect the spark plug cable *(page 58)*.

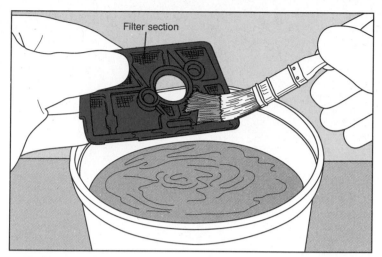

Filter section

2 **Cleaning the air filter.** If the air filter is of paper, tap it against a hard surface to knock off embedded dirt; if it is still clogged, replace it with an exact duplicate. If the air filter is flocked or of sponge, foam or mesh, wash off embedded dirt using a solution of mild household detergent and water; first pry apart any sections of the air filter, as in the model shown, with an old screwdriver. Wearing rubber gloves, apply the solution using a small paintbrush *(above)*; if the air filter is of sponge, immerse it in the solution and squeeze it out several times. Rinse off the air filter and let it dry thoroughly. Snap together any sections pried apart, screw the air filter onto the carburetor, and reconnect the spark plug cable *(page 58)*.

ADJUSTING THE CHAIN TENSION

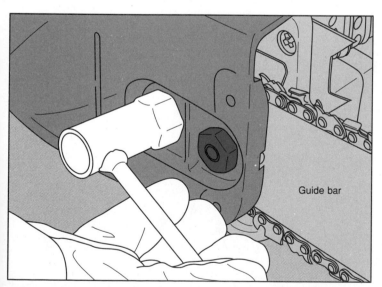

Guide bar

1 **Loosening the guide bar.** Check the chain tension before each use of the chain saw, 10 minutes after starting it and periodically during its operation; the chain usually sags as it warms up. Turn off the chain saw and disconnect the spark plug cable *(page 58)*. Wearing work gloves, carefully pull the chain along the guide bar; it should slide smoothly and stay in the groove. If the chain binds or moves stiffly, it is too tight; if the chain slips out of the groove, it is too loose. To adjust the chain tension, use the socket wrench supplied with the chain saw to loosen the guide bar mounting nuts *(above)*.

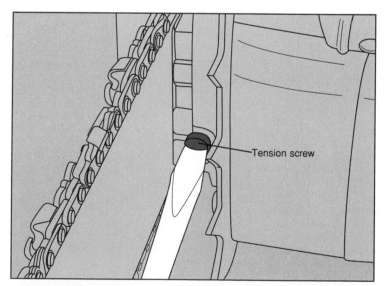

Tension screw

2 **Resetting the tension screw.** Locate the tension screw on the guide bar, typically on the side opposite the mounting nuts, as in the model shown, or between them. Tilt the chain saw slightly to raise the nose of the guide bar and use a screwdriver to reset the tension screw; turn clockwise to tighten *(above)* or counterclockwise to loosen the chain. Reset the tension screw until the chain slides smoothly along the guide bar without slipping out of the groove; it should sag only slightly along the bottom of the guide bar. Tighten the guide bar mounting nuts and check the chain tension; readjust it, if necessary. Reconnect the spark plug cable *(page 58)*. Loosen the chain before storing the chain saw.

DRAINING THE FUEL TANK

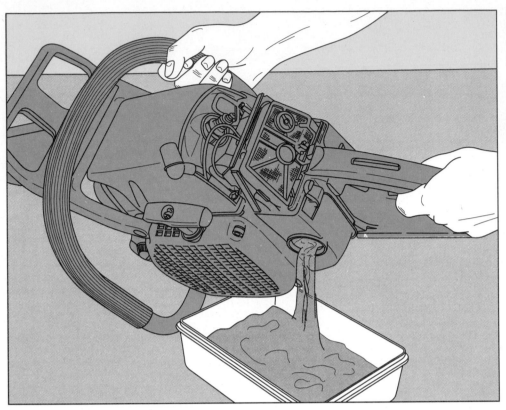

Emptying the fuel tank. For safety, you should always drain the fuel from the chain saw before testing the spark plug, performing a repair, or storing the chain saw for the season. Turn off the chain saw and disconnect the spark plug cable *(page 58)*. Allow the chain saw to cool for at least 15 minutes, then put the chain guard on it. Staying outdoors, move the chain saw at least 10 feet away from the work area. Position a metal container large enough to catch and hold the fuel on a flat surface. Unscrew the cap of the fuel tank and set it to one side. Holding the chain saw firmly with both hands, tilt it slowly onto its side to pour the fuel into the container *(left)*. When the fuel tank is empty, set the chain saw upright and screw the cap back onto the fuel tank. Wipe up any spilled fuel, then dispose of the rags and the fuel safely *(page 11)*; do not reuse drained fuel. Staying outdoors, move the chain saw at least 10 feet away from the draining site. Reconnect the spark plug cable *(page 58)*, remove the chain guard and start the chain saw. Allow the chain saw to run until it uses up all the fuel remaining in it. Then, turn off the chain saw and disconnect the spark plug cable again.

SHARPENING THE CHAIN

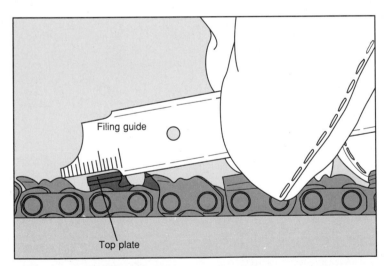

Filing guide

Top plate

1 **Measuring the top plate.** Sharpen the chain if the cutters are dull, producing sawdust that is powdery, or worn unevenly, causing the chain saw to chatter or pull. Turn off the chain saw and disconnect the spark plug cable *(page 58)*, then drain the fuel tank *(step above)*. Set the chain tension *(page 59)* loose enough to inspect the drive links; if they are severely worn or damaged or the guide bar is dirty or damaged, service the guide bar and chain *(page 61)*. Otherwise, reset the chain tension slightly tighter than required to use the chain saw. Set the chain saw on a firm, flat surface, with the guide bar and chain resting on a 2-by-4. Wearing work gloves, use the filing guide specified by the manufacturer to measure the length of each top plate *(above)*, then mark the cutter with the shortest top plate for reference using a felt-tipped pen.

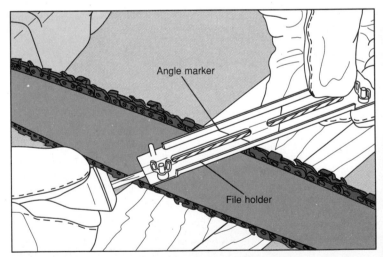

Angle marker

File holder

2 **Sharpening the cutting edge.** Sharpen the cutting edge of each cutter using the file specified by the manufacturer. Slide the file into its holder and tighten the wing nuts. Position yourself with the reference cutter curving toward you. Wearing work gloves, lay the file against the beveled cutting edge of the reference cutter, using the appropriate angle marker to align the holder with the guide bar. Steadying the holder with both hands, use moderate pressure to push the file away from you 2 or 3 times *(above)*, without applying pressure on the return stroke. Measure the top plate of the cutter *(step 1)*, then sharpen the cutting edge of each cutter facing toward you until its top plate is the same length; turn the chain as necessary. Reposition yourself on the other side of the reference cutter and use the same procedure to sharpen the cutting edge of each cutter facing toward you.

SHARPENING THE CHAIN (continued)

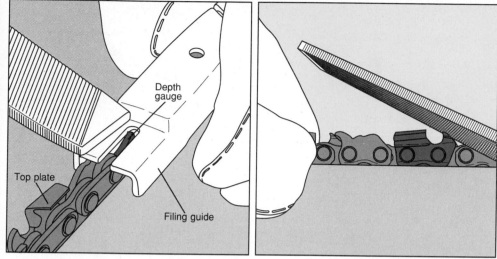

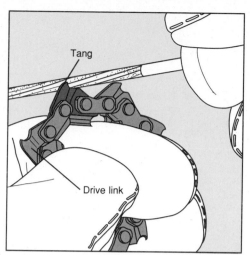

3 **Filing the depth gauges.** After sharpening the cutters, check each depth gauge using the filing guide specified by the manufacturer. Wearing work gloves, position the filing guide on the top plates of the chain, fitting its slot over the depth gauge of the reference cutter. Use a flat metal file to file off any edge of the depth gauge that protrudes through the slot of the filing guide *(above, left)*; apply only light pressure and avoid contact with any other part of the cutter. Then, take the file guide off the chain and slightly round off the outside edge of the depth gauge with a few light strokes of the file *(above, right)*. Repeat the procedure in turn with the depth gauge of each cutter, turning the chain as necessary. If the drive links of the cutters are slightly worn, file them *(step 4)*; otherwise, adjust the chain tension *(page 59)*, refuel the chain saw *(page 121)* and reconnect the spark plug cable *(page 58)*.

4 **Filing the drive links.** Wearing work gloves, remove the guide bar and take the chain off it *(step 1, below)*. If the tangs of the drive links are cracked, nicked or severely worn, buy an exact duplicate chain and guide bar and install them *(page 61)*. If the tangs of the drive links are worn only slightly, reshape them by filing lightly with the file used to sharpen the cutting edges of the cutters *(above)*. Then, reinstall the chain and guide bar *(page 62)*.

SERVICING THE GUIDE BAR AND CHAIN

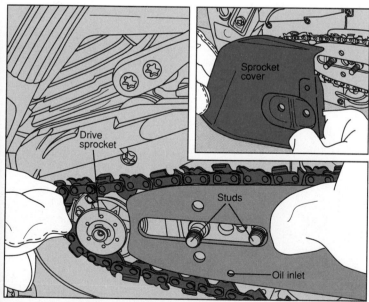

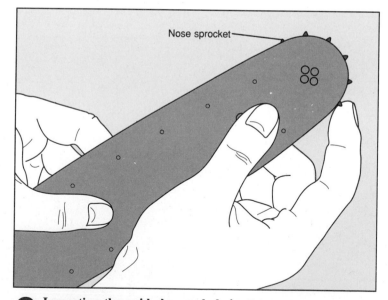

1 **Removing the guide bar and chain.** Turn off the chain saw and disconnect the spark plug cable *(page 58)*, then drain the fuel tank *(page 60)*. Set the chain saw on a firm, flat surface. Wearing work gloves, set the chain tension loose *(page 59)*, then remove the mounting nuts and lift off the sprocket cover *(inset)*. Holding the guide bar with one hand, pull the chain off the drive sprocket with the other hand *(above)*. Lift the guide bar and chain off the mounting studs, then pull the chain off the guide bar. Clean any gummy debris off the drive sprocket with a small paintbrush.

2 **Inspecting the guide bar and chain.** If the tangs of the drive links on the chain are worn flat, buy an exact duplicate chain and guide bar and install them *(step 4)*; if the tangs are worn only slightly, you can lightly file them *(step 4, above)*. If the guide bar is bent or cracked or its rails are crimped, replace the guide bar with an exact duplicate. Rotate the nose sprocket of the guide bar by hand *(above)*; it should turn smoothly. Apply a little lubricant to any oil inlet for the nose sprocket, if necessary, following the manufacturer's instructions. If the nose sprocket does not turn smoothly or its teeth are worn or otherwise damaged, replace the guide bar.

SERVICING THE GUIDE BAR AND CHAIN (continued)

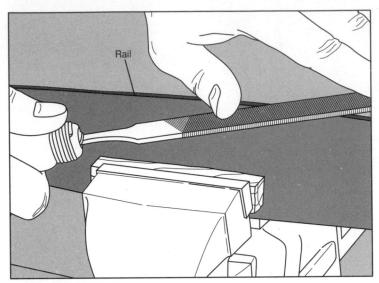

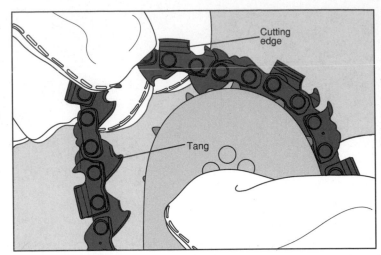

3 **Cleaning and filing the guide bar.** Use a short, stiff wire to clear each oil inlet at the end of the guide bar that fits near the drive sprocket. Use a small stick or an old screwdriver to clean gummy debris out of the groove along the guide bar, then wipe off the guide bar with a damp cloth. If the rails of the guide bar are uneven in height or burred, use a flat metal file to even and smooth them. Secure the guide bar in a vise, protecting it with wood blocks, and file it using light pressure: first, at a 45 degree angle across the rails to even them *(above)*; then, parallel to each rail along its outside edge to smooth it. If the groove of the guide bar is too shallow to hold the drive links of the chain, replace the guide bar.

4 **Reinstalling the chain and guide bar.** If the guide bar is symmetrical, you may reinstall it upside down to even wear on the rails. Wearing work gloves, hold the guide bar with its nose sprocket up and position the chain, fitting the tangs of the drive links between the teeth of the nose sprocket *(above)*; make sure the cutting edges on the top of the guide bar will face away from the chain saw when the guide bar is installed. Fit the chain into the groove along the guide bar, then position the guide bar on the mounting studs and the chain around the drive sprocket. Holding the guide bar with one hand, use a screwdriver in the other hand to tighten the tension screw until the chain fits snugly. Put back the sprocket cover and mounting nuts. Adjust the chain tension *(page 59)*, refuel the chain saw *(page 121)* and reconnect the spark plug cable *(page 58)*.

SERVICING THE DRIVE SPROCKET AND CLUTCH ASSEMBLY

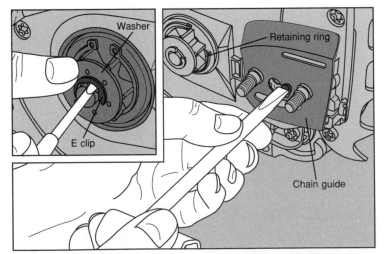

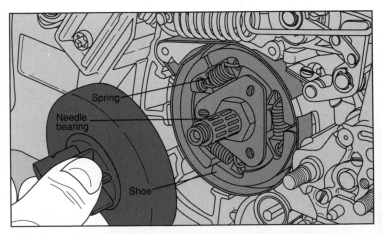

1 **Accessing the drive sprocket and clutch assembly.** Turn off the chain saw and disconnect the spark plug cable *(page 58)*, then drain the fuel tank *(page 60)*. Remove the guide bar and chain *(page 61)* and unscrew the chain guide *(above)*. Wearing safety goggles, pry the E clip off the drive shaft using a small screwdriver *(inset)*. Take off the washer, use external snap-ring pliers to remove the retaining ring and take off the sprocket washer; note the order of each component for reassembly. Unscrew the clutch cover, then lift out the oil-pump gears. Wearing rubber gloves, use a cloth dipped in denatured alcohol to clean off plastic gears; in paint thinner to clean off metal gears. Replace any damaged gear with an exact duplicate.

2 **Inspecting the drive sprocket and clutch assembly.** Pull off the drive sprocket and clutch drum *(above)*; if it is damaged, replace it with an exact duplicate. Slide off the needle bearing; replace it if it is damaged. If a clutch shoe or spring is damaged, take the chain saw for professional service. Otherwise, wearing rubber gloves, use a small paintbrush dipped in paint thinner to clean the needle bearing, drive shaft, drive sprocket and clutch drum, and other metal parts. Lubricate the needle bearing with a dab of white grease or the manufacturer's specified lubricant, then reinstall it and the drive sprocket and clutch drum. Put back the gears and screw on the clutch cover. Wearing safety goggles, reinstall the sprocket washer, retaining ring, washer and E clip, reversing the sequence used to remove them, and screw on the chain guide. Reinstall the chain and guide bar *(step 4, above)*.

SERVICING THE CARBURETOR

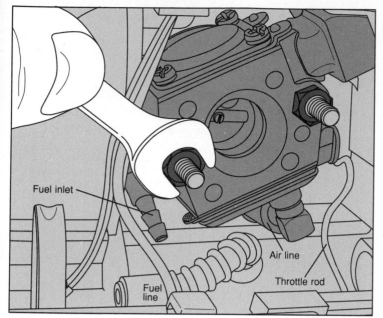

Fuel inlet

Air line

Fuel line

Throttle rod

1 **Removing the carburetor.** Turn off the chain saw and disconnect the spark plug cable *(page 58)*, then drain the fuel tank *(page 60)*. Remove the air filter *(page 59)* and note all carburetor connections, drawing a diagram, if necessary, for reassembly. Pull the fuel line off the carburetor and take the throttle rod off the throttle lever; it may lift or snap off. Use a wrench to remove the nuts holding the carburetor *(above)* and gently pull it out; as you remove it, push the air line off the crankcase. Remove the gasket between the carburetor and intake manifold; buy an exact duplicate for reassembly.

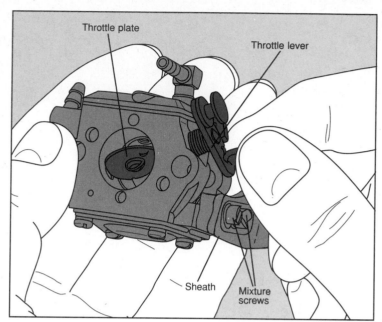

Throttle plate

Throttle lever

Sheath

Mixture screws

2 **Inspecting the throttle.** If the screw of the throttle plate is loose, tighten it. To check the throttle plate, flip the throttle lever back and forth *(above)*. If the throttle plate sticks, wear rubber gloves to spray it with carburetor and choke cleaner, then wipe or dry it off following the cleaner instructions. If the throttle plate does not move smoothly or is bent, unscrew it and install an exact duplicate. Before disassembling the carburetor *(step 3)*, buy the basic carburetor rebuilding kit for your chain saw make and model, including replacement gaskets, diaphragms and other parts; the carburetor may have its number stamped on it. Otherwise, reinstall the carburetor *(step 5)*.

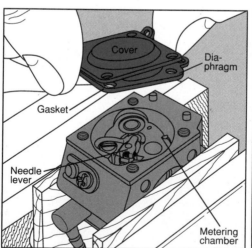

Cover

Diaphragm

Gasket

Needle lever

Metering chamber

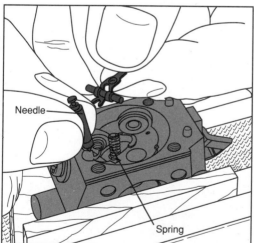

Needle

Spring

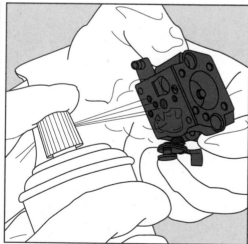

3 **Disassembling and cleaning the carburetor.** To reach the pump chamber, secure the carburetor upside down in a vise, protecting it with wood blocks. Unscrew the cover and lift it off, along with the gasket and the diaphragm. To reach the metering chamber, secure the carburetor upright in the vise, as shown, and remove the cover, along with the diaphragm and the gasket *(above, left)*. Press the needle lever with a fingertip, remove the needle screw and slowly lift your fingertip to release the needle spring. Then, take out the needle lever and the needle *(above, center)* and remove the needle spring. Take the rubber sheath off the high- and low-speed mixture screws and use a small screwdriver to remove them and their springs; note their placement. If a mixture screw or its spring is damaged, buy an exact duplicate for reassembly. Remove the carburetor from the vise. Wearing rubber gloves, spray inside the pump chamber *(above, right)* and the metering chamber with carburetor and choke cleaner, taking care not to drip any on plastic parts. Wipe or dry off the cleaner following its instructions. Resecure the carburetor in the vise with its metering chamber up. Install the high- and low-speed mixture springs and screws, and put back the rubber sheath; turn each screw clockwise until it is snug, then counterclockwise 1 1/4 turns. Reassemble the carburetor *(step 4)*.

CHAIN SAWS

SERVICING THE CARBURETOR (continued)

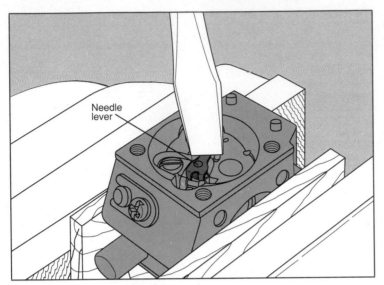

Needle lever

4 **Reassembling the carburetor.** Replace any damaged part using your carburetor rebuilding kit; never reuse a gasket or diaphragm. For the metering chamber, position the needle, the needle spring and the needle lever; press the needle lever with a finger-tip and install the needle screw with a small screwdriver. Depending on the carburetor, the needle lever should sit even with the floor or top of the chamber; check it with the floor by sitting a screwdriver blade across it *(above)* or with the top by placing a straight edge across it. If necessary, gently bend the needle lever into place. Position the new diaphragm and gasket, then screw on the cover; tighten each screw a little in turn. Secure the carburetor in the vise with the pump chamber up, position its new gasket and diaphragm, and screw on its cover.

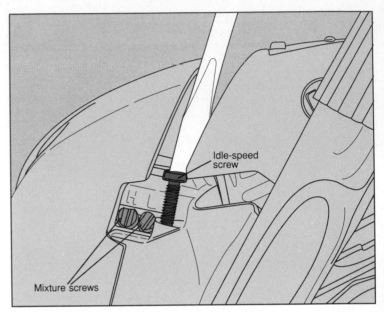

Idle-speed screw

Mixture screws

5 **Reinstalling the carburetor and setting the idle-speed screw.** Place the new gasket between the carburetor and intake manifold, position the carburetor, reconnecting the air line to the crankcase, and reinstall the nuts. Reconnect the throttle rod and the fuel line, then put back the air filter. Refuel the chain saw *(page 121)* and reconnect the spark plug cable *(page 58)*. Start the chain saw and allow it to idle for a few minutes. To set the idle-speed screw, slowly turn it clockwise *(above)* until the chain begins rotating; then, slowly turn it counterclockwise until the chain stops rotating. To adjust the high- and low-speed mixture screws, refer to your owner's manual.

SERVICING THE FUEL LINE AND FUEL FILTER

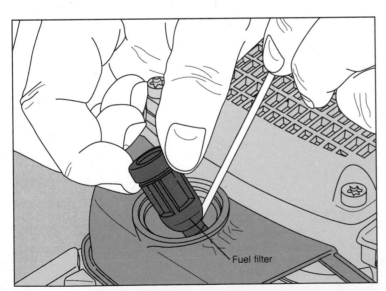

Fuel filter

1 **Removing the fuel filter.** Turn off the chain saw and disconnect the spark plug cable *(page 58)*, then drain the fuel tank *(page 60)*. Set the chain saw on a firm, flat surface and take the cap off the fuel tank. Shape a stiff wire into a hook at one end and use it to fish the fuel filter out of the fuel tank *(above)*. To avoid dropping the fuel line, bend the sire securely around it and across the opening of the fuel tank, if necessary. Pry the cap off the fuel filter housing, then remove the weight and the foam.

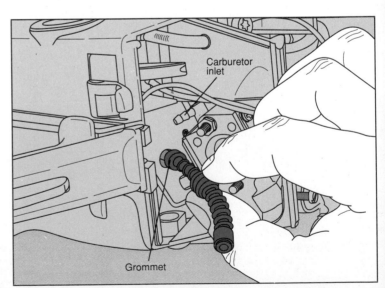

Carburetor inlet

Grommet

2 **Removing the fuel line.** Remove the air filter *(page 59)* and pull the fuel line off the carburetor. If the fuel line is not damaged, clean it and the fuel filter *(step 4)*. If the fuel line is stretched, hardened or cracked, replace it with an exact duplicate; if necessary, use a flashlight to check the portion of the fuel line inside the fuel tank. Feed the fuel line into the fuel tank, pushing through the grommet *(above)*, then fish it out using the wire *(step 1)*. After removing the fuel line, pry the fuel filter housing off it.

64

SERVICING THE FUEL LINE AND FUEL FILTER (continued)

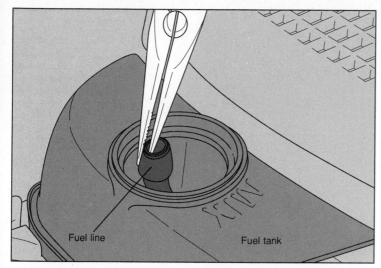

Fuel line

Fuel tank

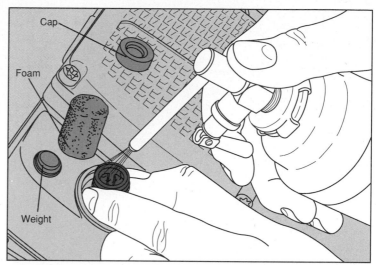

Cap

Foam

Weight

3 **Installing a new fuel line.** Feed the new fuel line into the fuel tank through its opening near the carburetor. Push the grommet on the fuel line firmly into place, compressing it with your fingers, if necessary; be careful not to damage it. Fish the end of the fuel line out of the fuel tank through its opening for the cap using the wire *(step 1)*. Grip the end of the fuel line with long-nose pliers to hold it *(above)* and pull it out, then push the fuel filter housing securely onto it. To avoid dropping the fuel line, bend the wire securely around it and across the opening of the fuel tank, if necessary.

4 **Cleaning the fuel filter and the fuel line.** Wearing rubber gloves, wash the fuel filter cap, weight and foam using paint thinner; immerse the foam and squeeze it out several times. Wearing safety goggles, dry the cap and the weight with compressed air; if you did not replace the fuel line, use compressed air to clear it *(above)*. If the foam is clogged with embedded dirt or damaged, replace it. Install the foam, the weight and the cap, then drop the fuel filter into the fuel tank. Reconnect the fuel line to the carburetor and reinstall the air filter. Refuel the chain saw *(page 121)* and reconnect the spark plug cable *(page 58)*.

SERVICING THE SWITCH

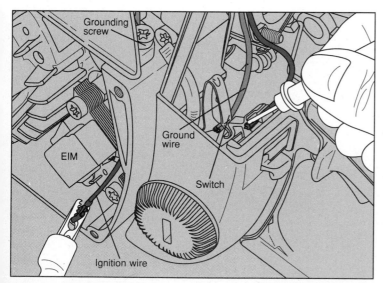

Grounding screw

Ground wire

EIM

Switch

Ignition wire

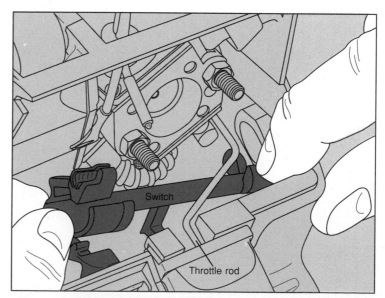

Switch

Throttle rod

1 **Testing the switch wires.** Turn off the chain saw and disconnect the spark plug cable *(page 58)*, then drain the fuel tank *(page 60)*. To reach the switch and its wires, remove the air filter *(page 59)* and the starter assembly housing *(page 66)*. To test the switch wires, set a multitester to test for continuity *(page 113)* and set the switch control to the start position. Pull the ignition wire off the electronic ignition module (EIM), clip one tester probe to its connector and touch the other tester probe to its other connector at the switch terminal *(above)*; the multitester should register continuity. Unscrew the grounding wire from the housing and repeat the test. If a wire tests faulty or its insulation is damaged, replace it with an identical wire. Otherwise, reconnect the wires.

2 **Cleaning and replacing the switch.** Clean the switch contacts by rubbing with fine emery paper, then wipe them off with a piece of paper. If the switch is damaged, replace it with an exact duplicate. To remove the switch, disconnect the wires from it; note their terminals or label them for reassembly. Unscrew the switch and slide it out *(above)*; depress the throttle trigger, if necessary, to manipulate the switch past the throttle rod. To install a new switch, screw it in and reconnect the wires to its terminals. Reinstall the starter assembly housing and the air filter. Refuel the chain saw *(page 121)* and reconnect the spark plug cable *(page 58)*.

SERVICING THE STARTER ASSEMBLY

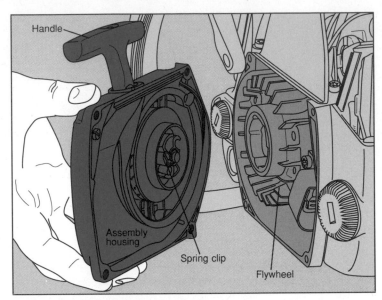

Handle
Assembly housing
Spring clip
Flywheel

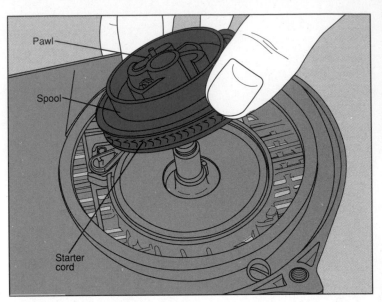

Pawl
Spool
Starter cord

1 **Removing the starter assembly housing.** Turn off the chain saw and disconnect the spark plug cable *(page 58)*, then drain the fuel tank *(page 60)*. Unscrew the starter assembly housing and lift it off the chain saw *(above)*; the starter assembly is secured inside it. Set the starter assembly housing on a flat, firm surface with the starter assembly facing up.

2 **Removing the spool and the starter cord.** Wearing safety goggles, pry the spring clip off the shaft with a small screwdriver. Take off the washer, then lift out the spool *(above)*. If the starter cord is damaged, pull the knot out of the handle and cut it off. Unwind the starter cord from the spool, cutting off or freeing the knot at the other end of it. If the rewind spring is unhooked, broken or otherwise damaged, replace it *(step 3)*. Otherwise, replace the starter cord and reset the rewind spring tension *(step 4)*.

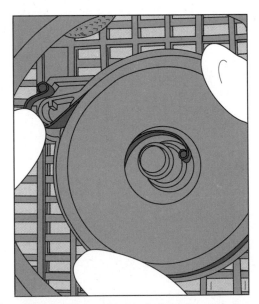

3 **Replacing the rewind spring.** Wearing work gloves and safety goggles, un-hook the rewind spring from the starter assembly housing; then, lift out the rewind spring housing—be prepared for the rewind spring to fly out. Buy an exact duplicate rewind spring, coiled in its housing, and lubricate it with a few drops of light machine oil or the manufacturer's specified lubricant. Position the rewind spring housing and hook the rewind spring to the starter assembly housing *(above)*.

4 **Replacing the starter cord and setting the rewind spring tension.** If the starter cord is damaged, replace it with an exact duplicate. Thread one end of the starter cord through the opening in the spool using long-nose pliers *(above)*, then knot it. Thread the other end of the starter cord through the opening in the starter assembly housing and the handle, then knot it. Cauterize each knot, holding a flame under it without touching it *(inset)*. Fit the knot into the spool and wind all but the last 6 inches of the starter cord clockwise around the spool.

Position the spool in the starter assembly housing, then reinstall the washer. Wearing safety goggles, put back the spring clip. Hold the end of the wound starter cord against the spool and pull it clockwise, rotating the spool 3 or 4 turns. Hold the spool and pull the handle to straighten the unwound starter cord. Then, holding the handle, release the spool and let the unwound starter cord wind slowly onto it. If the handle droops, repeat the procedure, rotating the spool 1 extra turn. If the spool cannot be rotated clockwise at least 2 full turns when the starter cord is extended, repeat the procedure, rotating the spool 1 less turn. Otherwise, reinstall the starter assembly housing. Refuel the chain saw *(page 121)* and reconnect the spark plug cable *(page 58)*.

SERVICING THE ELECTRONIC IGNITION MODULE (EIM)

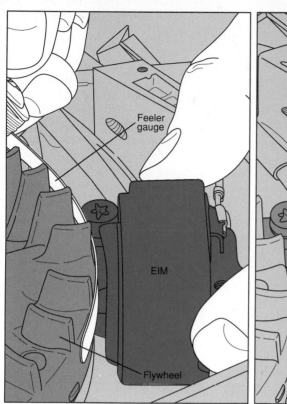

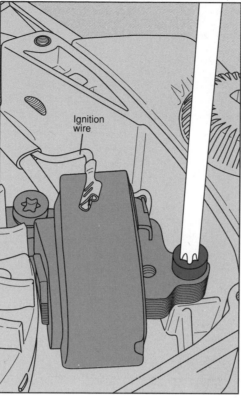

Gapping and replacing the electronic ignition module (EIM). Turn off the chain saw and disconnect the spark plug cable *(page 58)*, then drain the fuel tank *(page 60)*. Remove the starter assembly housing *(page 66)*, locate the EIM and identify it *(page 121)*.

To gap the EIM, use a brass or plastic feeler gauge that matches the gap specified by the manufacturer. Rotate the flywheel until its magnets are as far as possible from the EIM. Loosen the EIM screws and slide the EIM enough to fit the feeler gauge horizontally between it and the flywheel *(far left)*. Rotate the flywheel until its magnets are aligned with the EIM. Tighten the EIM screws and pull out the feeler gauge. Reinstall the starter assembly housing, refuel the chain saw *(page 121)* and reconnect the spark plug cable *(page 58)*. If the problem persists, replace the EIM and spark plug cable.

To replace the EIM and spark plug cable, also remove the air filter *(page 59)* and the engine housing. Use long-nose pliers to pull the ignition wire off the EIM, then slide it out of any sheath holding it against the spark plug cable. Unscrew the EIM *(near left)* and lift it out. Install an exact duplicate EIM, reconnect the ignition wire, and put back the engine housing and air filter. Then, gap the EIM.

SERVICING THE MUFFLER

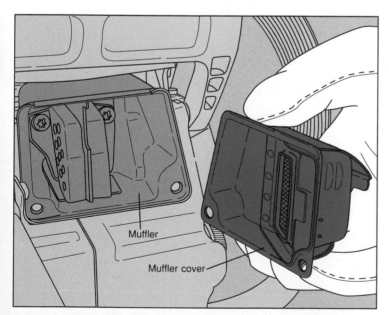

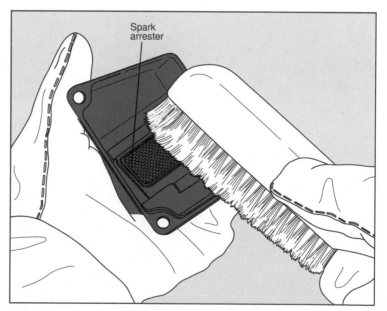

1 Cleaning the muffler. Turn off the chain saw and disconnect the spark plug cable *(page 58)*, then drain the fuel tank *(page 60)*. Wearing work gloves, unscrew the muffler cover and pull it off *(above)*. Inspect the muffler and its cover for cracks and weakened areas; replace any part that is damaged. Make sure each screw inside the muffler is tight. Use a wire brush to clean off any carbon deposits and other debris; to loosen a stubborn carbon deposit, first apply a small amount of decarbonizing spray.

2 Servicing the spark arrester. The spark arrester is the screen located inside the muffler cover. Wearing work gloves, carefully clean off the spark arrester with a wire brush *(above)* and inspect it for tears, corrosion and other damage. If the spark arrester is damaged, replace it with an exact duplicate. Screw back on the muffler cover, refuel the chain saw *(page 121)* and reconnect the spark plug cable *(page 58)*. Start the chain saw and let it run for 1 or 2 minutes; then, turn it off, disconnect the spark plug cable and tighten each screw of the muffler cover.

LAWN MOWERS

The fuel-powered lawn mowers common today are a technological advance from the push-type lawn mowers that preceded them. By far the most popular kind of fuel-powered lawn mower, the rotary lawn mower has a single cutting blade driven by the engine crankshaft. As the blade spins, the cutting edge at each end of it mows the lawn; the height of the blade above the ground is adjusted by raising or lowering the deck of the lawn mower using the lever at each wheel. Illustrated below are two typical rotary lawn mowers, one with a two-cycle engine and one with a four-cycle engine; both engines have a single cylinder and differ principally only in how they produce the power stroke of the piston.

With proper care and routine maintenance, a lawn mower can last a lifetime; read your owner's manual thoroughly to familiarize yourself with the specific requirements of your model. To prevent damaging the lawn mower and injuring yourself, clear the lawn of all obstructions before turning on and starting the lawn mower. Fill the fuel tank only with clean fuel; if the engine is two cycle, mix the fuel of gasoline and oil according to the manufacturer's instructions. If the engine is four cycle, check its oil level regularly; after every 25 hours of use, drain the crankcase *(page 72)* and refill it *(page 120)*. Clean off clumps of grass clippings and dirt after using the lawn mower. Keep the blade sharp and balanced *(page 73)*.

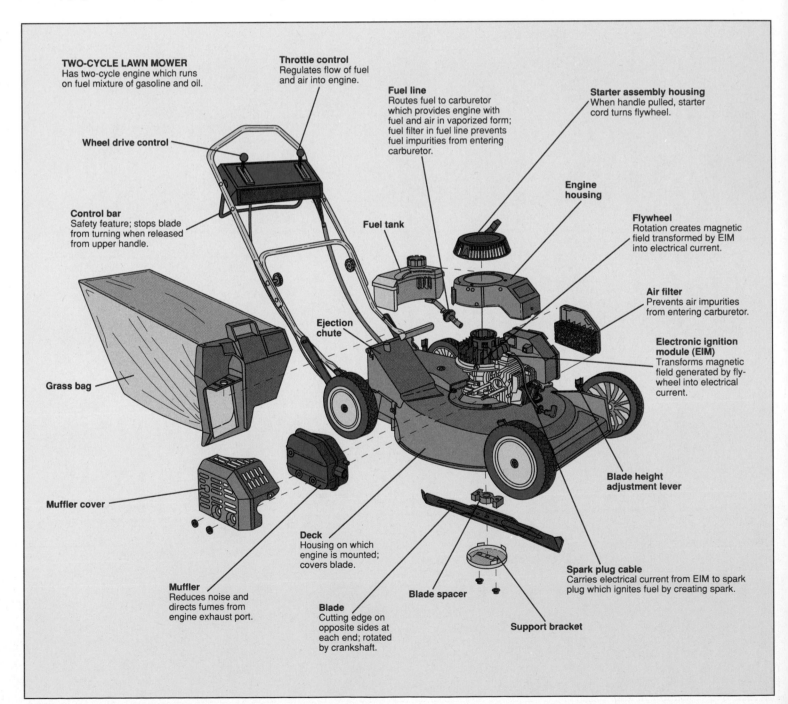

TWO-CYCLE LAWN MOWER
Has two-cycle engine which runs on fuel mixture of gasoline and oil.

Throttle control
Regulates flow of fuel and air into engine.

Fuel line
Routes fuel to carburetor which provides engine with fuel and air in vaporized form; fuel filter in fuel line prevents fuel impurities from entering carburetor.

Starter assembly housing
When handle pulled, starter cord turns flywheel.

Wheel drive control

Engine housing

Control bar
Safety feature; stops blade from turning when released from upper handle.

Fuel tank

Flywheel
Rotation creates magnetic field transformed by EIM into electrical current.

Air filter
Prevents air impurities from entering carburetor.

Ejection chute

Electronic ignition module (EIM)
Transforms magnetic field generated by flywheel into electrical current.

Grass bag

Muffler cover

Blade height adjustment lever

Deck
Housing on which engine is mounted; covers blade.

Muffler
Reduces noise and directs fumes from engine exhaust port.

Blade
Cutting edge on opposite sides at each end; rotated by crankshaft.

Blade spacer

Support bracket

Spark plug cable
Carries electrical current from EIM to spark plug which ignites fuel by creating spark.

When a problem occurs with your lawn mower, consult the Troubleshooting Guide on page 70; even if the lawn mower does not start, diagnosing is seldom difficult and most repairs are easy to undertake. Starting problems are less frequent with the electronic ignition module (EIM) of a contemporary lawn mower; if your model has a system of points and a condenser, you may update it by having an EIM installed. Remember to clean the air filter on a regular basis *(page 74)*. Perform all routine adjusting, cleaning and maintenance tasks before tackling a repair to the carburetor *(page 75)*; disassembling it requires patience and attention to detail. Service the controls and cables at least once each season *(page 81)*.

In most instances, only basic tools are needed to service a lawn mower; for some repairs, however, special tools are called for. A feeler gauge, for example, is necessary to gap the EIM. And to remove the flywheel, you will need a strap wrench and the tool specified by the manufacturer; to install the flywheel, you will need the strap wrench and a torque wrench. To prevent damage to the engine, avoid substituting another tool for any special tool you are instructed to use. Refer to Tools & Techniques *(page 110)* to identify the ignition system and type of carburetor in your lawn mower, as well as for information on refueling, the diagnosis of spark plugs and seasonal storage.

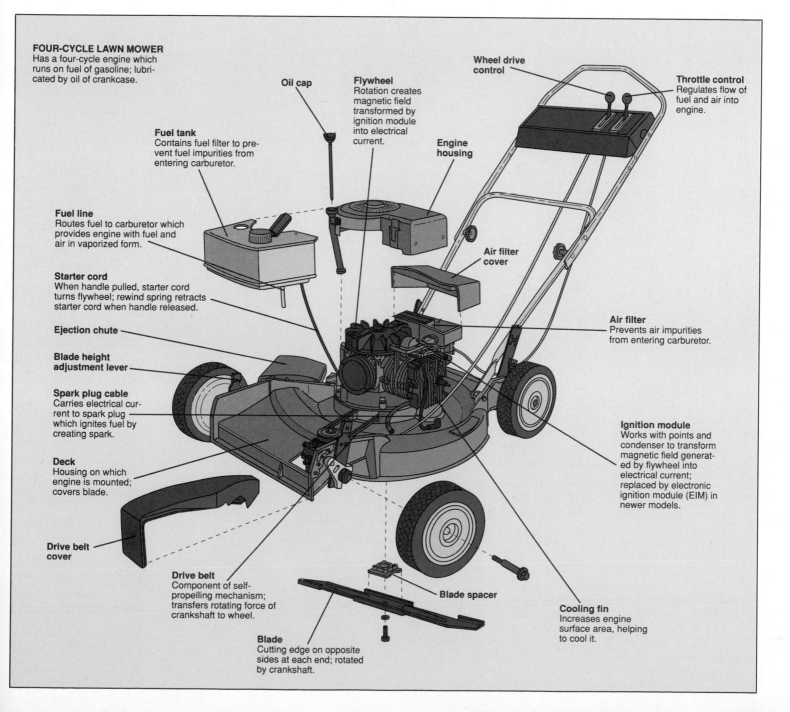

FOUR-CYCLE LAWN MOWER
Has a four-cycle engine which runs on fuel of gasoline; lubricated by oil of crankcase.

Oil cap

Flywheel
Rotation creates magnetic field transformed by ignition module into electrical current.

Wheel drive control

Throttle control
Regulates flow of fuel and air into engine.

Fuel tank
Contains fuel filter to prevent fuel impurities from entering carburetor.

Engine housing

Fuel line
Routes fuel to carburetor which provides engine with fuel and air in vaporized form.

Air filter cover

Starter cord
When handle pulled, starter cord turns flywheel; rewind spring retracts starter cord when handle released.

Air filter
Prevents air impurities from entering carburetor.

Ejection chute

Blade height adjustment lever

Spark plug cable
Carries electrical current to spark plug which ignites fuel by creating spark.

Ignition module
Works with points and condenser to transform magnetic field generated by flywheel into electrical current; replaced by electronic ignition module (EIM) in newer models.

Deck
Housing on which engine is mounted; covers blade.

Drive belt cover

Drive belt
Component of self-propelling mechanism; transfers rotating force of crankshaft to wheel.

Blade spacer

Cooling fin
Increases engine surface area, helping to cool it.

Blade
Cutting edge on opposite sides at each end; rotated by crankshaft.

TROUBLESHOOTING GUIDE

SYMPTOM	POSSIBLE CAUSE	PROCEDURE
Lawn mower does not start	Control set incorrectly	Consult manual to start lawn mower
	Starter cord or rewind spring broken	Service starter assembly (p. 77) ◨●
	Fuel contaminated or fuel tank empty	Drain fuel tank (p. 72) □○; refuel lawn mower (p. 121) □○
	Spark plug faulty or cable disconnected	Service spark plug (p. 71) □○
	Fuel line or fuel filter dirty or damaged	Service fuel line and fuel filter (p. 74) ◨●
	Throttle control or cable dirty or faulty	Service controls and cables (p. 81) ◨○
	Carburetor adjusted incorrectly or faulty	Consult manual to adjust carburetor; service carburetor (p. 75) ■●
	Muffler clogged	Service muffler (p. 82) □○
	EIM gapped incorrectly or faulty	Service EIM (p. 78) ◨○▲
	Flywheel damaged or engine faulty	Service flywheel (p. 79) ■●▲; take lawn mower for service
Lawn mower starts, but power diminished	Fuel tank cap vents blocked	Clear vents with toothpick
	Air filter dirty	Service air filter (p. 74) □○
	Fuel contaminated or mixed incorrectly	Drain fuel tank (p. 72) □○ and refuel lawn mower (p. 121) □○
	Fuel line or fuel filter dirty or damaged	Service fuel line and fuel filter (p. 74) ◨●
	Throttle control or cable dirty or faulty	Service controls and cables (p. 81) ◨○
	Carburetor adjusted incorrectly or faulty	Consult manual to adjust carburetor; service carburetor (p. 75) ■●
	Muffler or exhaust port (two-cycle) clogged	Service muffler (p. 82) □○; clean exhaust port (p. 83) □○
	EIM gapped incorrectly or faulty	Service EIM (p. 78) ◨○▲
	Engine faulty	Take lawn mower for service
Lawn mower runs erratically or stalls	Fuel tank cap vents blocked	Clear vents with toothpick
	Air filter dirty	Service air filter (p. 74) □○
	Fuel contaminated or mixed incorrectly	Drain fuel tank (p. 72) □○ and refuel lawn mower (p. 121) □○
	Oil contaminated or low (four-cycle)	Drain crankcase (p. 72) □○; refill crankcase (p. 120) □○
	Fuel line or fuel filter dirty or damaged	Service fuel line and fuel filter (p. 74) ◨●
	Carburetor adjusted incorrectly or faulty	Consult manual to adjust carburetor; service carburetor (p. 75) ■●
	Muffler or exhaust port (two-cycle) clogged	Service muffler (p. 82) □○; clean exhaust port (p. 83) □○
	Flywheel damaged or engine faulty	Service flywheel (p. 79) ■●▲; take lawn mower for service
Lawn mower overheats	Engine cooling fins dirty	Clean engine cooling fins with wire brush
	Air filter dirty	Service air filter (p. 74) □○
	Fuel contaminated or mixed incorrectly	Drain fuel tank (p. 72) □○ and refuel lawn mower (p. 121) □○
	Oil contaminated or low (four-cycle)	Drain crankcase (p. 72) □○; refill crankcase (p. 120) □○
	Muffler or exhaust port (two-cycle) clogged	Service muffler (p. 82) □○; clean exhaust port (p. 83) □○
	Flywheel damaged or engine faulty	Service flywheel (p. 79) ■●▲; take lawn mower for service
Lawn mower rattles or vibrates excessively	Housing fastener loose	Tighten housing fasteners
	Blade unbalanced or damaged	Service blade (p. 73) ◨○
	Muffler clogged	Service muffler (p. 82) □○
	Flywheel damaged or engine faulty	Service flywheel (p. 79) ■●▲; take lawn mower for service
Lawn mower cuts unevenly	Blade height set incorrectly	Set blade height at each wheel
	Blade dirty, dull or damaged	Service blade (p. 73) ◨○
	Engine faulty	Take lawn mower for service
Self-propelling mechanism does not work	Drive belt damaged	Service drive belt (p. 80) ◨●
	Wheel drive control or cable faulty	Service controls and cables (p. 81) ◨○
	Mechanism faulty	Take lawn mower for service

DEGREE OF DIFFICULTY: □ Easy ◨ Moderate ■ Complex
ESTIMATED TIME: ○ Less than 1 hour ● 1 to 3 hours ● Over 3 hours   ▲ Special tool required

LAWN MOWER USE AND MAINTENANCE

Lever

Operating a lawn mower. When using the lawn mower, wear work gloves, long pants and heavy shoes; tie back your hair if it is long. Before starting the lawn mower, remove all rocks, sticks and other foreign objects from the lawn. Mix fuel, if necessary, and add it at least 10 feet away from the lawn *(page 121)*; if the engine is four cycle, check the oil level *(page 120)*. Set the cutting height, adjusting the lever at each wheel *(inset)*. Attach the grass bag or discharge chute securely; if it is damaged, repair or replace it.

Connect the spark plug cable *(step 1, below)* and start the lawn mower according to the manufacturer's instructions. Gripping the handle bar with both hands and keeping your weight balanced, walk at a steady pace *(left)*, mowing the lawn in parallel rows that overlap by 1/4 row. On a slope, mow at an angle across it rather than straight up and down it. Turn off the lawn mower and disconnect the spark plug cable to reset the cutting height or to clean off the lawn mower. Use a wire brush to clean off the engine cooling fins. Tilt the lawn mower onto the side recommended in the owner's manual and use a stick to scrape clumps of grass clippings and dirt off the blade and the bottom of the deck; keep your hands clear of the blade.

SERVICING THE SPARK PLUG

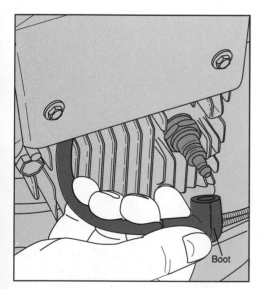

Boot

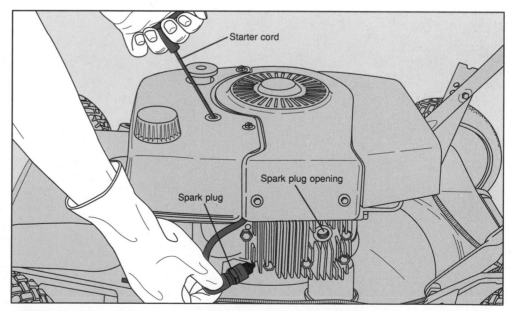

Starter cord

Spark plug opening

Spark plug

1 **Disconnecting and reconnecting the spark plug cable.** Move the lawn mower to a level surface and turn it off. Grasp the spark plug cable by the boot and pull it off the spark plug *(above)*; set the boot well away from the spark plug. If necessary, test and replace the spark plug *(step 2)*. To reconnect the spark plug cable, fit the boot back onto the spark plug.

2 **Testing the spark plug.** Loosen the spark plug using a socket wrench, then unscrew it by hand; clean and gap it *(page 123)*. To test the spark plug and other parts of the ignition system, drain the fuel tank *(page 72)*. Push the spark plug into the boot and set the controls to the start position. Wearing a heavy rubber glove, hold only the boot and touch the spark plug threads to an exposed metal part of the engine block as far as possible from the spark plug opening. Pull the starter cord 2 or 3 times *(above)*. If there is a bright, snapping spark, the spark plug and other parts of the ignition system are not faulty. Otherwise, repeat the test with a new spark plug. If there is still no spark, service the EIM *(page 78)*. Pull the boot off the spark plug and screw in the spark plug. Refuel the lawn mower *(page 121)* and reconnect the spark plug cable *(step 1)*.

DRAINING THE FUEL TANK

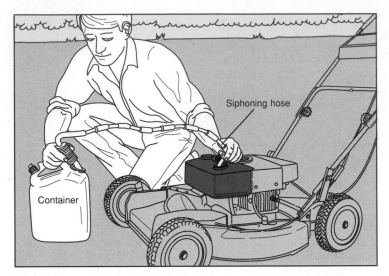

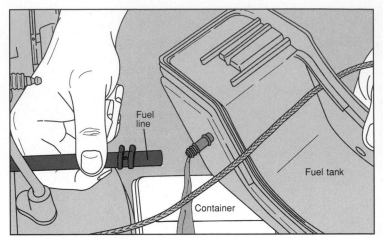

Siphoning the fuel. Turn off the lawn mower and disconnect the spark plug cable *(page 71)*. Let the engine cool. It may be easiest to drain the fuel by disconnecting the fuel line *(step right)*. Otherwise, work outdoors with a siphoning hose. Unscrew the fuel tank cap, feed one end of the hose onto the bottom of the fuel tank and the other end into a fuel container for disposal. Pump the bulb until fuel flows through the hose *(above)*; continue until the fuel is drained. Wipe up any spill and dispose of the fuel safely *(page 11)*. Screw the cap onto the fuel tank, move the lawn mower at least 10 feet away from the draining site and reconnect the spark plug cable *(page 71)*. Start the lawn mower and let it run to use up any remaining fuel; turn it off and disconnect the spark plug cable.

Disconnecting the fuel line. Turn off the lawn mower and disconnect the spark plug cable *(page 71)*. Let the engine cool. For safety, drain the fuel using a siphoning hose *(step left)*. Otherwise, work outdoors to disconnect the fuel line; you may have to remove the oil cap, unscrew the fuel tank and lift it away from the engine housing, as shown. Set a metal container under the fuel tank at the fuel line connection. Slide the clamp along the fuel line with utility pliers, then disconnect the fuel line *(above)*. Allow the fuel to drain. Wipe up any spill and dispose of the fuel safely *(page 11)*. Reconnect the fuel line, screw on the fuel tank and put back the oil cap. Move the lawn mower at least 10 feet away from the draining site and reconnect the spark plug cable *(page 71)*. Start the lawn mower and let it run to use up any remaining fuel; turn it off and disconnect the spark plug cable.

DRAINING THE CRANKCASE (Four-cycle engine)

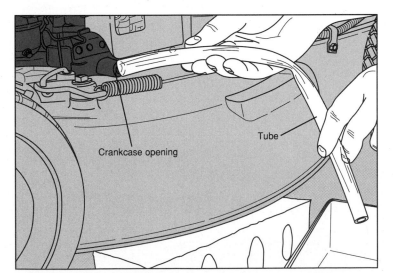

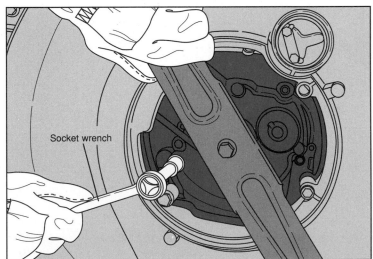

Draining oil from a side drain. Turn off the lawn mower and disconnect the spark plug cable *(page 71)*, then drain the fuel tank *(step above)*. If the crankcase drain plug is on the bottom of the deck, drain the oil from it *(step right)*. If the crankcase drain plug is on one side of the engine, drain the oil using the tube supplied with the lawn mower. Prop up the deck with a brick, as shown, and use a socket wrench to remove the drain plug. Fit one end of the tube onto the crankcase opening and run the other end into a metal container *(above)*. Pull away the brick and let the oil drain; tilt the lawn mower toward the container, if necessary. Wipe up any spill, then dispose of the rags and the oil safely *(page 11)*. Reinstall the drain plug and refill the crankcase *(page 120)*.

Draining oil from a bottom drain. Turn off the lawn mower and disconnect the spark plug cable *(page 71)*, then drain the fuel tank *(step above)*. If the crankcase drain plug is on one side of the engine, drain the oil from it *(step left)*. If the crankcase drain plug is on the bottom of the deck, tilt the lawn mower onto the side recommended in the owner's manual; support it with wood blocks, if necessary. Set a metal container on the ground near the drain plug. Wearing work gloves, hold the blade out of the way and use a socket wrench to remove the drain plug *(above)*. Set the lawn mower upright over the container and let the oil drain. Wipe up any spill, then dispose of the rags and the oil safely *(page 11)*. Reinstall the drain plug and refill the crankcase *(page 120)*.

SERVICING THE BLADE

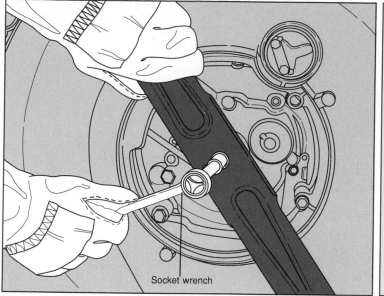

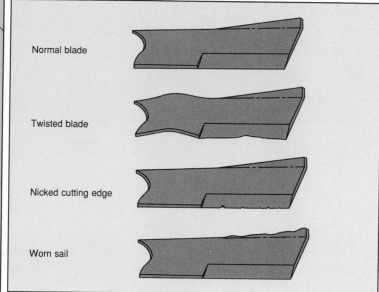

1 Removing and inspecting the blade. Turn off the lawn mower and disconnect the spark plug cable *(page 71)*, then drain the fuel tank *(page 72)*. Tilt the lawn mower onto the side recommended in the owner's manual; support it with wood blocks, if necessary. Wearing work gloves, hold the blade steady and use a socket wrench to take off each bolt or nut securing it onto the crankshaft *(above, left)*. Remove any support bracket and washer, then pull off the blade; note the placement of each part removed for reassembly. Use a stick to scrape any clumps of grass clippings and dirt off the blade, then wipe it with a cloth.

Set the blade down on a level surface to inspect it; it should lie flat. Replace any bolt or nut that is damaged or has been reinstalled 4 times. If a cutting edge of the blade is dull or slightly nicked, sharpen the blade *(step 2)*. If the blade is cracked or twisted, a cutting edge is severely nicked or a sail is worn *(above, right)*, replace the blade with an exact duplicate. Position the blade and put back any washer and support bracket removed. Lightly grease the threads of each bolt or nut and install it; tighten each bolt or nut in turn with the socket wrench. Refuel the lawn mower *(page 121)* and reconnect the spark plug cable *(page 71)*.

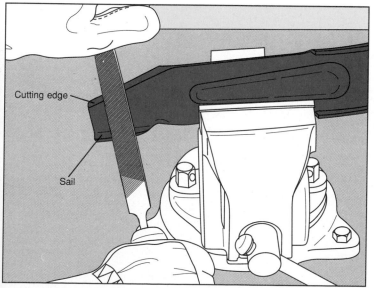

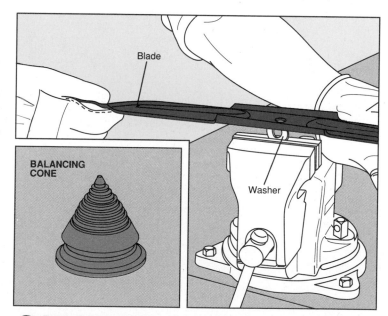

2 Sharpening the blade. Wearing work gloves, secure the blade in a vise and face the bevel of the cutting edge at one end of it. Use a flat, medium file first to clean off the flat edge of the blade, scraping once or twice along it, then to sharpen the cutting edge of the blade. Lay the file against the cutting edge at the original angle of the bevel, usually about 30 degrees. Push the file with strong, even pressure for 4 or 5 strokes along the cutting edge *(above)*, without exerting pressure on the return stroke. Knock the file to clean off shavings. When the cutting edge is shiny, take any burr off it by running the file once more along the flat edge of the blade. Use the same procedure to sharpen the other end of the blade.

3 Balancing the blade. To balance the blade, buy a special balancing cone *(inset)* or use a 1/2-inch metal washer; an unbalanced blade cuts unevenly and can damage the engine. Wearing work gloves, secure the washer in a vise and seat the center hole of the blade on it *(above)*. The blade should balance evenly. If one end of the blade tips down, file a little off the flat end of its cutting edge and repeat the procedure. When the blade is balanced, put it back and reposition any washer and support bracket removed. Lightly grease the threads of each bolt or nut and install it; tighten each bolt or nut in turn with the socket wrench. Refuel the lawn mower *(page 121)* and reconnect the spark plug cable *(page 71)*.

SERVICING THE AIR FILTER

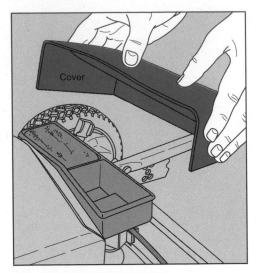

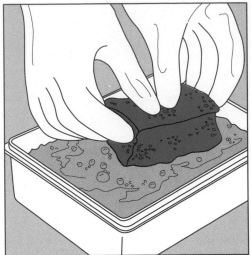

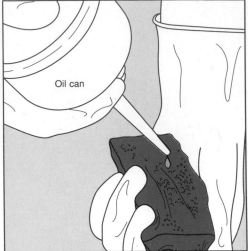

1 **Removing the air filter cover.** Turn off the lawn mower and disconnect the spark plug cable *(page 71)*. Locate the air filter near the engine housing; consult the owner's manual, if necessary. To remove the air filter cover on most models, pull it off *(above)*; on other models, you may have to first lift up its tabs or remove its screws.

2 **Cleaning the air filter.** Lift the air filter out of the housing. Wipe off any dirt inside the housing with a clean cloth. If the air filter is of paper, tap it against a hard surface to dislodge any loose dirt. Wearing rubber gloves, wash the air filter using a solution of mild household detergent and water; if the air filter is of sponge, immerse it in the solution and squeeze it out several times *(above, left)*. Rinse off the air filter and let it dry thoroughly; if it is still clogged with embedded dirt or damaged, replace it with an exact duplicate. If the air filter is of sponge, wrap a clean cloth around it and squeeze out excess moisture, then apply 5 teaspoons of SAE 30 oil *(above, right)* and squeeze it to distribute the oil. Reinstall the air filter and put back the air filter cover. Reconnect the spark plug cable *(page 71)*.

SERVICING THE FUEL LINE AND FUEL FILTER

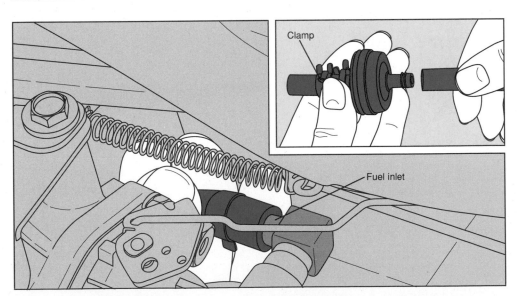

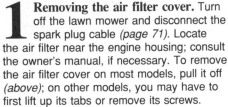

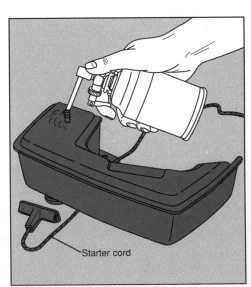

1 **Cleaning the fuel line and replacing an external fuel filter.** Turn off the lawn mower and disconnect the spark plug cable *(page 71)*, then drain the fuel tank and disconnect the fuel line *(page 72)*. Locate the end of the fuel line at the carburetor. Use utility pliers to slide the clamp along the fuel line, then disconnect it *(above)*. If there is a fuel filter along the fuel line, remove it *(inset)*. Wearing safety goggles, blow compressed air through the fuel line to clear it; if the fuel line is damaged, replace it with an exact duplicate. If there is no external fuel filter, clean the internal fuel filter *(step 2)*. If there is an external fuel filter, replace it with an exact duplicate if you suspect it is faulty. Install the external fuel filter along the fuel line and reconnect the fuel line. Refuel the lawn mower *(page 121)* and reconnect the spark plug cable *(page 71)*.

2 **Cleaning an internal fuel filter.** Unscrew the fuel tank and turn it upside down. Wearing safety goggles, blow compressed air through the fuel outlet *(above)*. Holding the fuel tank upright over a metal container, pour in a small amount of fuel, swirl it around and empty it. Wipe up any spill and dispose of the fuel safely *(page 11)*. Reinstall the fuel tank and reconnect the fuel line. Refuel the lawn mower *(page 121)* and reconnect the spark plug cable *(page 71)*.

SERVICING THE CARBURETOR

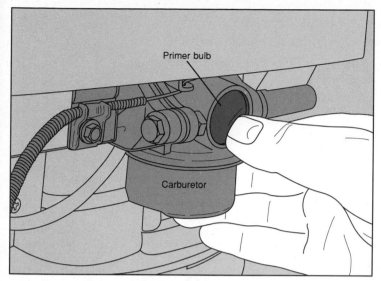

1 **Priming the carburetor.** Often, there is a primer bulb for forcing fuel into the carburetor. If your model does not have a primer bulb, access the carburetor *(step 2)*. If your model has a primer bulb, set the controls to the start position. Press the primer bulb once *(above)*, wait a few seconds and then press it again. Following the manufacturer's instructions, start the lawn mower; if the problem persists, access the carburetor to service its internal components.

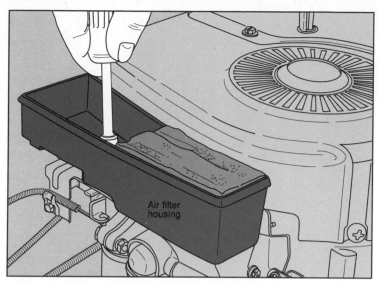

2 **Accessing the carburetor.** Turn off the lawn mower and disconnect the spark plug cable *(page 71)*, then drain the fuel tank *(page 72)*. Locate the end of the fuel line at the carburetor. Use utility pliers to slide the clamp along the fuel line, then disconnect the fuel line from the carburetor. Remove the air filter cover *(page 74)*, then unscrew the air filter housing *(above)* and lift it off the carburetor. Set the air filter housing carefully aside.

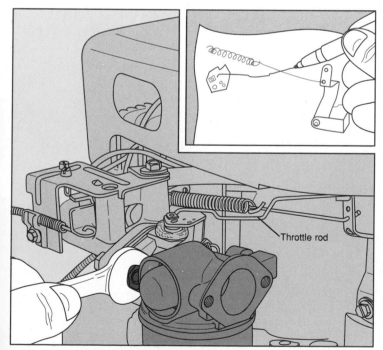

3 **Removing the carburetor.** Note all carburetor connections, drawing a diagram for reassembly *(inset)*; in particular, sketch the throttle linkage, showing the position of the throttle rod, the throttle lever, the governor bracket and each spring. Avoid handling any spring; if a spring is stretched, bent or otherwise damaged, take the lawn mower for professional service. Supporting the carburetor in one hand, if necessary, use a wrench to remove each nut securing it to the intake manifold *(above)*. Carefully pull out the carburetor enough to disconnect the throttle rod *(step 4)*.

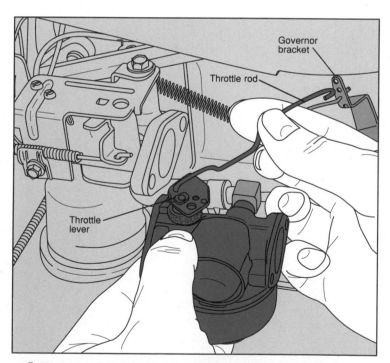

4 **Disconnecting the throttle rod.** Supporting the carburetor in one hand, gently turn it to unhook the end of the throttle rod from the governor bracket *(above)*; work carefully to avoid bending the throttle rod and make sure its position on the governor bracket is correctly noted on your diagram. Unhook the end of the throttle rod from the throttle lever the same way, likewise noting its position. Remove the gasket between the carburetor and the intake manifold, and buy an exact duplicate for reassembly.

SERVICING THE CARBURETOR (continued)

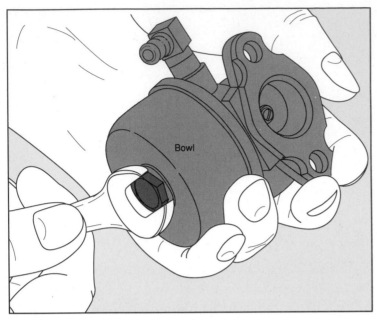

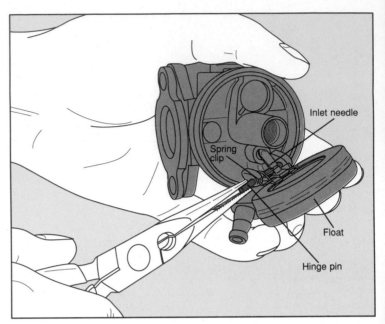

5 **Draining the carburetor.** Holding the carburetor over a metal container, loosen the bolt or screw on the float bowl *(above)*; allow the fuel to drain from the carburetor. Then, remove the bolt or screw and take off the float bowl along with its gasket; buy an exact duplicate gasket for reassembly. If there is a small hole in the bolt or screw, wear safety goggles and blow compressed air through it to clear it. Before disassembling the carburetor *(step 6)*, buy the basic carburetor rebuilding kit for your lawn mower make and model; the carburetor may have its number stamped on it. Otherwise, clean the carburetor and inspect the throttle *(step 7)*.

6 **Disassembling the carburetor.** Open the float on its hinge; carefully note the position of each part, especially the spring clip, for reassembly. Using long-nose pliers, remove the hinge pin *(above)*, releasing the float, the inlet needle and the spring clip. Use a small hooked wire to pull any rubber seat out of the inlet; replace it with an exact duplicate when reassembling the carburetor. Inspect the float, the inlet needle and the spring clip for wear and other damage; listen for fuel sloshing in the float, indicating it leaks. Use your carburetor rebuilding kit, along with any exploded diagram it contains, to replace any damaged part when reassembling the carburetor.

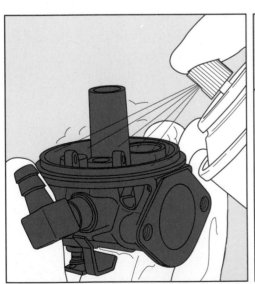

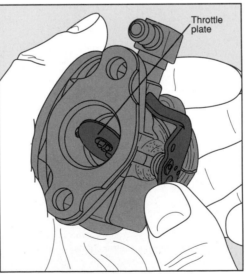

7 **Cleaning the carburetor and inspecting the throttle.** Wearing rubber gloves, spray the carburetor *(above, left)* and the float bowl with carburetor and choke cleaner, taking care not to drip any on plastic parts. Wipe or dry off the cleaner following its instructions. If the screw of the throttle plate is loose, tighten it. To check the throttle plate, flip the throttle lever back and forth *(above, right)*. If the throttle plate does not move smoothly or is bent, replace it with an exact duplicate; align the new throttle plate using any guidelines on it and the carburetor. Use the same procedure to inspect any choke plate on the other side of the carburetor. If you disassembled the carburetor, reassemble it *(step 8)*. Otherwise, install the gasket and float bowl, reconnect the throttle rod, and install the gasket and carburetor. Refuel the lawn mower *(page 121)* and reconnect the spark plug cable *(page 71)*. Adjust the carburetor as instructed in your owner's manual.

8 **Reassembling the carburetor.** Position any rubber seat, the inlet needle and the spring clip, then install the hinge pin. Close the float and check it is level using a special float-setting tool *(above)*, usually supplied with the carburetor rebuilding kit. To close any gap between the float and the float-setting tool, reopen the float and adjust the hinge tab with a small screwdriver. Then, install the gasket and float bowl, reconnect the throttle rod, and install the gasket and carburetor. Refuel the lawn mower *(page 121)* and reconnect the spark plug cable *(page 71)*. Adjust the carburetor as instructed in your owner's manual.

SERVICING THE STARTER ASSEMBLY

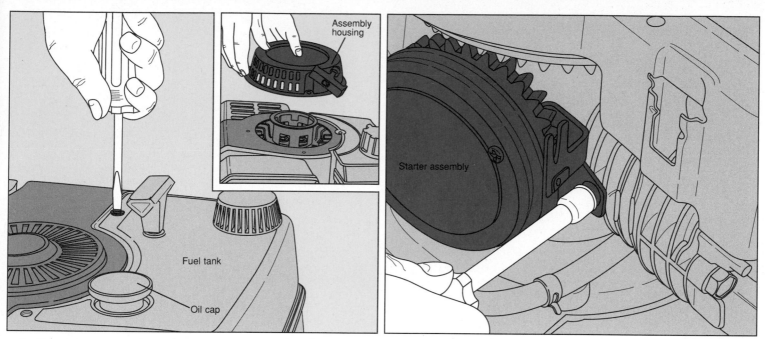

1 **Removing the starter assembly.** Turn off the lawn mower and disconnect the spark plug cable *(page 71)*, then drain the fuel tank *(page 72)*. If the starter cord pulls out horizontally, unscrew the starter assembly housing and lift it off the engine housing *(inset)*; service this type of starter assembly as you would for a snow thrower *(page 108)*. If the starter cord pulls out vertically, unscrew the fuel tank *(above, left)*, remove the oil cap, disconnect the fuel line and lift off the fuel tank; note that the starter cord is threaded through an opening in the fuel tank and attached to the handle. Then, use a nut driver to remove the starter assembly from the engine block *(above, right)*. If the starter cord is damaged, replace it *(step 2)*. If you suspect the rewind spring is damaged, remove it *(step 3)*.

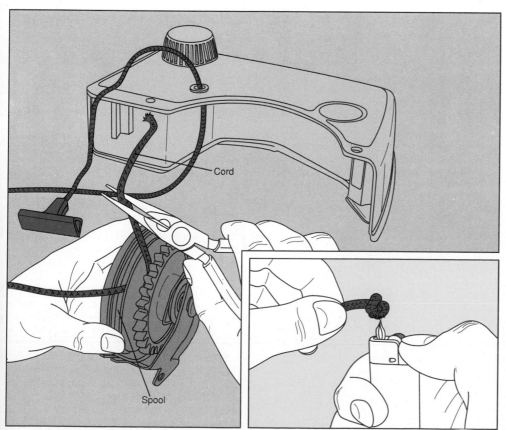

2 **Replacing the starter cord.** Holding the starter assembly in one hand, pull out enough of the starter cord to unwind it from the spool; as the starter cord is unwound, the rewind spring will release its tension. Pull the knot at the end of the starter cord out of the spool using long-nose pliers, then cut it off with scissors. Thread the starter cord out through the opening in the spool and the opening in the fuel tank. Replace the starter cord with an exact duplicate; it usually comes attached to a handle.

Use long-nose pliers to thread the end of the new starter cord in through the opening in the fuel tank and the opening in the spool *(left)*. Pull out a few inches of the starter cord and knot the end of it. Cauterize the knot well away from the fuel tank by holding a flame under it without touching it *(inset)*. Then, wind the starter cord counterclockwise onto the spool. If you suspect the rewind spring is damaged, remove it *(step 3)*.

To put tension on the rewind spring, hold the starter assembly in one hand and pull out 12 inches of the starter cord; then, wind it onto the spool and reinstall the starter assembly. Reconnect the fuel line, reinstall the fuel tank and put back the oil cap. Refuel the lawn mower *(page 121)* and reconnect the spark plug cable *(page 71)*.

SERVICING THE STARTER ASSEMBLY (continued)

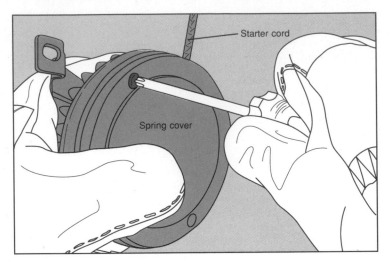

Starter cord

Spring cover

3 **Removing the rewind spring.** Wearing work gloves and safety goggles, hold the starter assembly in one hand and unscrew the rewind spring cover *(above)*. **Caution:** Do not pull the starter cord or rotate the spool once the rewind spring cover is loosened. Carefully turn over the starter assembly and take off the rewind spring cover— be prepared for the rewind spring to uncoil and pop out. If the rewind spring is damaged, use long-nose pliers to unhook each end of it from the spool lug. Replace any rewind spring that is damaged or uncoils and pops out with an exact duplicate; a new rewind spring usually comes coiled and bound with a wire or string.

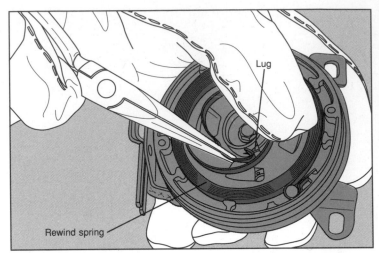

Lug

Rewind spring

4 **Installing the rewind spring.** Wearing work gloves and safety goggles, position the rewind spring and use long-nose pliers to hook its outside end to the spool lug. Holding the rewind spring in place, cut the wire or string binding it and hook its inside end to the spool lug *(above)*; rotate it clockwise, if necessary. Lubricate the rewind spring with a few drops of light machine oil or the manufacturer's specified lubricant and reinstall the rewind spring cover. To put tension on the rewind spring, pull out about 12 inches of the starter cord; then, wind it onto the spool and reinstall the starter assembly. Reconnect the fuel line, reinstall the fuel tank and put back the oil cap. Refuel the lawn mower *(page 121)* and reconnect the spark plug cable *(page 71)*.

SERVICING THE ELECTRONIC IGNITION MODULE (EIM)

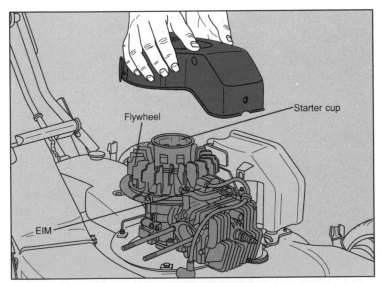

Flywheel

Starter cup

EIM

1 **Accessing the engine.** Turn off the lawn mower and disconnect the spark plug cable *(page 71)*, then drain the fuel tank *(page 72)*. To reach the electronic ignition module (EIM) and the flywheel, remove any component necessary to unscrew the engine housing and lift it off *(above);* on the model shown, you have to remove the starter assembly *(page 77)*, disconnect the fuel line and take off the fuel tank, and remove the side-mounted muffler *(page 83)*. After removing the engine housing, locate the EIM and identify it *(page 121)*.

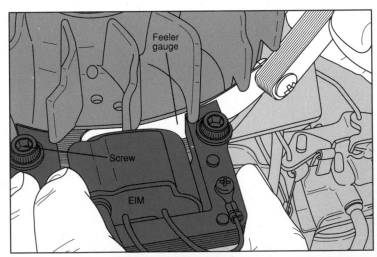

Feeler gauge

Screw

EIM

2 **Gapping the EIM.** To gap the EIM, use a brass or plastic feeler gauge that matches the gap specified by the manufacturer. Rotate the flywheel until its magnets are as far as possible from the EIM. Loosen the EIM screws and slide the EIM enough to fit the feeler gauge horizontally between it and the flywheel. Rotate the flywheel until its magnets are aligned with the EIM. Then, tighten the EIM screws and pull out the feeler gauge. If the feeler gauge is too short to fit across the EIM *(above)*, perform the procedure on each side of the EIM, loosening and tightening one EIM screw at a time. Put back the engine housing and other components removed, reversing the disassembly sequence used. Refuel the lawn mower *(page 121)* and reconnect the spark plug cable *(page 71)*. If the problem persists, access the engine *(step 1)* and remove the EIM *(step 3)*.

SERVICING THE ELECTRONIC IGNITION MODULE (EIM) (continued)

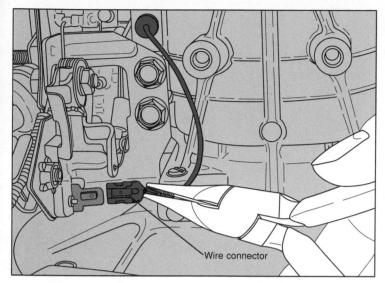

Wire connector

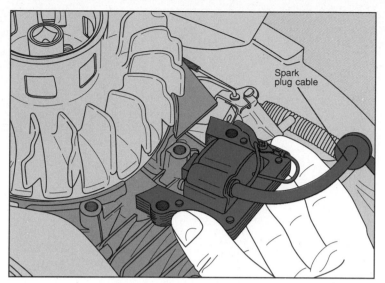

Spark plug cable

3 **Disconnecting the EIM.** If possible, disconnect each wire from the EIM, noting its terminal for reassembly. Otherwise, as in the model shown, trace each wire connected to the EIM to its other terminal and disconnect it, using long-nose pliers to pull off its connector *(above)*; note the terminal. Gently remove each wire from any retaining clip or bracket, noting its route. Then, unscrew the EIM and lift it out, along with any wires connected to it and the spark plug cable.

4 **Replacing the EIM.** Buy an exact duplicate EIM, position it *(above)* and screw it loosely in place. Route each wire to its terminal, fitting it into any retaining clip or bracket, and connect it. Gap the EIM *(step 2)*. Put back the engine housing and other components removed, reversing the disassembly sequence used. Refuel the lawn mower *(page 121)* and reconnect the spark plug cable *(page 71)*.

SERVICING THE FLYWHEEL

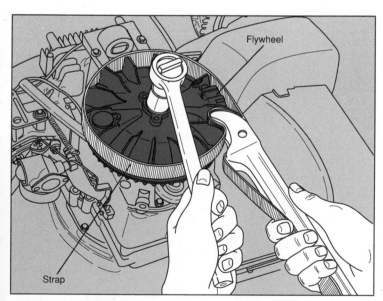

Flywheel

Strap

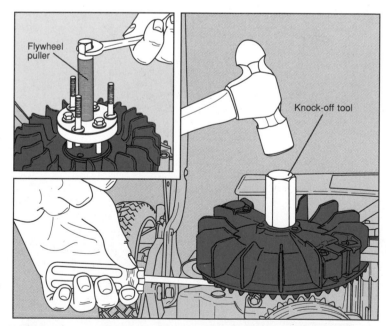

Flywheel puller

Knock-off tool

1 **Removing the flywheel nut.** Turn off the lawn mower and disconnect the spark plug cable *(page 71)*, then drain the fuel tank *(page 72)*. Access the engine *(page 78)* and take the starter cup off the flywheel. To hold the flywheel steady, use a strap wrench; wrap the strap counterclockwise around the flywheel, thread it through the opening at the top of the wrench and grip it tightly against the handle, as shown. Then, use a socket wrench to loosen the flywheel nut *(above)*, applying force counterclockwise. If the flywheel nut does not loosen, it may be reverse-threaded; reorient the strap wrench and apply force clockwise with the socket wrench. When the flywheel nut is loosened, turn it by hand to remove it.

2 **Removing the flywheel.** To loosen the flywheel, use the tool recommended by the manufacturer. With a knock-off tool, first screw it onto the crankshaft until it touches the flywheel, then unscrew it 1 or 2 turns. Slide an old, flat screwdriver under the flywheel. Wearing safety goggles, strike the tool squarely and sharply with a ball-peen hammer while prying up the flywheel with the screwdriver *(above)*. With a flywheel puller, position it into the flywheel holes, then use a wrench *(inset)* or locking pliers to screw it down until it touches the crankshaft. When the flywheel is loose, carefully lift it off.

SERVICING THE FLYWHEEL (continued)

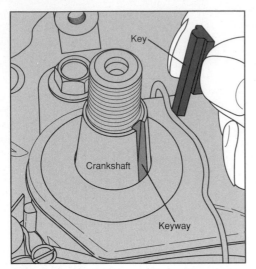

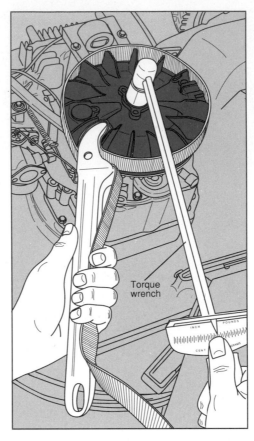

4 **Replacing the flywheel.** If the flywheel is damaged, replace it with an exact duplicate. With the flywheel key fitted into place in its keyway, position the flywheel on the crankshaft; make sure it sits evenly and is balanced. Screw on the flywheel nut by hand. Then, hold the flywheel steady with a strap wrench, reversing the orientation used to loosen the flywheel nut *(step 1)*, as shown; using a torque wrench, tighten the flywheel nut to the torque specifications of the manufacturer *(left)*. After tightening the flywheel nut, gap the EIM *(page 78)*. Put back the starter cup, the engine housing and other components removed, reversing the disassembly sequence used. Refuel the lawn mower *(page 121)* and reconnect the spark plug cable *(page 71)*.

3 **Inspecting the crankshaft and the flywheel key.** If the threads of the crankshaft are worn or it is otherwise damaged, take the lawn mower for professional service. Otherwise, locate the flywheel key in its keyway at the end of the crankshaft. Pull the flywheel key out of the keyway *(above)*, examine it carefully and reposition it. If the flywheel key is cracked, twisted or bent, or if it fits loosely in the keyway, replace it with an exact duplicate.

SERVICING THE DRIVE BELT

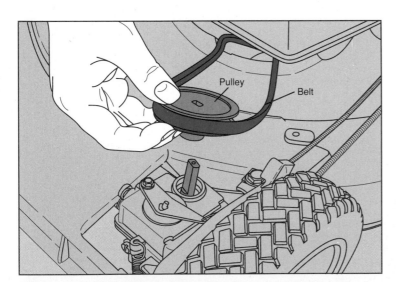

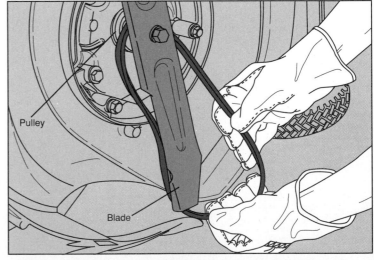

1 **Removing the drive belt.** Turn off the lawn mower and disconnect the spark plug cable *(page 71)*, then drain the fuel tank *(page 72)*. To reach the drive belt, unscrew the drive belt cover and take it off the deck. Inspect the drive belt by rotating it around the drive pulley. If the drive belt is not damaged, reinstall the drive belt cover and service the wheel drive cable *(page 81)*. If the drive belt is cracked, split or otherwise damaged, pry the retaining clip off the drive pulley with an old screwdriver, lift off the drive pulley *(above)* and take the drive belt off it.

2 **Replacing the drive belt.** Wearing work gloves, tilt the lawn mower onto the side recommended in the owner's manual. Take the drive belt off the crankshaft pulley *(above)* and pull it out around the blade. Buy an exact duplicate drive belt. Fit the drive belt around the blade and onto the crankshaft pulley, push it through the opening in the deck and turn the lawn mower upright. Then, fit the drive belt around the drive pulley, position the drive pulley and reinstall the retaining clip. Put back the drive belt cover. Refuel the lawn mower *(page 121)* and reconnect the spark plug cable *(page 71)*.

SERVICING THE CONTROLS AND CABLES

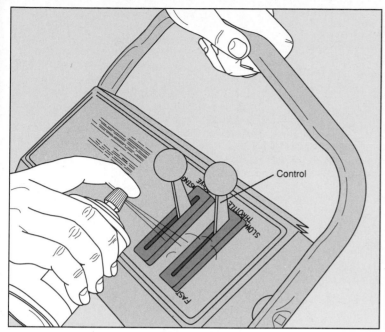

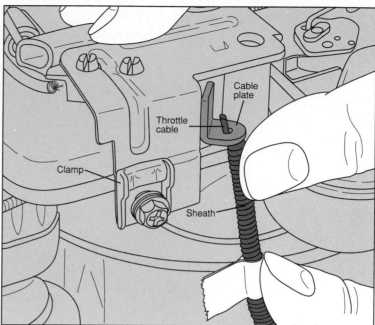

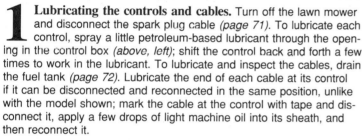

1 **Lubricating the controls and cables.** Turn off the lawn mower and disconnect the spark plug cable *(page 71)*. To lubricate each control, spray a little petroleum-based lubricant through the opening in the control box *(above, left)*; shift the control back and forth a few times to work in the lubricant. To lubricate and inspect the cables, drain the fuel tank *(page 72)*. Lubricate the end of each cable at its control if it can be disconnected and reconnected in the same position, unlike with the model shown; mark the cable at the control with tape and disconnect it, apply a few drops of light machine oil into its sheath, and then reconnect it.

Trace each cable from its control to its other end; for access, you may have to remove components: with the throttle cable, the air filter cover and housing; with the wheel drive cable, the drive belt cover. If the cable is damaged, free it from its clamp, disconnect it from its plate, and remove it *(step 2)*. Otherwise, mark the cable at its clamp with tape, then free it from the clamp and disconnect it from its plate *(above, right)*. Apply a few drops of light machine oil into the cable sheath. Reconnect the cable to its plate and reinstall it in its clamp using the tape as reference. Put back any component removed, refuel the lawn mower *(page 121)* and reconnect the spark plug cable *(page 71)*.

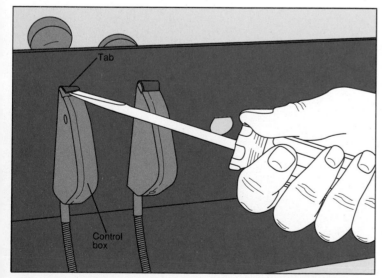

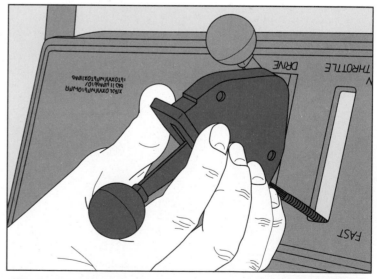

2 **Removing the cable.** If possible, disconnect the cable from its control. Otherwise, as in the model shown, remove the cable and its control box from the control panel. Working from the back of the control box, pry up any tab holding it in place using an old screwdriver *(above)* or unscrew it. Then, push the back of the control box through its opening or work from the front of the control box to pull it out. Note the route of the cable for reassembly and carefully thread it out, releasing it from any retaining clip or bracket. Buy an exact duplicate cable or cable and control box.

3 **Positioning the new cable.** If you disconnected the cable from the control, connect the new cable to it; first apply a few drops of light machine oil into the cable sheath. Otherwise, as in the model shown, thread in the new cable and fit its control box into the control panel *(above)*; tap it into position with a rubber mallet, if necessary. Working from the back of the control box, push down any tab to hold it using an old screwdriver or screw it in place. Set the control to its highest operating position. Then, route the cable to its plate, securing it in any retaining clip or bracket.

SERVICING THE CONTROLS AND CABLES (continued)

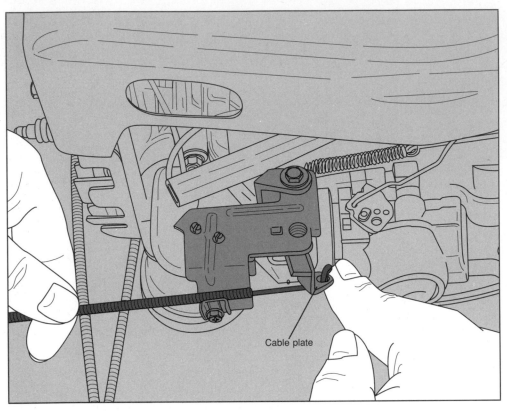

Cable plate

4 **Installing the new cable.** Apply a few drops of light machine oil into the cable sheath and connect the cable to its plate. Setting the plate to its highest operating position, keep the cable taut and fit it into its clamp *(left)*, then tighten the clamp screw. To check the cable, shift the control back and forth several times between its highest and lowest operating positions; the plate should move between its highest and lowest operating positions with the control. If necessary, reset the control to its highest operating position, then remove and reconnect the cable. Reinstall any component removed, refuel the lawn mower *(page 121)* and reconnect the spark plug cable *(page 71)*.

SERVICING THE MUFFLER

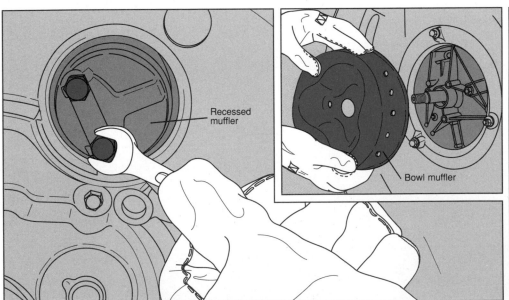

Recessed muffler

Bowl muffler

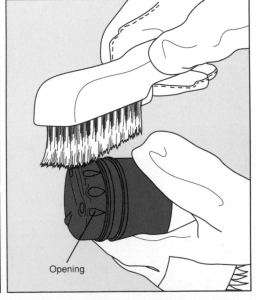

Opening

Removing and inspecting a bottom-mounted muffler. Turn off the lawn mower and disconnect the spark plug cable *(page 71)*, then drain the fuel tank *(page 72)*. If the muffler is mounted on the side of the engine, remove and inspect it *(page 83)*. Otherwise, wear work gloves and tilt the lawn mower onto the side recommended in the owner's manual; support it, if necessary, with bricks or wood blocks. For a recessed muffler, unscrew it *(above, left)* and take it off. For a bowl muffler, first remove the blade *(page 73)*, then unscrew it and take it off *(inset)*.

Remove any gasket and buy an exact duplicate for reassembly. If the muffler is rusted or otherwise damaged, replace it with an exact duplicate. To clean clumps of grass clippings, dirt and carbon deposits off the muffler, use a wire brush *(above, right)*, making sure each opening is clear. For stubborn carbon deposits, apply a small amount of decarbonizing spray and scrub with the brush. Position the gasket and screw on the muffler; reinstall the blade if you removed it. Turn the lawn mower upright, refuel it *(page 121)* and reconnect the spark plug cable *(page 71)*.

SERVICING THE MUFFLER (continued)

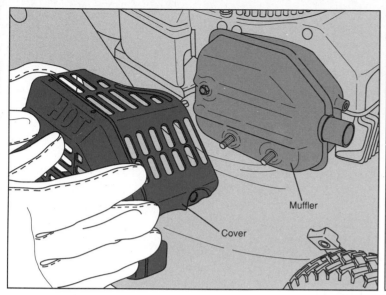

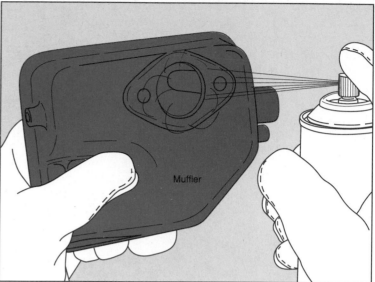

Removing and inspecting a side-mounted muffler. Turn off the lawn mower and disconnect the spark plug cable *(page 71)*, then drain the fuel tank *(page 72)*. If the muffler is mounted on the bottom of the engine, remove and inspect it *(page 82)*. Otherwise, wear work gloves to remove the nuts and screws holding the muffler cover, then lift it off *(above, left)*. Use a socket wrench to take off the muffler. Remove any gasket and buy an exact duplicate for reassembly. If the engine is two cycle, service the exhaust port *(steps below)*.

If the muffler is rusted or otherwise damaged, replace it with an exact duplicate. To clean clumps of grass clippings, dirt and carbon deposits off the muffler, use a wire brush; for stubborn carbon deposits, first apply a small amount of decarbonizing spray *(above, right)*. Position the gasket and screw on the muffler, then reinstall the muffler cover. Refuel the lawn mower *(page 121)* and reconnect the spark plug cable *(page 71)*. Start the lawn mower and let it run for 1 or 2 minutes; then, turn it off, disconnect the spark plug cable and tighten each nut and screw of the muffler cover.

CLEANING THE EXHAUST PORT (Two-cycle engine)

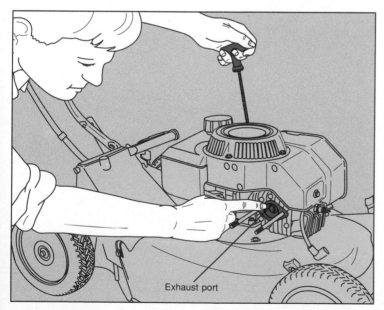

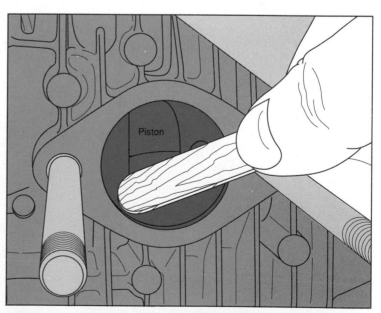

1 Blocking the exhaust port with the piston. Turn off the lawn mower and disconnect the spark plug cable *(page 71)*, then drain the fuel tank *(page 72)*. To reach the exhaust port, remove the side-mounted muffler *(step above)*. Watching for the piston through the exhaust port, slowly pull out the starter cord *(above)*; stop pulling out the starter cord when the piston completely blocks the exhaust port.

2 Scraping deposits out of the exhaust port. To keep particles from falling against the piston, raise the side of the lawn mower opposite the exhaust port; support it in place with bricks or wood blocks. Carefully scrape deposits out of the exhaust port with a stick *(above)*; do not use a metal tool or touch the piston. Reinstall the muffler and the muffler cover. Refuel the lawn mower *(page 121)* and reconnect the spark plug cable *(page 71)*.

GARDEN TILLERS

A garden tiller can work wonders, breaking new ground for planting, preparing a seedbed or working amendments into the soil. Shown below is a common front-tine garden tiller, the type popular with homeowners; it is powered by a four-cycle engine. The crankshaft rotates the forward drive pulley and, through a series of gears, the reverse drive pulley. When the forward clutch lever is depressed, its control rod engages the forward idler pulley with the forward drive belt, which is turned by the forward drive pulley; the forward drive belt then rotates the driven pulley, engaging the gears that turn the drive shaft of the tines. The same principles are applied in the opposite direction when the reverse clutch lever is depressed.

A garden tiller is vulnerable to the dusty conditions in which it is operated. Read the owner's manual for the special maintenance requirements of your garden tiller; wipe it off after each use. Remember to clean the air filter on a regular basis *(page 87)*. When a problem occurs, consult the Troubleshooting Guide *(page 85)*; diagnosing and fixing a problem is rarely difficult. Before undertaking any repair, make sure you disconnect the spark plug cable *(page 87)* and, when instructed, drain the fuel tank *(page 88)*. Refer to Tools & Techniques *(page 110)* for information on identifying ignition systems and types of carburetors, as well as on refueling, the diagnosis of spark plugs and seasonal storage.

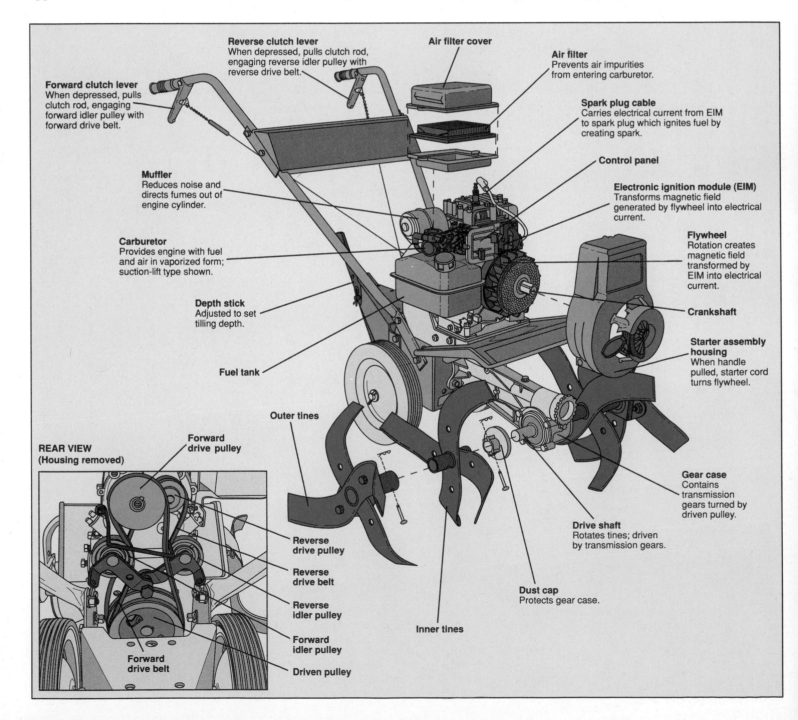

Reverse clutch lever
When depressed, pulls clutch rod, engaging reverse idler pulley with reverse drive belt.

Air filter cover

Air filter
Prevents air impurities from entering carburetor.

Forward clutch lever
When depressed, pulls clutch rod, engaging forward idler pulley with forward drive belt.

Spark plug cable
Carries electrical current from EIM to spark plug which ignites fuel by creating spark.

Control panel

Muffler
Reduces noise and directs fumes out of engine cylinder.

Electronic ignition module (EIM)
Transforms magnetic field generated by flywheel into electrical current.

Carburetor
Provides engine with fuel and air in vaporized form; suction-lift type shown.

Flywheel
Rotation creates magnetic field transformed by EIM into electrical current.

Crankshaft

Depth stick
Adjusted to set tilling depth.

Starter assembly housing
When handle pulled, starter cord turns flywheel.

Fuel tank

Outer tines

REAR VIEW
(Housing removed)

Forward drive pulley

Gear case
Contains transmission gears turned by driven pulley.

Reverse drive pulley

Drive shaft
Rotates tines; driven by transmission gears.

Reverse drive belt

Reverse idler pulley

Dust cap
Protects gear case.

Forward idler pulley

Forward drive belt

Inner tines

Driven pulley

TROUBLESHOOTING GUIDE

SYMPTOM	POSSIBLE CAUSE	PROCEDURE
Garden tiller does not start	Control set incorrectly	Consult manual to start garden tiller
	Starter cord or rewind spring broken	Service starter assembly (p. 94) ■◕
	Fuel contaminated or fuel tank empty	Drain fuel tank (p. 88) □○; refuel garden tiller (p. 121) □○
	Spark plug faulty or cable disconnected	Service spark plug (p. 87) □○
	Carburetor adjusted incorrectly	Consult manual to adjust carburetor
	Fuel line or carburetor dirty or faulty	Service fuel line and carburetor (p. 91) ■●
	Muffler clogged	Service muffler (p. 93) ■◕
	EIM gapped incorrectly or faulty	Service EIM (p. 95) ■○▲
	Engine faulty	Take garden tiller for professional service
Garden tiller starts, but power diminished	Fuel tank cap vents blocked	Clear vents with toothpick
	Air filter dirty	Service air filter (p. 87) □○
	Fuel contaminated	Drain fuel tank (p. 88) □○ and refuel garden tiller (p. 121) □○
	Carburetor adjusted incorrectly	Consult manual to adjust carburetor
	Fuel line or carburetor dirty or faulty	Service fuel line and carburetor (p. 91) ■●
	Muffler clogged	Service muffler (p. 93) ■◕
	EIM gapped incorrectly or faulty	Service EIM (p. 95) ■○▲
	Engine faulty	Take garden tiller for professional service
Garden tiller runs erratically or stalls	Fuel tank cap vents blocked	Clear vents with toothpick
	Air filter dirty	Service air filter (p. 87) □○
	Fuel contaminated	Drain fuel tank (p. 88) □○ and refuel garden tiller (p. 121) □○
	Oil contaminated or low	Drain crankcase (p. 88) □○; refill crankcase (p. 120) □○
	Carburetor adjusted incorrectly	Consult manual to adjust carburetor
	Fuel line or carburetor dirty or faulty	Service fuel line and carburetor (p. 91) ■●
	Muffler clogged	Service muffler (p. 93) ■◕
	Engine faulty	Take garden tiller for professional service
Garden tiller overheats	Engine cooling fins dirty	Clean engine cooling fins (p. 93) □○
	Air filter dirty	Service air filter (p. 87) □○
	Fuel contaminated	Drain fuel tank (p. 88) □○ and refuel garden tiller (p. 121) □○
	Oil contaminated or low	Drain crankcase (p. 88) □○; refill crankcase (p. 120) □○
	Tine or drive shaft damaged	Service tines (p. 88) □○
	Gear case oil contaminated or low	Change gear case oil (p. 89) □○ or replace gear case (p. 89) ■◕▲
	Muffler clogged	Service muffler (p. 93) ■◕
	Engine faulty	Take garden tiller for professional service
Garden tiller rattles or vibrates excessively	Housing fastener loose	Tighten housing fasteners
	Muffler clogged	Service muffler (p. 93) ■◕
	Engine faulty	Take garden tiller for professional service
Tines do not rotate or do not penetrate ground	Control set incorrectly	Consult manual to set controls
	Depth stick set incorrectly	Adjust depth stick (p. 86) □○
	Tines jammed	Clear tines (p. 86) □○
	Tine or drive shaft damaged	Service tines (p. 88) □○
	Drive belt loose or damaged	Service drive assembly (p. 89) ◕■
	Gear case oil contaminated or low	Change gear case oil (p. 89) □○ or replace gear case (p. 89) ■◕▲

DEGREE OF DIFFICULTY: □ Easy ■ Moderate ■ Complex
ESTIMATED TIME: ○ Less than 1 hour ◕ 1 to 3 hours ● Over 3 hours ▲ Special tool required

GARDEN TILLER USE AND MAINTENANCE

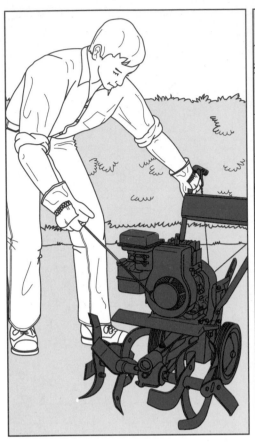

Operating a garden tiller. When using the garden tiller, wear work gloves, long pants and heavy shoes; tie back your hair if it is long. Before starting the garden tiller, remove all large rocks, sticks and other foreign objects from the work area. Set the handle bars to a comfortable operating height. Add fuel *(page 121)* and oil *(page 120)* at least 10 feet away from the work area. Then, wheel the garden tiller to the work area to adjust the tilling depth *(step below, left)*.

Connect the spark plug cable *(page 87)* and start the garden tiller according to the manufacturer's instructions. To pull the starter cord, stand beside the garden tiller and rest one hand on the handle bar, without depressing the clutch lever *(far left)*. To till, stand behind the garden tiller and depress the forward clutch lever; then, walking slowly behind the garden tiller, hold it back to let the tines penetrate the soil *(near left)*. Turn off the garden tiller and disconnect the spark plug cable to reset the tilling depth or to clean off the garden tiller. Use a stick to clean clumps of dirt off the tines. Clean the cooling fins with a wire brush *(page 93)*. If the tines jam, clear them *(step below, right)*.

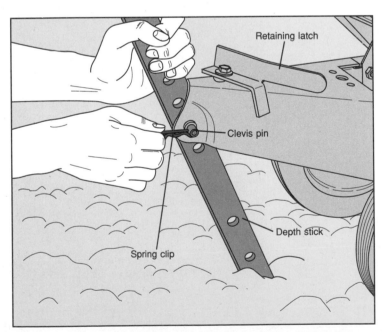

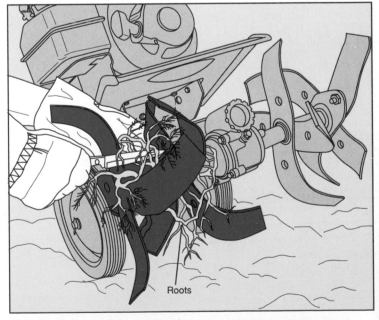

Setting the tilling depth. Always set the tilling depth at the work area before starting the garden tiller. Shift the retaining latch to release the depth stick, then remove the spring clip and the clevis pin. Push the depth stick into the soil to the tilling depth; if the soil is compacted, till first at a depth that just penetrates it, then at the depth desired. Reinstall the clevis pin and the spring clip *(above)*. Turn off the garden tiller and disconnect the spark plug cable *(page 87)* to reset the tilling depth and when finished tilling. Before wheeling the garden tiller from the work area, swing up the depth stick and shift the retaining latch to lock it.

Clearing jammed tines. If the tines jam, release the forward clutch lever. To clear the tines, depress the reverse clutch lever for a few seconds and then release it; if your model has no reverse clutch lever or the tines still jam, turn off the garden tiller and disconnect the spark plug cable *(page 87)*. Wearing work gloves, pull off any roots or vegetation tangled in the tines; if necessary, use a knife to cut them off *(above)*, having a helper tilt the garden tiller back slightly. If a tine is damaged, replace it *(page 88)*. Otherwise, set the garden tiller upright and reconnect the spark plug cable *(page 87)*.

DRAINING THE FUEL TANK AND THE CRANKCASE

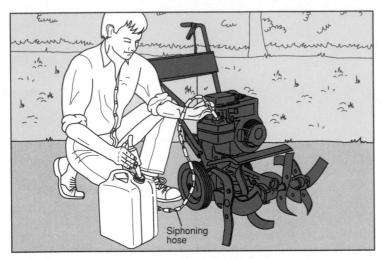

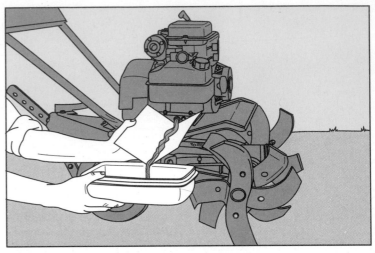

Siphoning the fuel. Turn off the garden tiller and disconnect the spark plug cable *(page 87)*. Let the engine cool, then drain the fuel tank using a siphoning hose. Working outdoors, unscrew the fuel tank cap, feed one end of the hose onto the bottom of the fuel tank and the other end into a fuel container for disposal. Pump the bulb until fuel flows through the hose *(above)*; continue until the fuel is drained. Wipe up any spill and dispose of the fuel safely *(page 11)*; do not reuse drained fuel. Screw the cap onto the fuel tank, wheel the garden tiller at least 10 feet away from the draining site and reconnect the spark plug cable *(page 87)*. Start the garden tiller and let it run to use up any remaining fuel; turn it off and disconnect the spark plug cable.

Draining the oil. Turn off the garden tiller and disconnect the spark plug cable *(page 87)*, then drain the fuel tank *(step left)*. Locate the drain plug on one side of the engine and set a metal container below it. Fold a piece of heavy cardboard in half and hold it under the drain plug, then remove the drain plug with a wrench and channel the oil into the container *(above)*; have a helper tilt the garden tiller toward the container, if necessary. Wipe up any spill, then dispose of the rags, the oil and the cardboard safely *(page 11)*. Reinstall the drain plug and refill the crankcase *(page 120)*. Refuel the garden tiller *(page 121)* and reconnect the spark plug cable *(page 87)*.

SERVICING THE TINES

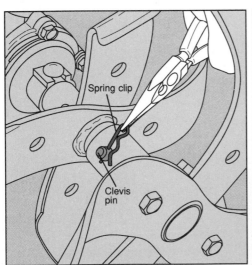

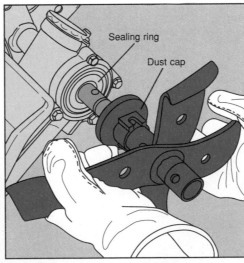

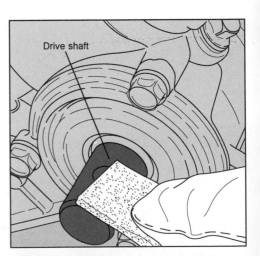

1 **Removing the tines.** Turn off the garden tiller and disconnect the spark plug cable *(page 87)*, then drain the fuel tank *(step above)*. Wearing work gloves, tilt the garden tiller back onto its handles. To remove each set of outer tines, use long-nose pliers to pull out the spring clip *(above, left)*, then pull out the clevis pin; if the tines are installed with a shear bolt and nut, remove the nut with a socket wrench and pull out the bolt. Pull off the outer tines, working them back and forth, if necessary; they may be joined, as in the model shown, or come off individually. To remove each set of inner tines, use the same procedure *(above, right)*; the dust cap may come off with the inner tines, as shown, or have to be pulled off after taking off the inner tines. Wipe off each tine, dust cap, sealing ring and drive shaft using a damp cloth. If a drive shaft is loose in the gear case, service the gear case *(page 90)*. If a tine or dust cap is damaged, buy an exact duplicate for reassembly.

2 **Smoothing the drive shafts and reinstalling the tines.** Rub each drive shaft lightly with emery paper *(above)* to smooth any burrs and rough edges, then apply a small amount of white grease or the manufacturer's specified lubricant. Reposition each dust cap and set of tines in turn, reversing the disassembly sequence used, and reinstall its clevis pin and spring clip or shear bolt and nut; make sure the top beveled edge of each tine faces away from the garden tiller. Refuel the garden tiller *(page 121)* and reconnect the spark plug cable *(page 87)*.

SERVICING THE DRIVE ASSEMBLY

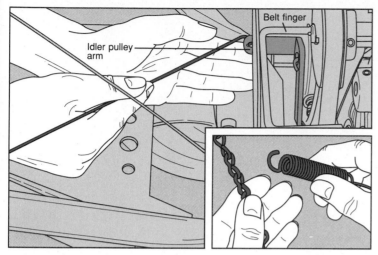

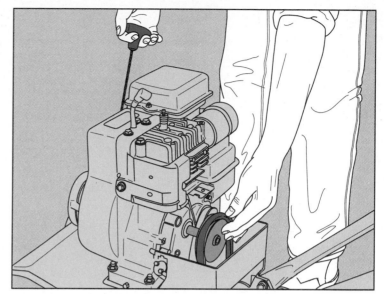

1 **Accessing the drive assembly.** Turn off the garden tiller and disconnect the spark plug cable *(page 87)*, then take off the drive belt cover. To check the tension of a drive belt, depress its clutch lever and pull it with your finger; there should be about 1/2 inch of play. To adjust the tension of a drive belt, rehook the spring of its clutch rod onto the chain of its clutch lever: higher to increase *(inset)*; lower to reduce. If a drive belt is damaged, replace it. To take off a drive belt, drain the fuel tank *(page 88)*, unhook each clutch rod from the chain of its clutch lever and the arm of its idler pulley *(above)*, and unscrew the belt finger; then, remove the forward drive belt *(step 2)*. Otherwise, reinstall the drive belt cover and reconnect the spark plug cable *(page 87)*.

2 **Replacing the forward drive belt.** Pull the starter cord slowly to rotate the forward drive pulley and guide the forward drive belt off it *(above)*. Take the forward drive belt off the driven pulley on the shaft of the gear case, noting its position, and push its idler pulley out of the way to free it. If necessary, remove the reverse drive belt *(step 3)*. If the forward drive belt is damaged, buy an exact duplicate. To install the forward drive belt, fit it into place around the driven pulley and against its idler pulley. Pull the starter cord slowly to rotate the forward drive pulley and guide the forward drive belt onto it. Reinstall the belt finger and each clutch rod. Refuel the garden tiller *(page 121)* and reconnect the spark plug cable *(page 87)*.

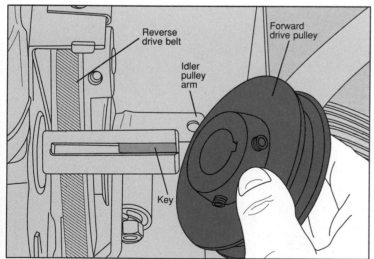

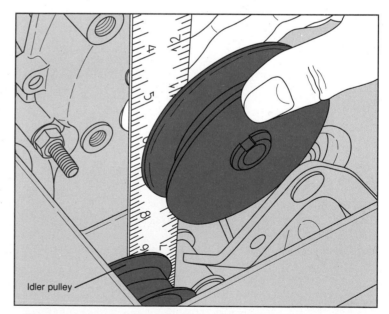

3 **Replacing the reverse drive belt.** Loosen the screws of the forward drive pulley using a hex wrench and pull the forward drive pulley off the crankshaft *(above)*. Take the key out of its keyway in the crankshaft and reposition it; if it fits loosely or is otherwise damaged, replace it with an exact duplicate. Pull the starter cord to rotate the reverse drive pulley and guide the reverse drive belt off it. Take the reverse drive belt off the driven pulley on the shaft of the gear case, noting its position, and push its idler pulley to one side to free it. If the reverse drive belt is damaged, buy an exact duplicate. To install the reverse drive belt, fit it into place around the driven pulley and against its idler pulley. Pull the starter cord slowly to rotate the reverse drive pulley and guide the reverse drive belt onto it.

4 **Realigning the forward drive pulley.** Push the forward drive pulley onto the crankshaft and align it with its idler pulley using a straight edge. Placing the straight edge against the inside edge of the forward drive pulley and its idler pulley, adjust the forward drive pulley until the straight edge is vertical *(above)*; then, tighten the screws of the forward drive pulley. Fit the forward drive belt into place around the driven pulley and against its idler pulley. Pull the starter cord slowly to rotate the forward drive pulley and guide the forward drive belt onto it. Reinstall the belt finger and each clutch rod. Refuel the garden tiller *(page 121)* and reconnect the spark plug cable *(page 87)*.

SERVICING THE GEAR CASE

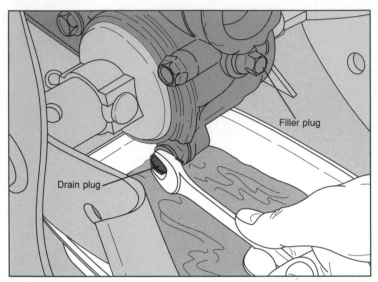

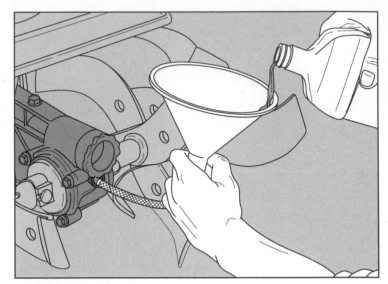

1 **Draining the gear case.** Turn off the garden tiller and disconnect the spark plug cable *(page 87)*, then drain the fuel tank *(page 88)*. Locate the drain plug on the gear case; there may be a drain plug and a filler plug, as in the model shown, or only one drain and filler plug. Set a metal container under the drain opening and use a wrench to remove the drain plug *(above)*. Allow the oil to drain; tilt the garden tiller toward the container, if necessary. If there is a separate filler plug, reinstall the drain plug. Wipe up any spill, then check the oil and dispose of it safely *(page 11)*; if it contains metal shavings, remove the driven pulley *(step 3)*.

2 **Refilling the gear case.** Set a metal container under the filler opening and use a wrench to remove the filler plug. Slide one end of a flexible tube onto a funnel and the other end onto the filler opening. Slowly pour the oil specified by the manufacturer into the funnel *(above)*; if necessary, stop periodically to check the oil level. After filling the gear case, reinstall the filler plug. Wipe up any spill and dispose of the oil safely *(page 11)*. Refuel the garden tiller *(page 121)* and reconnect the spark plug cable *(page 87)*. If the problem persists, turn off the garden tiller, disconnect the spark plug *(page 87)* and drain the fuel tank *(page 88)*; then, remove the driven pulley *(step 3)*.

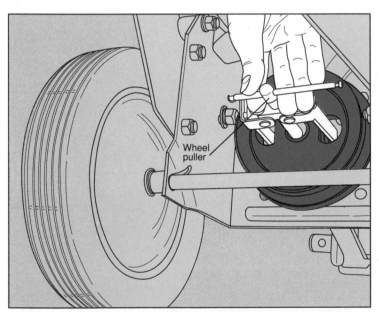

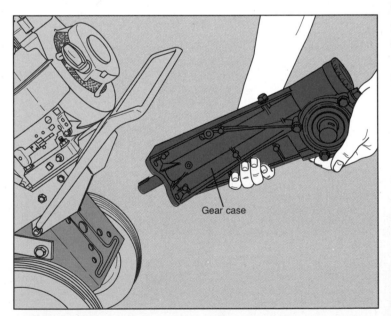

3 **Removing the driven pulley.** Remove the tines *(page 88)* and each drive belt *(page 89)*. Tilt the garden tiller forward, resting it on the gear case. To remove the driven pulley, use a special wheel puller. Loosen the screws of the driven pulley with a hex wrench and fit the wheel puller into the openings of the driven pulley. Turn the handle of the wheel puller clockwise *(above)* until its center arm is firmly seated on the shaft of the gear case; then, continue turning until the driven pulley pulls off. Take the key out of its keyway in the shaft of the gear case and reposition it; if it fits loosely or is otherwise damaged, replace it with an exact duplicate.

4 **Replacing the gear case.** To reach the gear case, set the garden tiller upright and then tilt it back, resting it on its handles. Having a helper on hand to catch the gear case, remove the bolts securing it; take off each bolt using a socket wrench, steadying its nut with a wrench, if necessary. Take the gear case for professional service or replace it with an exact duplicate. Working with a helper, position the gear case *(above)* and install its bolts and nuts; tighten each bolt with the socket wrench. Reinstall the driven pulley, each drive belt and the tines, reversing the sequence used to remove them. Fill the gear case with oil *(step 2)*, then refuel the garden tiller *(page 121)* and reconnect the spark plug cable *(page 87)*.

SERVICING THE FUEL LINE AND THE CARBURETOR

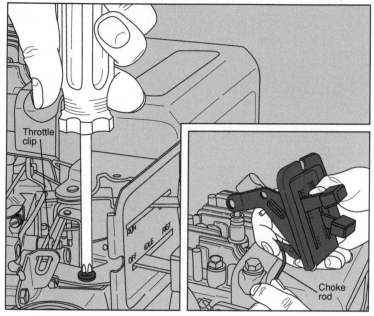

Throttle clip

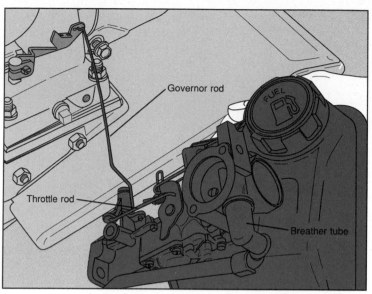

Choke rod

Governor rod

Throttle rod

Breather tube

1 **Removing the control panel and controls.** Turn off the garden tiller and disconnect the spark plug cable *(page 87)*, then drain the fuel tank *(page 88)*. Remove the air filter *(page 87)*, then unscrew and lift off the air filter housing. Disconnect the grounding wire from the throttle control, noting its terminal. Unscrew the control panel *(above)* and pull it away from the fuel tank, angling it to clear the throttle clip; take the choke rod off the choke control *(inset)*, noting its position for reassembly. Set the control panel and controls aside.

2 **Removing the fuel tank and the carburetor.** Draw a sketch of the carburetor showing each linkage for reassembly. In particular, note the position of each governor rod at the fuel tank and the carburetor; in the model shown, there are two governor rods. If possible, first disconnect each governor rod from the carburetor using a small screwdriver, then disconnect the governor spring from the fuel tank and slide it off the governor lever. Otherwise, unscrew the carburetor and the fuel tank, carefully lift them away from the engine block *(above)*, and pull the breather tube off the crankcase; then, disconnect each governor rod and remove the governor spring. Remove the gasket between the carburetor and the engine block; buy an exact duplicate for reassembly.

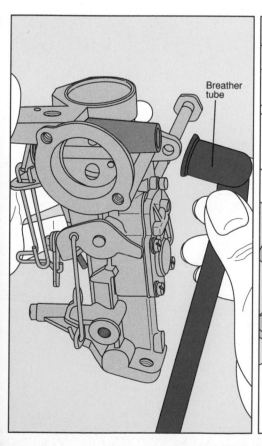

Breather tube

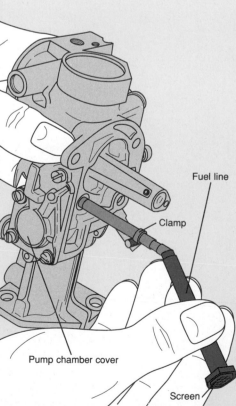

Fuel line

Clamp

Pump chamber cover

Screen

3 **Cleaning the fuel line.** Unscrew the carburetor and lift it along with the gasket off the fuel tank; buy an exact duplicate gasket for reassembly. Wearing safety goggles, pull the breather tube off the carburetor *(far left)* and blow compressed air through it. If dirt or debris flies out of the breather tube, take the garden tiller for professional service. Otherwise, carefully inspect the fuel line; unlike with the model shown, there may be two fuel lines. If the screen of the fuel line is dirty or the fuel line is damaged, slide the clamp off it using an old screwdriver, soak it in a cup of hot water for a few minutes to soften it, and pull it off the carburetor *(near left)*. To clean off the screen of the fuel line, wear safety goggles and blow compressed air through it; to replace the fuel line, buy an exact duplicate for reassembly.

SERVICING THE FUEL LINE AND THE CARBURETOR (continued)

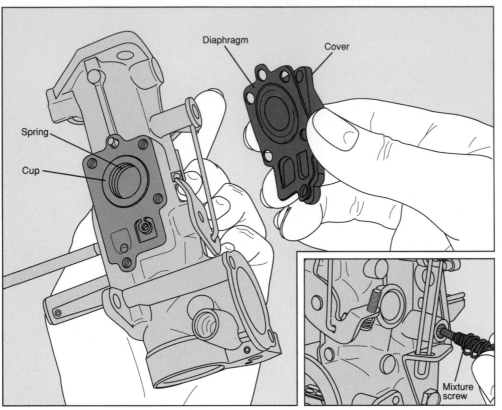

Diaphragm

Cover

Spring

Cup

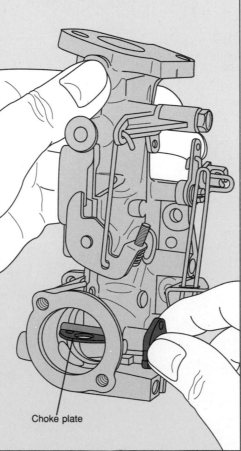

Mixture screw

4 **Inspecting the mixture screw and disassembling the carburetor.** Locate the mixture screw and remove it along with its spring *(inset)*. If the tip of the mixture screw is bent, grooved or otherwise damaged or if the spring is damaged, buy an exact duplicate for reassembly. Before disassembling the carburetor, buy the basic carburetor rebuilding kit for your garden tiller make and model, including a replacement diaphragm and other parts required for reassembly; the carburetor may have its number stamped on the starter assembly housing or the carburetor. Otherwise, clean the carburetor and inspect the choke *(step 5)*. To disassemble the carburetor, locate the cover of the pump chamber, unscrew it and take it off, along with the diaphragm *(left)* and any gasket. Then, lift the cup and the spring out of the pump chamber.

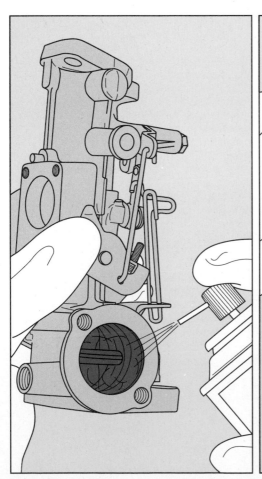

5 **Cleaning the carburetor and inspecting the choke.** Wearing rubber gloves, clean off the carburetor by spraying it with carburetor and choke cleaner, taking care not to drip any on plastic parts; be sure to spray the choke plate *(far left)*, the throttle plate and inside the pump chamber. Wipe or dry off the cleaner following its instructions. If the screw of the choke plate is loose, tighten it. To check the choke plate, flip the choke lever back and forth several times *(near left)*. If the choke plate does not move smoothly or is bent or otherwise damaged, remove it and install an exact duplicate; align the new choke plate using any guidelines on it and the carburetor. Use the same procedure to check the throttle plate, if possible; on the model shown, the screw of the throttle plate cannot be reached for tightening or removing.

Choke plate

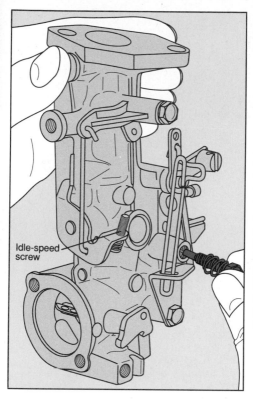

Idle-speed screw

6 **Reassembling and reinstalling the carburetor.** Reassemble and reinstall the carburetor, reversing the disassembly sequence used. Using your carburetor rebuilding kit, place the spring and the cup in the pump chamber, position the diaphragm and any gasket, and screw on the pump chamber cover; tighten each screw a little in turn. Install the mixture screw along with its spring *(left)*. Soak the fuel line in a cup of hot water for a few minutes and wipe it dry; then, push it onto the carburetor and slide the clamp onto it. Push the breather tube onto the carburetor, position the gasket and screw the carburetor onto the fuel tank. Using your sketch of the carburetor and each linkage, reinstall the governor spring and reconnect each governor rod; then, push the breather tube onto the crankcase, position the gasket, and reinstall the fuel tank and the carburetor. Reconnect the choke rod and put back the control panel, angling it into position and screwing it in place; then, reconnect the grounding wire. Reinstall the air filter housing and the air filter.

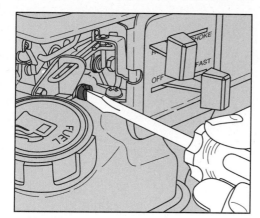

7 **Setting the mixture screw.** Use a screwdriver to turn the mixture screw clockwise until it is snug, then counterclockwise 1 1/2 turns *(above)*. Refuel the garden tiller halfway *(page 121)* and reconnect the spark plug cable *(page 87)*. Start the garden tiller and allow it to idle for a few minutes. To adjust the mixture screw and the idle-speed screw, refer to the garden tiller owner's manual.

SERVICING THE COOLING FINS AND THE MUFFLER

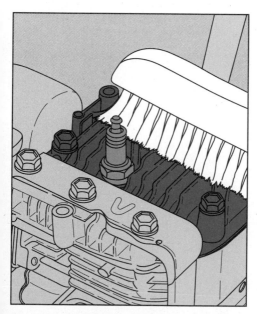

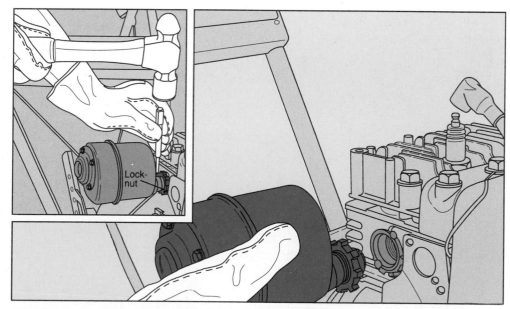

Locknut

Cleaning the engine cooling fins. Turn off the garden tiller and disconnect the spark plug cable *(page 87)*. After each use of the garden tiller, clean off the exposed portion of the fins with a wire brush *(above)*. After extensive use of the garden tiller in dusty conditions, remove the starter assembly housing and clean off the covered portion of the fins; then, reinstall the starter assembly housing.

Cleaning and replacing the muffler. Turn off the garden tiller and disconnect the spark plug cable *(page 87)*, then drain the fuel tank *(page 88)*. Wearing work gloves, unscrew the muffler cover and use a wire brush to clean off the spark arrester—the screen or holes on the muffler. If the muffler is damaged, remove the control panel and controls, along with the fuel tank and the carburetor *(page 91)*, and replace the muffler. To loosen the locknut of a pipe-threaded muffler, as in the model shown, wear safety goggles and set a punch against it; strike the punch sharply with a ball-peen hammer *(inset)*. Then, unscrew the muffler by hand. Buy an exact duplicate muffler and install it *(above)*. Using your sketch of the carburetor and each linkage, reinstall the fuel tank and the carburetor, along with the control panel and controls, reversing the disassembly sequence used. Refuel the garden tiller *(page 121)* and reconnect the spark plug cable *(page 87)*.

SERVICING THE STARTER ASSEMBLY

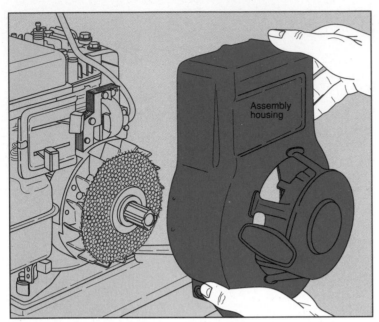

1 **Removing the starter assembly.** Turn off the garden tiller and disconnect the spark plug cable *(page 87)*, then drain the fuel tank *(page 88)*. Unscrew the starter assembly housing and lift it off the garden tiller *(above)*; the starter assembly is secured inside it. If the rewind spring is damaged, remove it *(step 3)*. If the starter cord is damaged, pull it out of the handle and cut off the knot with scissors; allow it to rewind slowly, releasing tension on the rewind spring. Unwind the starter cord from the spool, cutting off or freeing the other knot. Buy an exact duplicate starter cord, thread it through the opening in the handle and knot it; cauterize the knot by holding a flame under it without touching it.

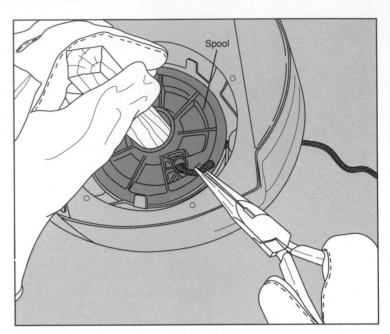

2 **Winding the starter cord.** To wind the starter cord onto the spool, wear work gloves to put tension on the rewind spring. Fit a stick into the center of the spool and rotate it counterclockwise 5 or 6 turns. Holding the spool in position with the stick, thread the starter cord through the opening in the starter assembly housing and the opening in the spool, pulling it out with long-nose pliers *(above)*. Have a helper knot the starter cord and cauterize the knot, holding a flame under it without touching it; then, fit the knot into the spool. Holding onto the starter cord, take the stick out of the spool and let the starter cord wind slowly onto it. Reinstall the starter assembly housing, refuel the garden tiller *(page 121)* and reconnect the spark plug cable *(page 87)*.

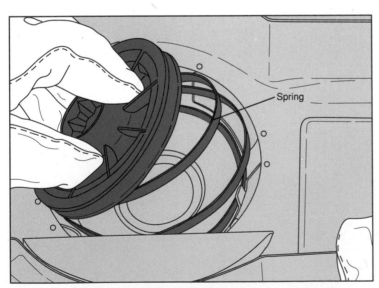

3 **Removing the rewind spring.** Pull the knot of the starter cord out of the spool and cut it off with scissors, releasing tension on the rewind spring. Unwind the starter cord from the spool by pulling the handle. Wearing work gloves and safety goggles, use long-nose pliers to pry up a tab holding the spool in place. Carefully lift the spool and slide it out of the starter assembly housing, allowing the rewind spring to uncoil *(above)*—be prepared for it to fly out. Unhook the rewind spring from its opening in the spool and its opening in the starter assembly housing. Buy an exact duplicate rewind spring.

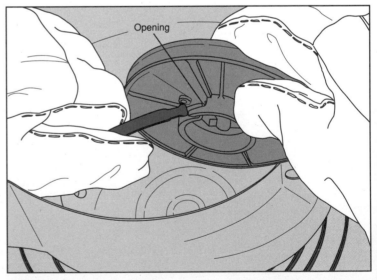

4 **Installing the rewind spring.** Apply a few drops of light machine oil or the manufacturer's specified lubricant on the center of the rewind spring. Wearing work gloves, feed the rewind spring through its opening in the starter assembly housing and hook it into its opening in the spool *(above)*. Position the spool in the starter assembly housing and use long-nose pliers to push the tab into place. Fit a stick into the center of the spool and turn it counterclockwise to coil the rewind spring; hook it into its opening in the starter assembly housing. Then, wind the starter cord onto the spool *(step 2)*.

SERVICING THE ELECTRONIC IGNITION MODULE (EIM)

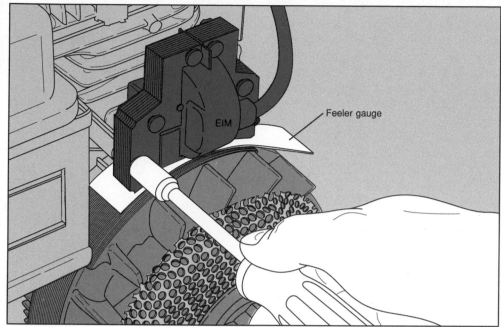

Feeler gauge

EIM

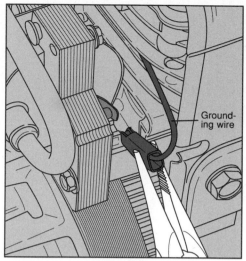

Grounding wire

1 **Accessing and gapping the electronic ignition module (EIM).** Turn off the garden tiller and disconnect the spark plug cable *(page 87)*, then drain the fuel tank *(page 88)*. To reach the EIM and the flywheel, unscrew and take off the starter assembly housing. Locate the EIM and identify it *(page 121)*. To gap the EIM, use a plastic or brass feeler gauge that matches the gap specified by the manufacturer. Rotate the flywheel until its magnets are as far as possible from the EIM. Loosen the EIM bolts using a nut driver and slide the EIM enough to fit the feeler gauge horizontally between it and the flywheel. Rotate the flywheel until its magnets are aligned with the EIM. Then, tighten the EIM bolts with the nut driver *(above)* and pull out the feeler gauge. Reinstall the starter assembly housing, refuel the garden tiller *(page 121)* and reconnect the spark plug cable *(page 87)*. If the problem persists, access the EIM again and remove it *(step 2)*.

2 **Removing the EIM.** Locate the grounding wire and disconnect it from the EIM, using long-nose pliers to pull off its connector *(above)*. Unscrew the EIM and lift it along with the spark plug cable out of the garden tiller. Buy an exact duplicate EIM and spark plug cable; if the new EIM and spark plug cable come with a new grounding wire, disconnect the old grounding wire from the throttle control and remove it.

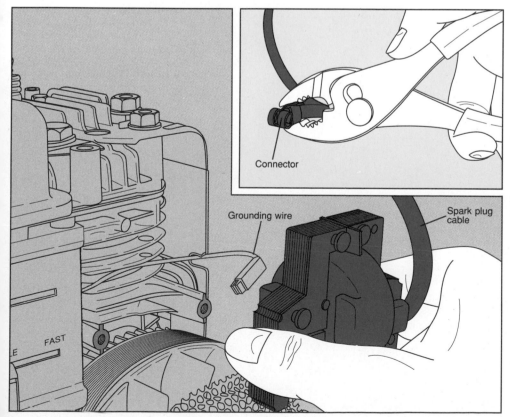

Connector

Grounding wire

Spark plug cable

FAST

3 **Replacing the EIM.** Position the new EIM *(left)* and screw it loosely into place. Reconnect the old grounding wire to the EIM or connect the new grounding wire to it and the throttle control. If necessary, prepare the new spark plug cable. Use wire cutters to cut the boot off the old spark plug cable and to cut the new spark plug cable to length. Apply a dab of white grease on the end of the new spark plug cable and slide the boot onto it. Push the new connector onto the spark plug cable and use pliers to crimp it *(inset)*, then slide the boot into place over it. Gap the EIM *(step 1)*, then reinstall the starter assembly housing, refuel the garden tiller *(page 121)* and connect the spark plug cable *(page 87)*.

SNOW THROWERS

Homeowners in northern regions appreciate the speed and efficiency of a snow thrower in clearing their walks and driveways after a snowfall. Two typical snow throwers are illustrated: the heavy-duty two stage *(below)*, powered by a four-cycle engine, and its lighter cousin, the one stage *(page 97)*, powered by a two-cycle engine. Both the two-stage snow thrower and the one-stage snow thrower are similar in design and operating principles, although their engines differ in how the power stroke of the piston is produced.

When the auger drive clutch lever is depressed, its control rod engages the auger idler pulley with the auger drive belt, which is turned by the crankshaft pulley; the auger drive pulley is then turned by the auger drive belt, engaging the auger assembly. Snow forced into the auger assembly is broken up by it and then thrown out through the discharge chute; the turning impeller, the other stage of the two-stage snow thrower, helps hurl out the snow. The two-stage snow thrower also features a wheel drive assembly for propelling it; when the wheel drive clutch lever is depressed, its control rod engages the wheel drive belt, which is also turned by the crankshaft pulley, with the wheel drive assembly, which then rotates the wheels. The one-stage snow thrower is not equipped with a wheel drive assembly for propelling it and must be pushed by the operator.

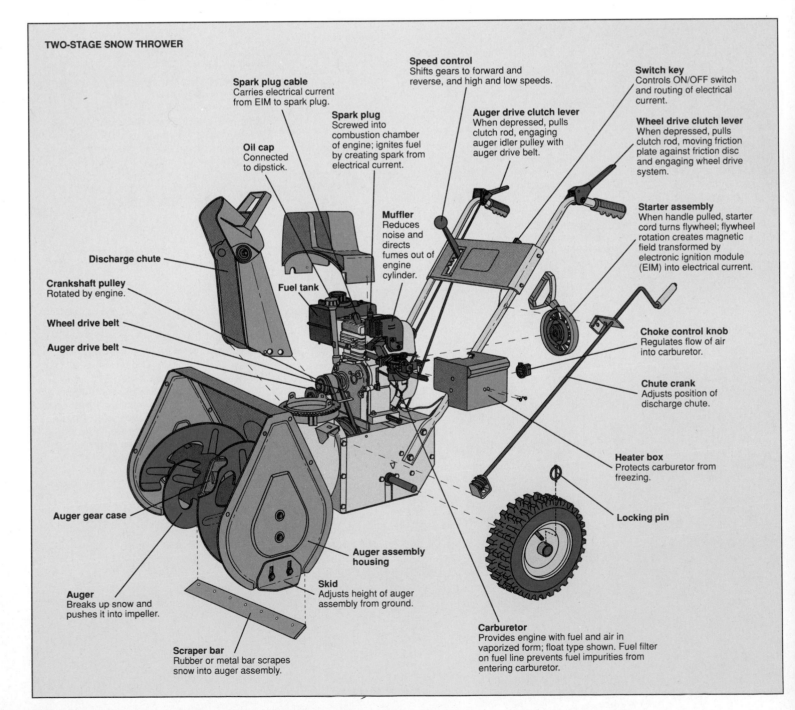

TWO-STAGE SNOW THROWER

Speed control
Shifts gears to forward and reverse, and high and low speeds.

Switch key
Controls ON/OFF switch and routing of electrical current.

Spark plug cable
Carries electrical current from EIM to spark plug.

Spark plug
Screwed into combustion chamber of engine; ignites fuel by creating spark from electrical current.

Auger drive clutch lever
When depressed, pulls clutch rod, engaging auger idler pulley with auger drive belt.

Wheel drive clutch lever
When depressed, pulls clutch rod, moving friction plate against friction disc and engaging wheel drive system.

Oil cap
Connected to dipstick.

Muffler
Reduces noise and directs fumes out of engine cylinder.

Starter assembly
When handle pulled, starter cord turns flywheel; flywheel rotation creates magnetic field transformed by electronic ignition module (EIM) into electrical current.

Discharge chute

Fuel tank

Crankshaft pulley
Rotated by engine.

Choke control knob
Regulates flow of air into carburetor.

Wheel drive belt

Auger drive belt

Chute crank
Adjusts position of discharge chute.

Heater box
Protects carburetor from freezing.

Auger gear case

Locking pin

Auger
Breaks up snow and pushes it into impeller.

Auger assembly housing

Skid
Adjusts height of auger assembly from ground.

Scraper bar
Rubber or metal bar scrapes snow into auger assembly.

Carburetor
Provides engine with fuel and air in vaporized form; float type shown. Fuel filter on fuel line prevents fuel impurities from entering carburetor.

With proper care and maintenance, a snow thrower can last a lifetime; read your owner's manual to familiarize yourself with the specific requirements of your model. Fill the fuel tank only with clean fuel; if the engine is two cycle, mix the fuel of gasoline and oil according to the manufacturer's instructions. If the engine is four cycle, check its oil level regularly; after every 25 hours of use, drain the crankcase *(page 101)* and refill it *(page 120)*. Although designed for the rigors of harsh winters, a snow thrower is still vulnerable to snow, ice and deicing salts; wipe it off after each use, then restart it and allow the engine to run until any remaining moisture evaporates.

When a problem occurs with your snow thrower, consult the Troubleshooting Guide *(page 98)*; diagnosing and fixing a problem is seldom difficult. Most repairs to snow throwers require only basic tools: a set of wrenches, screwdrivers and pliers. To service the switch, you will need a multitester; to gap the EIM, you will need a feeler gauge. Before undertaking any repair, make sure you disconnect the spark plug cable and, when instructed, drain the fuel tank *(page 100)*. Refer to Tools & Techniques *(page 110)* for information on identifying ignition systems and types of carburetors, as well as on refueling, the diagnosis of spark plugs, finding replacement parts and seasonal storage.

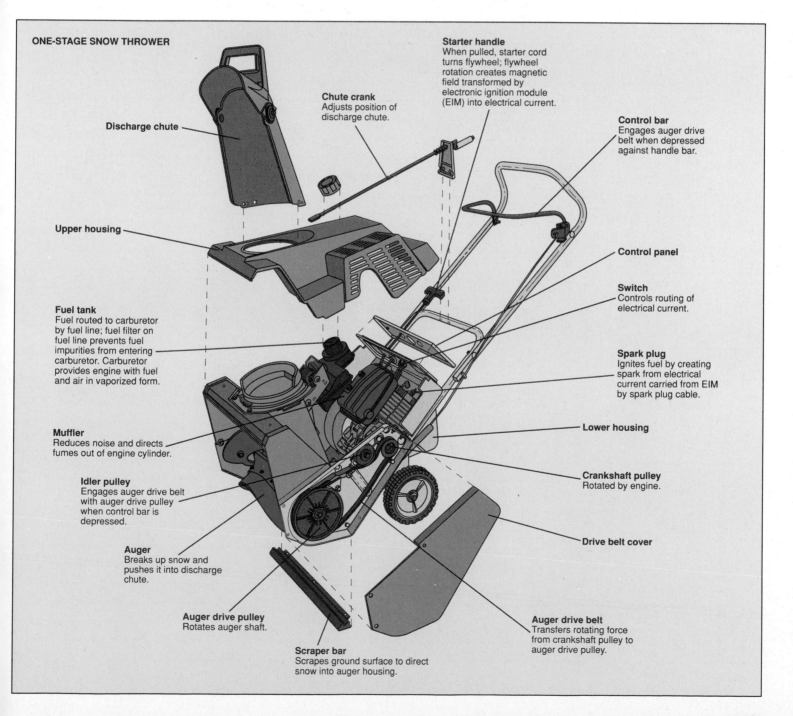

ONE-STAGE SNOW THROWER

Discharge chute

Chute crank
Adjusts position of discharge chute.

Starter handle
When pulled, starter cord turns flywheel; flywheel rotation creates magnetic field transformed by electronic ignition module (EIM) into electrical current.

Control bar
Engages auger drive belt when depressed against handle bar.

Upper housing

Control panel

Switch
Controls routing of electrical current.

Fuel tank
Fuel routed to carburetor by fuel line; fuel filter on fuel line prevents fuel impurities from entering carburetor. Carburetor provides engine with fuel and air in vaporized form.

Spark plug
Ignites fuel by creating spark from electrical current carried from EIM by spark plug cable.

Lower housing

Muffler
Reduces noise and directs fumes out of engine cylinder.

Idler pulley
Engages auger drive belt with auger drive pulley when control bar is depressed.

Crankshaft pulley
Rotated by engine.

Drive belt cover

Auger
Breaks up snow and pushes it into discharge chute.

Auger drive pulley
Rotates auger shaft.

Scraper bar
Scrapes ground surface to direct snow into auger housing.

Auger drive belt
Transfers rotating force from crankshaft pulley to auger drive pulley.

TROUBLESHOOTING GUIDE

SYMPTOM	POSSIBLE CAUSE	PROCEDURE
Snow thrower does not start	Control set incorrectly	Consult manual to start snow thrower
	Starter cord or rewind spring broken	Service starter assembly *(p. 108)* ▬◖
	Fuel contaminated or fuel tank empty	Drain fuel tank *(p. 100)* □○; refuel snow thrower *(p. 121)* □○
	Spark plug faulty or cable disconnected	Service spark plug *(p. 100)* □○
	Fuel line or fuel filter dirty or damaged	Service fuel line and fuel filter *(p. 107)* ▬◖
	Switch faulty	Service switch *(p. 109)* ▬◖▲
	Carburetor adjusted incorrectly or faulty	Consult manual to adjust carburetor; service carburetor *(p. 104)* ■◖
	Muffler faulty	Replace muffler with exact duplicate
	EIM gapped incorrectly or faulty	Service EIM *(p. 109)* ▬○▲
	Engine faulty	Take snow thrower for professional service
Snow thrower starts, but power diminished	Fuel tank cap vents blocked	Clear vents with toothpick
	Fuel contaminated or fuel tank empty	Drain fuel tank *(p. 100)* □○ and refuel snow thrower *(p. 121)* □○
	Fuel line or fuel filter dirty or damaged	Service fuel line and fuel filter *(p. 107)* ▬◖
	Carburetor adjusted incorrectly or faulty	Consult manual to adjust carburetor; service carburetor *(p. 104)* ■◖
	Muffler faulty	Replace muffler with exact duplicate
	EIM gapped incorrectly or faulty	Service EIM *(p. 109)* ▬○▲
	Engine faulty	Take snow thrower for professional service
Snow thrower runs erratically or stalls	Fuel tank cap vents blocked	Clear vents with toothpick
	Fuel contaminated or mixed incorrectly	Drain fuel tank *(p. 100)* □○ and refuel snow thrower *(p. 121)* □○
	Oil contaminated or low (two-stage)	Drain crankcase *(p. 101)* □○; refill crankcase *(p. 120)* □○
	Fuel line or fuel filter dirty or damaged	Service fuel line and fuel filter *(p. 107)* ▬◖
	Carburetor adjusted incorrectly or faulty	Consult manual to adjust carburetor; service carburetor *(p. 104)* ■◖
	Muffler faulty	Replace muffler with exact duplicate
	Engine faulty	Take snow thrower for professional service
Snow thrower overheats	Engine cooling fins dirty	Clean engine cooling fins with wire brush
	Fuel contaminated or mixed incorrectly	Drain fuel tank *(p. 100)* □○ and refuel snow thrower *(p. 121)* □○
	Oil contaminated or low (two-stage)	Drain crankcase *(p. 101)* □○; refill crankcase *(p. 120)* □○
	Wheel drive assembly faulty (two-stage)	Service wheel drive assembly *(p. 102)* ▬◖
	Muffler faulty	Replace muffler with exact duplicate
	Engine faulty	Take snow thrower for professional service
Snow thrower rattles or vibrates excessively	Housing fastener loose	Tighten housing fasteners
	Auger assembly damaged	Service auger assembly *(p. 101)* □○
	Muffler faulty	Replace muffler with exact duplicate
	Engine faulty	Take snow thrower for professional service
Snow thrower does not clear snow	Discharge chute clogged	Unclog discharge chute *(p. 99)* □○
	Scraper bar damaged or skid height adjusted incorrectly	Inspect scraper bar and adjust skid height *(p. 99)* □○
	Auger assembly damaged	Service auger assembly *(p. 101)* □○
	Drive belt loose or damaged	Service one-stage belt *(p. 103)* ▬○; two-stage belts *(p. 103)* ▬◖
	Wheel drive assembly faulty (two-stage)	Service wheel drive assembly *(p. 102)* ▬◖
Snow thrower does not work in all speeds (two-stage)	Speed control set incorrectly	Consult manual to set speed control
	Wheel drive assembly faulty	Service wheel drive assembly *(p. 102)* ▬◖
Wheels do not turn smoothly	Tire flat	Consult manual to service tires
	Wheel drive belt loose (two-stage)	Service belts *(p. 103)* ▬◖
	Wheel drive assembly faulty (two-stage)	Service wheel drive assembly *(p. 102)* ▬◖

DEGREE OF DIFFICULTY: □ Easy ▬ Moderate ■ Complex
ESTIMATED TIME: ○ Less than 1 hour ◖ 1 to 3 hours ● Over 3 hours
▲ Special tool required

SNOW THROWER USE AND MAINTENANCE

Operating a snow thrower. When using the snow thrower, wear warm, close-fitting clothes, gloves and sturdy boots with a tread. Tie back any long hair and any dangling scarf. Before starting the snow thrower, remove sticks, toys, door mats and any other foreign objects from the work area. Mix fuel, if necessary, and add it at least 10 feet from the work area; *(page 121)*; if the engine is four cycle, check the oil level *(page 120)*. Inspect the discharge chute; if any part is damaged, repair or replace it. Check the scraper bar and adjust the height of any skids *(step below, left)*.

Connect the spark plug cable *(page 100)* and start the snow thrower outdoors according to the manufacturer's instructions; make sure the discharge chute is aimed away from you. Allow the engine to warm up for a few minutes. Gripping the handle bars with both hands and keeping your weight balanced, walk at a slow, steady pace behind the snow thrower; be on the lookout for potholes and other hidden hazards. On a slope, work straight up and down it rather than across it; do not tackle steep slopes. If the discharge chute clogs, clear it *(step below, right)*.

After each use of the snow thrower, turn it off and disconnect the spark plug cable *(page 100)*, then brush snow off the discharge chute, the auger assembly and the housing. Reconnect the spark plug cable and turn on the snow thrower, allowing it to run until any remaining snow melts and the water evaporates. Store the snow thrower in a clean, dry area; be sure to turn it off, disconnect the spark plug cable, close any fuel shutoff valve and remove the key.

Discharge chute

Skid

Checking the scraper bar and adjusting skid height. If the scraper bar is worn to less than 1/16 inch or otherwise damaged, replace it with an exact duplicate; for access on some models, you may have to remove the drive belt housing. To adjust skid height, loosen the bolts using a wrench *(above)*; if necessary, have a helper tilt the snow thrower back slightly. For a paved surface, set each skid as high as possible, lowering the auger assembly to 1/8 inch from the ground; for a graveled surface, set each skid as low as possible. Tighten each skid bolt with the wrench. To readjust the skid height, turn off the snow thrower and disconnect the spark plug cable *(page 100)*.

Unclogging the discharge chute. If the auger or the impeller jams, turn off the snow thrower and disconnect the spark plug cable *(page 100)*. Standing to one side of the snow thrower and keeping your feet clear of the auger assembly and the wheels, push a broom handle down through the discharge chute to force any ice or packed snow into the auger assembly *(above)*. **Caution:** Never put your hands into the discharge chute. If you cannot clear the discharge chute from the top or if the auger assembly or the impeller is still blocked, carefully push the broom handle up through the bottom of the discharge chute. Reconnect the spark plug cable *(page 100)*.

SERVICING THE SPARK PLUG

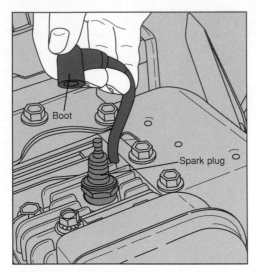

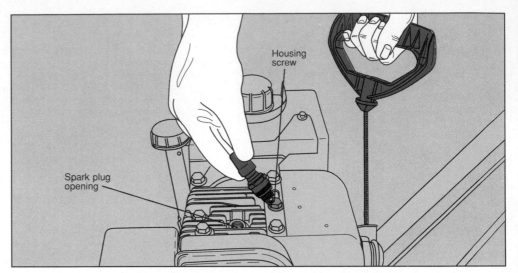

1 **Disconnecting and reconnecting the spark plug cable.** Move the snow thrower to a level surface and turn it off. To reach the spark plug on some models, you may have to unscrew the control panel. Grasp the cable by the boot and pull it off the spark plug (above); set the boot well away from the spark plug. If necessary, test and replace the spark plug (step 2). To reconnect the cable, fit the boot back onto the spark plug. Reinstall the control panel if you removed it.

2 **Testing the spark plug.** Loosen the spark plug using a socket wrench, then unscrew it by hand; clean and gap it (page 123). To test the spark plug and other parts of the ignition system, drain the fuel tank (step below). Push the spark plug into the boot and set the controls to the start position. Wearing a heavy rubber glove, hold only the boot and touch the spark plug threads to an exposed metal part of the engine block as far as possible from the spark plug opening; on the model shown, a housing screw. Pull the starter cord 2 or 3 times (above). If there is a bright, snapping spark, the spark plug and other parts of the ignition system are not faulty. Otherwise, repeat the test with a new spark plug. If there is still no spark, service the switch, then, if necessary, the EIM (page 109). Pull the boot off the spark plug and screw in the spark plug. Refuel the snow thrower (page 121) and reconnect the spark plug cable (step 1).

DRAINING THE FUEL TANK

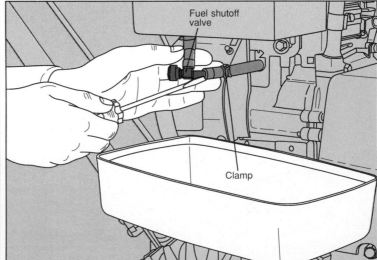

Emptying the fuel tank. Turn off the snow thrower and disconnect the spark plug cable (step 1, above). Allow the engine to cool for at least 15 minutes. Working outdoors or in a well-ventilated garage with the door to the outdoors open, drain the fuel tank using a siphoning hose or by disconnecting the fuel line. To siphon the fuel, unscrew the fuel tank cap, feed one end of the hose onto the bottom of the fuel tank and feed the other end into a fuel container for disposal. Pump the bulb until fuel flows through the hose (above, left); continue the procedure until the fuel is drained, then screw the cap back onto the fuel tank. To drain the fuel tank by disconnecting the fuel line, close any fuel shutoff valve and set a metal container under the end of the fuel line. Slide the clamp along the fuel line with utility pliers, then use an old screwdriver to pry the fuel line off the fuel tank (above, right). Open the shutoff valve, allow the fuel to drain and reconnect the fuel line. Wipe up any spill and dispose of the fuel safely (page 11). Move the snow thrower outdoors at least 10 feet from the draining site and reconnect the spark plug cable (step 1, above). Start the snow thrower and let it run to use up any remaining fuel. Then, turn it off and disconnect the spark plug cable.

DRAINING THE CRANKCASE (Two-stage snow thrower)

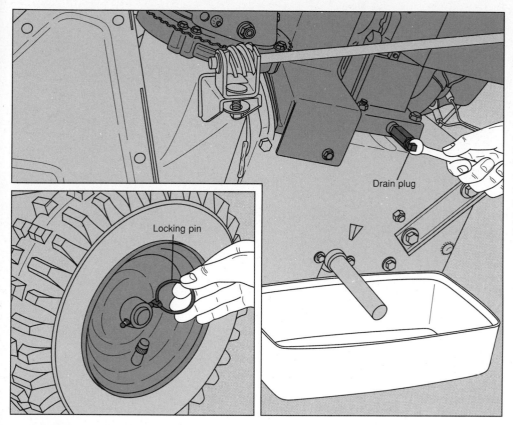

Drain plug

Locking pin

Draining the oil. Turn off the snow thrower, disconnect the spark plug cable and drain the fuel tank *(page 100)*. Locate the crankcase drain plug on the side of the engine; for easiest access to drain the oil on some models, you may need to remove a wheel. Having a helper support the snow thrower, pull out the locking pin *(inset)* and slide off the wheel. Place a metal container on the ground under the drain plug and set the snow thrower down gently, resting it as shown. Remove the drain plug using a wrench *(left)* and let the oil drain into the container. Reinstall the drain plug, tightening it with the wrench. Wipe up any spill and dispose of the oil safely *(page 11)*. Put back any wheel you removed. Refill the crankcase with the oil specified by the manufacturer *(page 120)*.

SERVICING THE AUGER ASSEMBLY

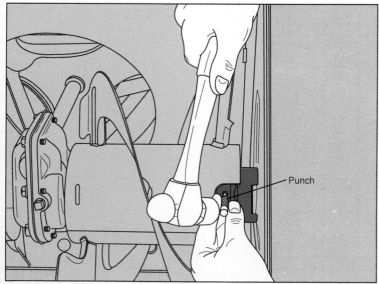

Punch

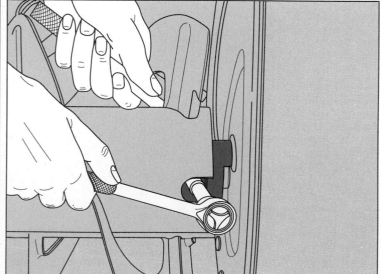

Inspecting the auger assembly and replacing shear bolts. Turn off the snow thrower, disconnect the spark plug cable and drain the fuel tank *(page 100)*. Engage the control bar and slowly pull the starter cord to rotate the auger assembly and inspect it. If the auger assembly is damaged extensively or broken, take the snow thrower for professional service. If a shear bolt is damaged or broken, remove it. Wearing safety goggles, position a punch on the end of the shear bolt opposite the nut

and tap sharply using a ball-peen hammer *(above, left)*, driving the shear bolt out of the shaft. Buy an exact duplicate shear bolt; never substitute a common bolt for a shear bolt. Apply a dab of white grease into the shaft opening, push the shear bolt into place and screw on the nut; using a socket wrench to steady the bolt, tighten the nut with another socket wrench *(above, right)*. Refuel the snow thrower *(page 121)* and reconnect the spark plug cable *(page 100)*.

SERVICING THE WHEEL DRIVE ASSEMBLY (Two-stage snow thrower)

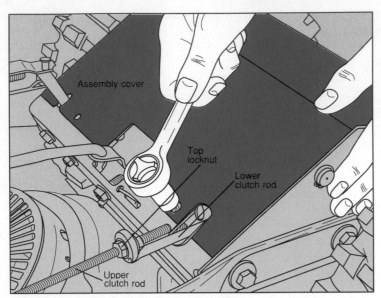

1 **Adjusting the friction disc and accessing the wheel drive assembly.** Turn off the snow thrower and disconnect the spark plug cable *(page 100)*. To increase the friction disc traction, reset the wheel drive clutch rod; on the model shown, turn the top locknut until it is 1/2 inch higher on the upper clutch rod, slide up the lower clutch rod and tighten the bottom locknut against it. Reverse the procedure to decrease the friction disc traction. Reconnect the spark plug cable *(page 100)*. If the problem persists, turn off the snow thrower, disconnect the spark plug and drain the fuel tank *(page 100)*. To reach the wheel drive assembly, tilt the snow thrower forward and turn it upside down; if necessary, support it with a 2-by-4. Unscrew the cover of the wheel drive assembly *(above)* and slide it off.

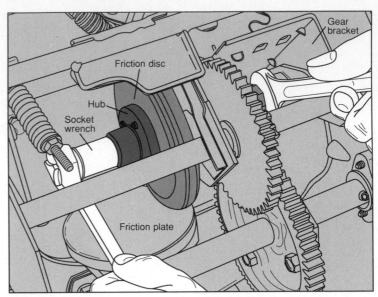

2 **Checking the friction disc.** Set the speed control in turn to each operating position, depressing and releasing the wheel drive control; the friction disc should contact the friction plate evenly when the control is depressed and clear it when the control is released. If the friction disc is not damaged, lubricate the wheel drive assembly *(step 4)*. If the friction disc is damaged, try readjusting it *(step 1)*. Otherwise, set the speed control to its highest operating position and use a socket wrench to take the nut off the hub of the friction disc, steadying the shaft with a wrench *(above)*. Slide the hub and the friction disc off the shaft. Take the key out of its keyway in the shaft and reposition it; if it fits loosely or is otherwise damaged, replace it with an exact duplicate.

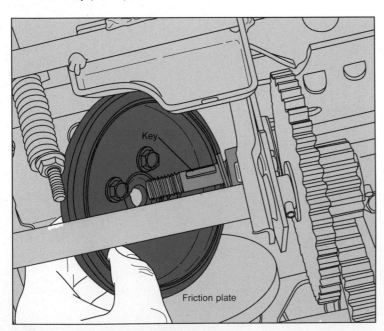

3 **Replacing the friction disc.** Unscrew the hub using a socket wrench and take it off the friction disc; keep the hub for reassembly. Buy an exact duplicate friction disc and screw it onto the hub with the socket wrench. With the speed control still set at its highest operating position, slide the friction disc and the hub into position on the shaft *(above)*. Then, steadying the shaft with a wrench, install the nut and use the socket wrench to tighten it against the hub. Check the friction disc *(step 2)* and, if necessary, adjust it *(step 1)*.

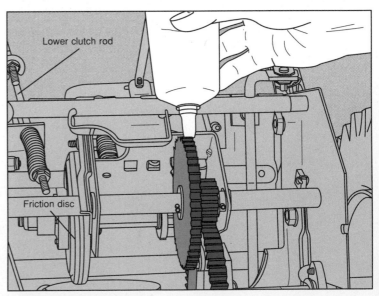

4 **Lubricating the wheel drive assembly.** Set the speed control to its lowest operating position, moving the friction disc out of the way; do not lubricate it or the friction plate. Turning a wheel as necessary to rotate the wheel drive assembly, apply a small amount of white grease or the manufacturer's specified lubricant to the teeth of each gear *(above)* and the openings in the gear bracket, as well as each end of the gear shaft and its contact points with the gears and the gear bracket. Also lubricate the connection of the wheel drive clutch rods. Reinstall the cover of the wheel drive assembly. Turn the snow thrower upright, refuel it *(page 121)* and reconnect the spark plug cable *(page 100)*.

SERVICING THE AUGER DRIVE BELT (One-stage snow thrower)

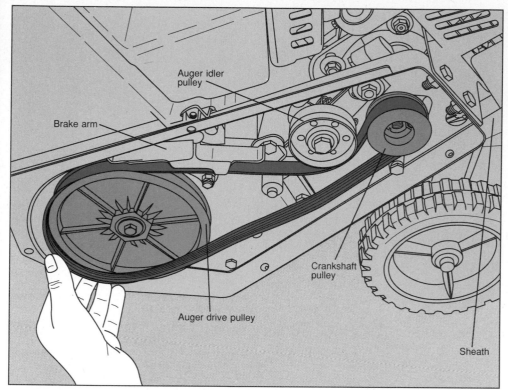

Auger idler pulley

Brake arm

Auger drive pulley

Crankshaft pulley

Sheath

Checking and replacing the auger drive belt.
Turn off the snow thrower and disconnect the spark plug cable *(page 100)*, then take off the drive belt cover. To check the tension of the auger drive belt, depress the control bar and pull it with a finger; there should be about 1/2 inch of play. To adjust the tension of the auger drive belt on the model shown, reset the auger drive clutch rod; on some models, you can adjust the auger idler pulley. Unhook the auger drive clutch rod at the top from the control bar, slide up the sheath at the bottom of it and rehook the spring onto it: higher to increase tension, lower to reduce tension. Then, rehook the auger drive clutch rod onto the control bar.

If the auger drive belt is damaged, slide it off the auger drive pulley *(left)*, the auger idler pulley and the crankshaft pulley, freeing it from the brake arm; if necessary, have a helper pull the starter cord slowly to rotate it or depress the control bar to clear it. Replace the auger drive belt with an exact duplicate, reversing the sequence used to remove it; if necessary, adjust the tension. Reinstall the drive belt cover and reconnect the spark plug cable *(page 100)*.

SERVICING THE AUGER AND WHEEL DRIVE BELTS (Two-stage snow thrower)

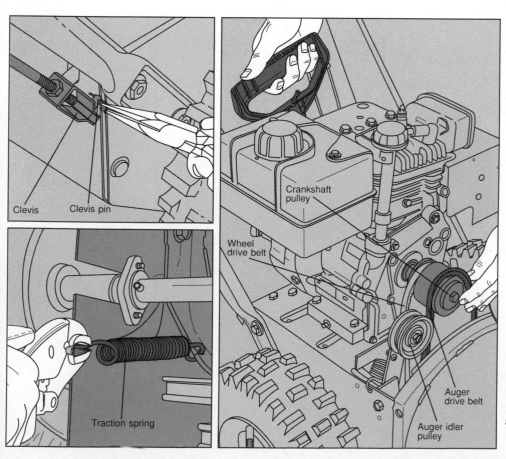

Clevis   Clevis pin

Crankshaft pulley

Wheel drive belt

Auger drive belt

Auger idler pulley

Traction spring

Checking and replacing the auger and wheel drive belts. Turn off the snow thrower and disconnect the spark plug cable *(page 100)*, then take off the drive belt housing. To check the tension of each drive belt, depress its clutch lever and pull it with a finger; there should be about 1/2 inch of play. To adjust the tension of the auger drive belt on the model shown, reset its clutch rod; on some models, you can adjust the auger idler pulley. Use long-nose pliers to pull the retaining pin out of the clevis pin *(far left, top)*, then remove the clevis pin and turn the nut along with the clevis: higher to increase tension, lower to reduce tension. On the model shown, the tension of the wheel drive belt cannot be adjusted.

If a drive belt is damaged, drain the fuel tank *(page 100)*. Pull the starter cord slowly to slide off the auger drive belt *(near left)*. To remove the wheel drive belt, access the wheel drive assembly *(page 102)*, then wear work gloves and safety goggles to unhook the traction spring from the housing using locking pliers. Turn the snow thrower upright and slide off the wheel drive belt. Replace the wheel or auger drive belt with an exact duplicate, reversing the disassembly sequence used; put back the traction spring *(far left, bottom)*, then turn over the snow thrower to reinstall the cover of the wheel drive assembly housing, if you removed them. Reinstall the drive belt housing, refuel the snow thrower *(page 121)* and reconnect the spark plug cable *(page 100)*.

ACCESS TO THE INTERNAL COMPONENTS (One-stage snow thrower)

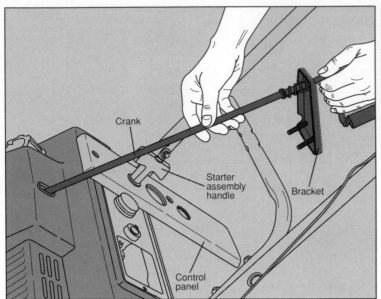

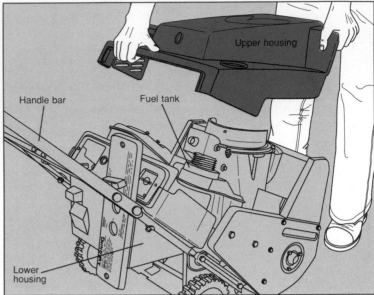

Removing and reinstalling the lower housing and upper housing.
Turn off the snow thrower, disconnect the spark plug cable and drain the fuel tank *(page 100)*. To reach the carburetor or the fuel line and fuel filter, unscrew the lower housing and take it off. To reach the starter assembly, the switch or the electronic ignition module (EIM), unscrew the crank bracket, pull out the crank *(above, left)* and take off the discharge chute. Remove the fuel tank cap, then unscrew the upper housing and lift it off *(above, right)*. To service the starter assembly, pull the starter cord out of its handle, cut off or untie its knot and allow it to

rewind slowly, releasing tension on the rewind spring; otherwise, leave the starter cord in place. Unscrew the fuel tank and lift it off its bracket, without pulling the fuel line, then remove the bracket. Unscrew the starter assembly housing and take it off. To service the switch or the EIM, remove the engine housing; on some models, further disassembly may also be required and you may wish to take the snow thrower for professional service. After servicing the snow thrower, reassemble it, reversing the disassembly sequence used. Refuel the snow thrower *(page 121)* and reconnect the spark plug cable *(page 100)*.

SERVICING THE CARBURETOR

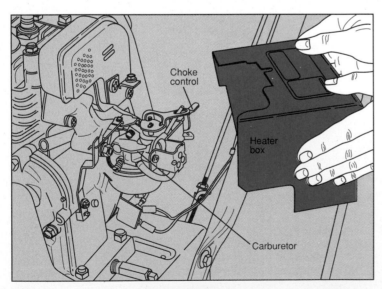

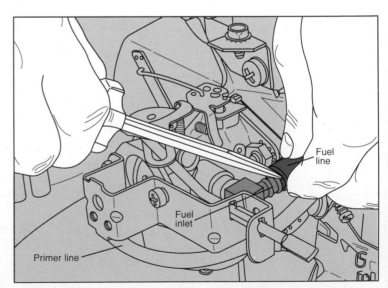

1 **Accessing the carburetor.** Turn off the snow thrower, disconnect the spark plug cable and drain the fuel tank *(page 100)*. To reach the carburetor on a two-stage snow thrower, first take the crank bracket off the auger assembly housing and set the crank aside. Then, pull the knob off the choke control, unscrew the heater box and lift it off the carburetor *(above)*. To reach the carburetor on a one-stage snow thrower, remove the lower housing *(step above)*.

2 **Disconnecting the fuel line and the primer line.** Locate the fuel line and the primer line, then trace them in turn to the carburetor and note their positions. To disconnect the fuel line from the carburetor, use utility pliers to slide the clamp off the fuel inlet and along the fuel line. Then, pry the fuel line off the fuel inlet with an old screwdriver *(above)*. To disconnect the primer line from the carburetor, slide off any clamp and pull it off its fuel inlet the same way.

SERVICING THE CARBURETOR (continued)

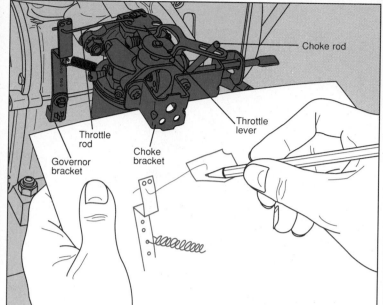
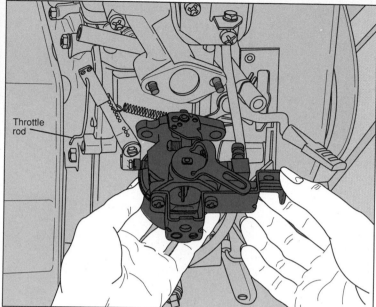

Choke rod

Throttle
lever

Throttle
rod

Governor
bracket

Throttle
rod

Choke
bracket

3 **Removing the carburetor.** Before removing the carburetor, draw a diagram of it showing each linkage for reassembly *(above, left)*. In particular, sketch the throttle linkage, noting the position of the throttle rod, the throttle lever, the governor bracket and each spring; as well, note the position of the choke rod and its connections. Avoid handling any spring; if a spring is damaged, take the snow thrower for professional service.

Supporting the carburetor in one hand, use a wrench to remove the nuts holding it onto the intake manifold, then take off the washers. Gently unhook the throttle rod from the throttle lever; make sure that its position is correctly noted on your diagram. Then, carefully lift the carburetor away from the intake manifold *(above, right)*. Remove the gasket between the intake manifold and the carburetor; buy an exact duplicate gasket for reassembly.

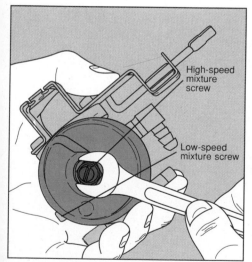
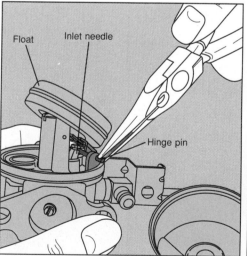
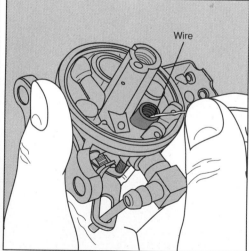

High-speed
mixture
screw

Low-speed
mixture
screw

Float

Inlet needle

Hinge pin

Wire

4 **Draining the carburetor.** Holding the carburetor over a metal container, loosen the high-speed mixture screw *(above)* and allow the fuel to drain. Remove the high-speed mixture screw and its spring and take off the float bowl along with its gasket; buy an exact duplicate gasket for reassembly. Wearing safety goggles, blow compressed air through each small hole in the high-speed mixture screw. Remove the low-speed mixture screw and its spring. If a mixture screw or its spring is damaged, buy an exact duplicate for reassembly.

5 **Disassembling the carburetor.** Before disassembling the carburetor, buy the basic carburetor rebuilding kit for your snow thrower make and model, containing the replacement parts needed for reassembly; the carburetor may have its number stamped on it or printed on the engine housing. Otherwise, clean the carburetor and inspect the throttle and the choke *(step 6)*. Open the float on its hinge; carefully note the position of each part, especially the spring clip, for reassembly. Using long-nose pliers, remove the hinge pin *(above, left)*, releasing the float, the inlet needle and the spring clip. Use a small hooked wire to pull any rubber seat out of the inlet *(above, right)*; note any markings on it for positioning a replacement when reassembling the carburetor. Inspect the float, the inlet needle and the spring clip for wear and other damage; listen for fuel sloshing in the float, indicating it leaks.

SERVICING THE CARBURETOR (continued)

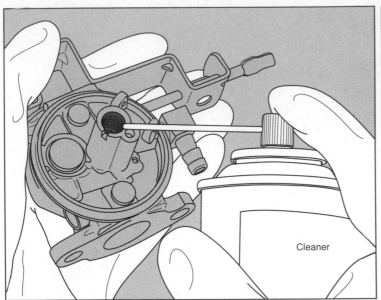

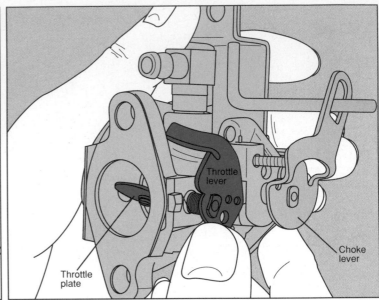

Cleaner

Throttle
lever

Choke
lever

Throttle
plate

6 **Cleaning the carburetor and inspecting the throttle and the choke.** Wearing rubber gloves, spray the carburetor *(above, left)* and the float bowl with carburetor and choke cleaner, taking care not to drip any on plastic parts. Wipe or dry off the cleaner following its instructions. If the screw of the throttle plate or the choke plate is loose, tighten it. To check the throttle plate, flip the throttle lever back and forth *(above, right)*. If the throttle plate does not move smoothly or is bent, replace it with an exact duplicate; align the new throttle plate using any guidelines on it and the carburetor. Use the same procedure to inspect the choke plate on the other side of the carburetor.

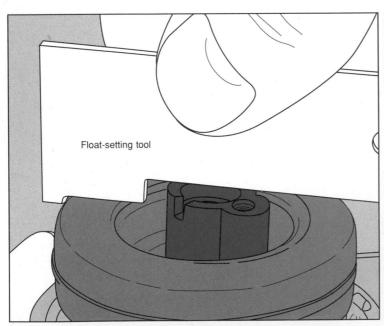

Float-setting tool

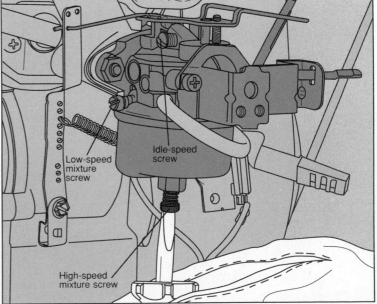

Idle-speed
screw

Low-speed
mixture
screw

High-speed
mixture screw

7 **Reassembling and reinstalling the carburetor.** If you disassembled the carburetor, reassemble it using your carburetor rebuilding kit. Position any rubber seat, the inlet needle and the spring clip, then use long-nose pliers to install the hinge pin. Close the float on its hinge and check it is level using a special float-setting tool *(above, left)*, usually supplied with the carburetor rebuilding kit. To close any gap between the float and the float-setting tool, reopen the float and adjust the hinge tab with a small screwdriver. To reinstall the carburetor, position the gasket and the float bowl, then install the high-speed mixture screw; turn it clockwise until it is snug but not tight, then turn it counterclockwise 1 turn. Install the low-speed mixture screw, turning it

clockwise until it is snug but not tight; then, turn it counterclockwise 1 1/2 turns. Position the gasket and the carburetor on the intake manifold, reconnect the throttle rod, and put back the washer and the nut; tighten the nut with a wrench. Reconnect the primer line and the fuel line. Move the snow thrower outdoors, refuel it *(page 121)* and reconnect the spark plug cable *(page 100)*. Start up the snow thrower and allow it to idle for a few minutes. To adjust the high-speed mixture screw *(above, right)*, the low-speed mixture screw and the idle-speed screw, consult your owner's manual. On a two-stage snow thrower, put back the heater box, the choke control knob and the crank; on a one-stage snow thrower, reinstall the lower housing *(page 104)*.

SERVICING THE FUEL LINE AND FUEL FILTER

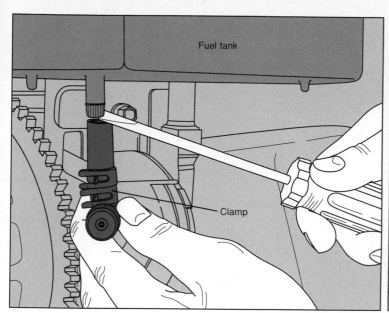

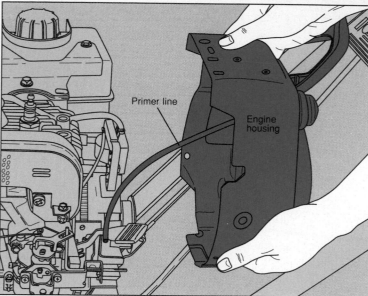

1 **Accessing the fuel line.** Turn off the snow thrower, disconnect the spark plug cable and drain the fuel tank *(page 100)*. To reach the fuel line and fuel filter on a two-stage snow thrower, first disconnect the fuel line from the fuel tank. Use utility pliers to slide the clamp along the fuel line, then pry off the fuel line with an old screwdriver *(above, left)*. Then, access the carburetor and disconnect the fuel line and the primer line from it *(page 104)*. To free the fuel line and fuel filter, unscrew the engine housing and lift it along with the primer line off the snow thrower *(above, right)*. To reach the fuel line and fuel filter on a one-stage snow thrower, remove the lower housing *(page 104)* and use the same procedure to disconnect the fuel line in turn from the fuel tank and the carburetor; leave the primer line in place.

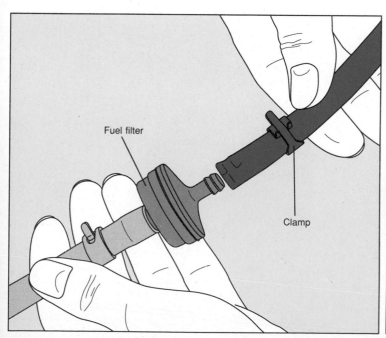

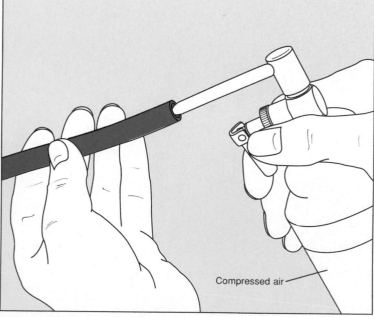

2 **Cleaning and replacing the fuel line and the fuel filter.** To remove the fuel filter, slide each clamp along the fuel line using utility pliers, then pull off the fuel filter *(above, left)*. If the fuel line is cracked, stretched or otherwise damaged, buy an exact duplicate. Otherwise, wearing safety goggles, spray compressed air through the fuel line to clear it *(above, right)*. If you suspect the fuel filter is blocked or faulty, replace it with an exact duplicate. Install the fuel filter on the fuel line and reconnect the fuel line to the fuel tank and the carburetor. On a two-stage snow thrower, also reconnect the primer line to the carburetor and reinstall the engine housing; then, put back the heater box, the choke control knob and the crank. On a one-stage snow thrower, reinstall the lower housing *(page 104)*. Refuel the snow thrower *(page 121)* and reconnect the spark plug cable *(page 100)*.

SERVICING THE STARTER ASSEMBLY

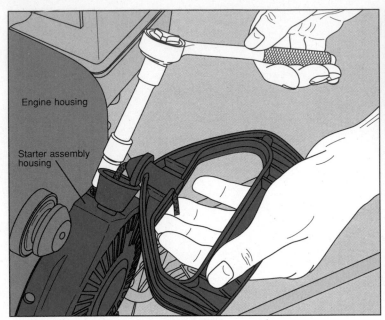

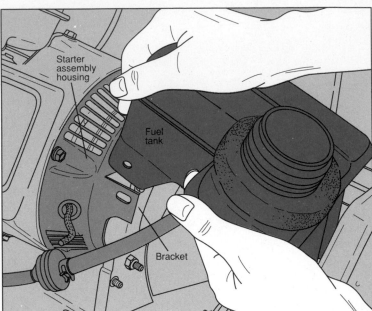

1 **Accessing the starter assembly.** Turn off the snow thrower and disconnect the spark plug cable *(page 100)*. To reach the starter assembly on a two-stage snow thrower, unscrew the starter assembly housing *(above, left)* and lift it off the engine housing; the starter assembly is secured inside it. Set the starter assembly housing on a flat, firm surface with the starter assembly facing up. Pull the starter cord out of the handle and cut off or untie the knot; allow it to rewind slowly, releasing tension on the rewind spring. To reach the starter assembly on a one-stage snow thrower, drain the fuel tank *(page 100)* and remove the upper housing *(page 104)*, taking the handle off the starter cord and then removing the fuel tank *(above, right)* and its bracket before unscrewing and taking off the starter assembly housing.

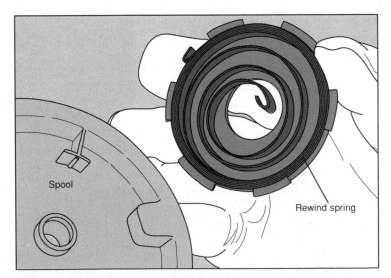

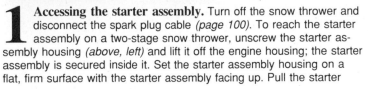

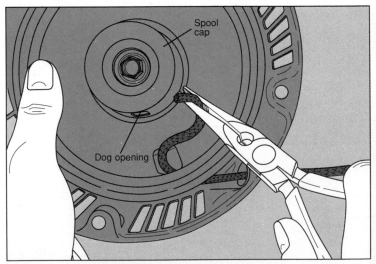

2 **Replacing the rewind spring.** Unwind the starter cord from the spool, cutting off or freeing the knot. If the starter cord is damaged, buy an exact duplicate; if the rewind spring is not damaged, wind it onto the spool *(step 3)*. Otherwise, wear work gloves and safety goggles to take off the spool cap; if you cannot remove it, take the starter assembly for professional service. Remove the spring and the dog, then lift out the spool. Carefully turn the rewind spring housing to remove it from the spool *(above)*—be prepared for it to uncoil and fly out. Buy an exact duplicate rewind spring coiled in its housing, apply a few drops of light machine oil or the manufacturer's specified lubricant to it and fit it onto the spool. Position the spool in the starter assembly housing and turn it clockwise to hook the rewind spring into place. Reinstall the dog, the spring and the spool cap.

3 **Winding the starter cord.** Thread one end of the starter cord through the opening in the handle and knot it. Cauterize the knot by holding a flame under it without touching it. Holding the starter assembly housing steady, rotate the spool counterclockwise 5 or 6 turns. Holding the spool in position, thread the other end of the starter cord through the opening in the starter assembly housing and the opening in the spool, then pull it out with long-nose pliers *(above)*. Have a helper knot the end of the starter cord and cauterize the knot, then position it in the spool. Release the spool, allowing the starter cord to wind slowly onto it. On a two-stage snow thrower, put back the starter assembly housing. On a one-stage snow thrower, reassemble it, reversing the disassembly sequence used *(page 104)*. Refuel the snow thrower *(page 121)* and reconnect the spark plug cable *(page 100)*.

SERVICING THE SWITCH

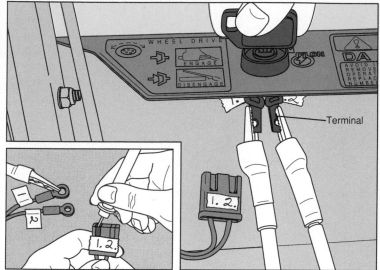

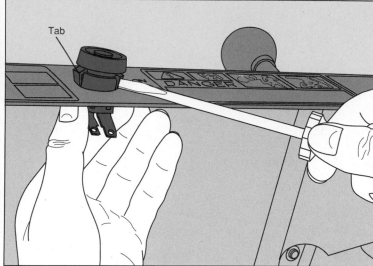

Testing and replacing the switch. Turn off the snow thrower, disconnect the spark plug cable and drain the fuel tank *(page 100)*; on a one-stage snow thrower, also remove the upper housing *(page 104)*. Locate the switch, label its wires and their corresponding terminals, then disconnect the wires from the switch. Set a multitester to test for continuity *(page 118)* and clip a tester probe to each switch terminal. Turn the key to the ON position, then to the OFF position *(above, left)*; there should be continuity only in the OFF position. If the switch does not test faulty, trace each wire to its other end, label it and its terminal, then disconnect it; if you cannot reach the end of the wires, you cannot test them.

To test the wires, clip one tester probe to the end of one wire and touch the other tester probe in turn to the other end of each wire *(inset)*; there should be continuity only once. Clip the tester probe to the end of the other wire and repeat the test. If a wire tests faulty, buy an exact duplicate. If the switch tests faulty, pry up its tabs or take off its nut, then remove it using an old screwdriver *(above, right)*; install an exact duplicate. Connect each wire to its switch terminal and its other terminal. On a one-stage snow thrower, reassemble it, reversing the disassembly sequence used *(page 104)*. Refuel the snow thrower *(page 121)* and reconnect the spark plug cable *(page 100)*.

SERVICING THE ELECTRONIC IGNITION MODULE (EIM)

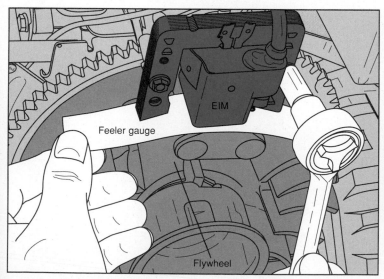

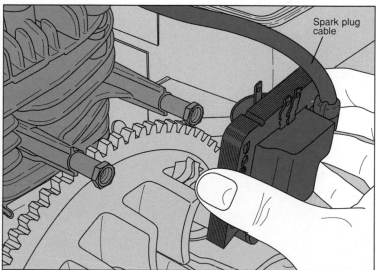

Gapping and replacing the EIM. Turn off the snow thrower, disconnect the spark plug cable and drain the fuel tank *(page 100)*. On a two-stage snow thrower, take off the engine housing; on a one-stage snow thrower, remove the lower housing *(page 104)*. Identify the EIM *(page 121)* and gap it using a brass or plastic feeler gauge that matches the gap specified by the manufacturer. Rotate the flywheel until its magnets are as far as possible from the EIM. Loosen the EIM screws and slide the EIM enough to fit the feeler gauge horizontally between it and the flywheel. Rotate the flywheel until its magnets are aligned with the EIM. Then, tighten the EIM screws *(above, left)* and pull out the feeler

gauge. On a two-stage snow thrower, put back the engine housing; on a one-stage snow thrower, reassemble it, reversing the disassembly sequence used *(page 104)*. Refuel the snow thrower *(page 121)* and reconnect the spark plug cable *(page 100)*.

If the problem persists, access the EIM again. Using long-nose pliers, disconnect each wire from the EIM; if a wire cannot be disconnected from the EIM, trace it to the other end and disconnect it. Unscrew the EIM and remove it along with the spark plug cable *(above, right)*. Buy an exact duplicate EIM, position it and screw it loosely into place. Then, connect each wire to its terminal and gap the EIM.

TOOLS & TECHNIQUES

This section introduces basic tests and procedures common to the use and repair of power tools and equipment, from using a multitester *(page 113)* and an extension cord *(page 115)* to servicing motor components *(page 118)* and spark plugs *(page 123)*. Many of the tools used for repairs can be found in an all-purpose tool kit *(below)*; for a specialized tool such as a feeler gauge or a flywheel puller, you may need to visit a service center or contact the manufacturer.

When an electrical tool stops working, determine whether or not the problem originates outside it before you take it apart. Carefully examine the power cord of the tool *(page 115)*; a frayed or broken power cord is a common cause of failure. When gas-powered equipment fails, check that there is fuel in the fuel tank and that the fuel is not contaminated; if the

engine is two-cycle, make sure the fuel mixture is the correct proportions of gasoline and oil. Fuel that is contaminated or mixed incorrectly can lead to serious engine damage.

Getting inside the tool or equipment to make a repair is often the most difficult part of the job. Refer to page 114 for tips on disassembly. Make diagrams of wire connections and carburetor linkages to make it easier to reassemble the tool or equipment later. Refer to the appropriate section in this chapter for information on servicing switches and brush assemblies *(page 117)*, bearings *(page 120)*, ignition systems *(page 121)* and carburetors *(page 122)*. Always replace a damaged or faulty component with an exact replacement; sources of replacement parts and professional service assistance appear on page 112.

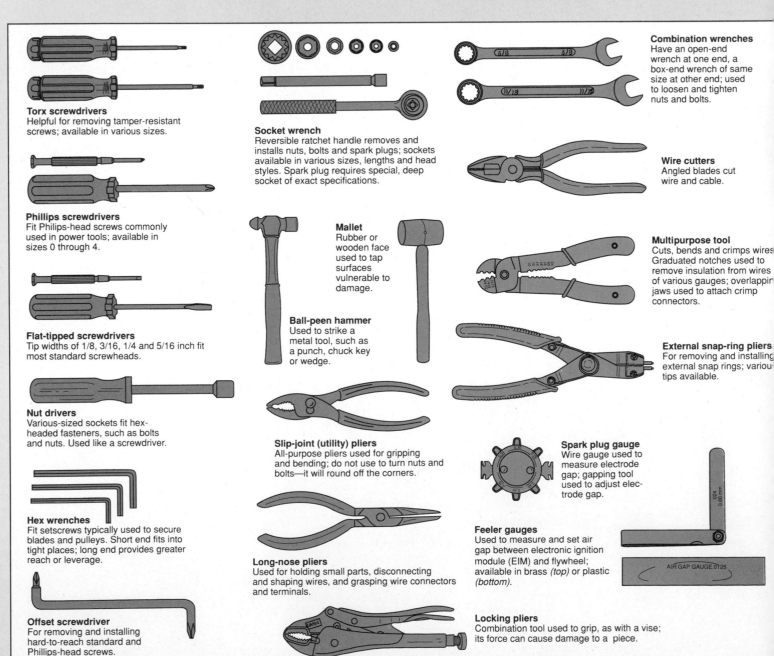

Torx screwdrivers
Helpful for removing tamper-resistant screws; available in various sizes.

Phillips screwdrivers
Fit Philips-head screws commonly used in power tools; available in sizes 0 through 4.

Flat-tipped screwdrivers
Tip widths of 1/8, 3/16, 1/4 and 5/16 inch fit most standard screwheads.

Nut drivers
Various-sized sockets fit hex-headed fasteners, such as bolts and nuts. Used like a screwdriver.

Hex wrenches
Fit setscrews typically used to secure blades and pulleys. Short end fits into tight places; long end provides greater reach or leverage.

Offset screwdriver
For removing and installing hard-to-reach standard and Phillips-head screws.

Socket wrench
Reversible ratchet handle removes and installs nuts, bolts and spark plugs; sockets available in various sizes, lengths and head styles. Spark plug requires special, deep socket of exact specifications.

Mallet
Rubber or wooden face used to tap surfaces vulnerable to damage.

Ball-peen hammer
Used to strike a metal tool, such as a punch, chuck key or wedge.

Slip-joint (utility) pliers
All-purpose pliers used for gripping and bending; do not use to turn nuts and bolts—it will round off the corners.

Long-nose pliers
Used for holding small parts, disconnecting and shaping wires, and grasping wire connectors and terminals.

Combination wrenches
Have an open-end wrench at one end, a box-end wrench of same size at other end; used to loosen and tighten nuts and bolts.

Wire cutters
Angled blades cut wire and cable.

Multipurpose tool
Cuts, bends and crimps wires Graduated notches used to remove insulation from wires of various gauges; overlappir jaws used to attach crimp connectors.

External snap-ring pliers
For removing and installing external snap rings; variou tips available.

Spark plug gauge
Wire gauge used to measure electrode gap; gapping tool used to adjust electrode gap.

Feeler gauges
Used to measure and set air gap between electronic ignition module (EIM) and flywheel; available in brass *(top)* or plastic *(bottom)*.

AIR GAP GAUGE.0125

Locking pliers
Combination tool used to grip, as with a vise; its force can cause damage to a piece.

Keep your work area clean and uncluttered to reduce the possibility of misplacing parts. Read the owner's manual for the power tool or equipment before undertaking any repairs; contact the manufacturer to find out if a service manual is available. To prevent accidents, always turn off the tool or equipment and unplug it or disconnect its spark plug cable and, when instructed, drain the fuel tank. Work slowly and methodically, taking notes and making diagrams whenever necessary to track your work. Wear work gloves and safety goggles when their use is recommended. When reassembling the tool or equipment, ensure all wire connections are made correctly and no wires are pinched. Always reinstall the housing and tighten the fasteners before attempting to use the tool or equipment.

Use the right tool for the job and use it properly. If you choose the wrong screwdriver or socket, for example, you may strip the fastener. Magnetize screwdrivers to avoid time-consuming hunts for a dropped screw. The electrical tests described in this book require a battery-powered multitester that can be obtained at most hardware stores; read the section on using a multitester *(page 113)* before testing for continuity or resistance and checking for leaking voltage.

Maintaining tools and equipment in good working order can eliminate most problems. Keep your tools and equipment clean; lubricate gears and other moving parts as often as recommended in the owner's manual. Store your tools and equipment in a clean, dry place; see page 124 for information on preparing gas-powered equipment for seasonal storage.

Wire brush
Used to scrape deposits, rust and dirt off metal surfaces.

Paintbrush
Used to clean fragile parts.

Work gloves
Protect hands from cutting edges; should be worn when working with blades or rewind springs.

Try square
Wooden handle sits flush against surface edge; metal blade indicates precise 90-degree angle.

Files
Flat, fine-toothed file used to remove burrs and sharpen large blades. Round file used to sharpen cutters of chain saw and cutting blade of hedge trimmer.

Safety goggles
Protect eyes from wood or metal debris; should be used when sawing, drilling or replacing rewind springs.

Rubber gloves
Thick rubber gloves worn to provide insulation and prevent shock when testing a spark plug.

C clamps
Hold material to workbench or table.

Funnel
May be plastic or metal.

Dust mask
Prevents inhalation of dust and debris.

Ear protectors
Worn when operating noisy equipment, such as chain saws and string trimmers, for extended periods of time.

Lubricating oil
Light machine oil used for lubricating pivot points, control cables, power tool parts.

White grease
All-purpose grease used to lubricate gears, bearings and other rotating parts.

Siphoning hose
Plastic tube used to drain fuel tank safely; pump bulb to create suction in tube.

Spray cleaner
Available in various formulations for cleaning or lubricating: decarbonizing spray to clean mufflers, cooling fins and engines; choke and carburetor cleaner to clean carburetors; petroleum-based lubricating spray to displace moisture and lubricate moving parts.

Compressed air
Aerosol can of air used to blow dirt and debris off and out of parts not accessible with brush or cloth; extension nozzle localizes spray.

CHECKING THE MAIN SERVICE PANEL

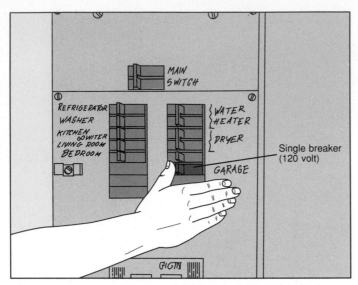

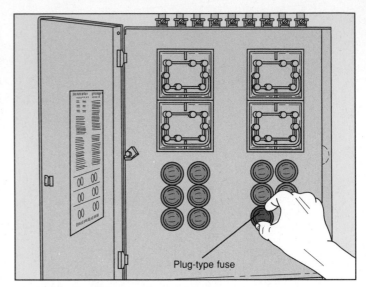

Resetting a tripped circuit breaker. If an electrical circuit is overloaded, the circuit breaker automatically trips; its toggle flips OFF or to an intermediate position, shutting off power. Before resetting the circuit breaker, turn off or unplug each tool, appliance and other electrical unit on the circuit. Then, push the circuit breaker toggle fully OFF, then back ON *(above)*. If the circuit breaker trips again, inspect the tool, especially its power cord *(page 115)*, for a short circuit. If necessary, have the tool or the circuit serviced professionally to correct the problem.

Replacing a fuse. Electrical circuits in an older system are protected by plug-type fuses. If a fuse blows, turn off or unplug each tool, appliance and other electrical unit on the circuit. Then, unscrew the fuse and replace it with one of identical amperage *(above)*. A visible break in the metal strip of the fuse indicates an overloaded circuit; move the tool to another circuit. A discolored or clouded fuse shows a short circuit; inspect the tool, especially its power cord *(page 115)*. If necessary, have the tool or the circuit serviced professionally to correct the problem.

GETTING HELP WHEN YOU NEED IT

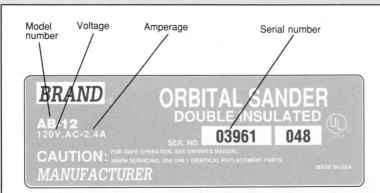

Finding what you need for effective repairs. The information you need for obtaining the correct replacement part or owner's manual can be found on the nameplate of your power tool or equipment *(above)*; check for the nameplate on the housing. Have the make, model number and serial number on hand before contacting a supply source. The owner's manual may include an exploded view and a parts list of the tool or equipment; if not, use the model number and the serial number to order them from the manufacturer. Armed with these references, you can pinpoint the part and part number you require.

When buying a replacment part, you have several sources from which to choose:

Authorized service centers. Many specialize in the repair of certain brands; if a part is not on hand, a service technician can usually order it for you. To locate the service center nearest you, contact the manufacturer; you can find the address and telephone number in the owner's manual, the telephone yellow pages or, for a toll-free number, through the 800 operator.

Tool rental agencies. Many perform their own repairs. If you cannot obtain a part, you may be directed to a retail source.

Parts dealers. Many supply specialized parts, such as carburetor rebuilding kits and electronic ignition modules (EIMs); a dealer may also provide you with a list of service centers authorized to repair the tool or equipment. For a particular engine or carburetor part, contact the engine or carburetor manufacturer; most engines and carburetors are made by independent manufacturers.

Hardware stores Many stock tools, wires, spark plugs, air filters and other common parts, but their salespeople may lack specialized knowledge.

You and your warranty. Before undertaking any repair, check the warranty provided by the manufacturer. If the warranty is still in effect, you may void it if you perform the repair yourself; take the power tool or equipment to an authorized service center.

TROUBLESHOOTING WITH A MULTITESTER

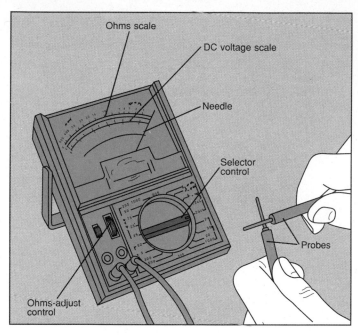

Ohms scale

DC voltage scale

Needle

Selector control

Probes

Ohms-adjust control

Testing for continuity, resistance or voltage. A multitester can be used for determining if a circuit is completed (continuity), for measuring in ohms the amount of resistance in a circuit (resistance) and for measuring in volts the strength of electrical current passing through a circuit (voltage). Before each test for continuity and resistance, ensure a precise reading by "zeroing" the multitester. Set the multitester to the ohms setting you plan to use and touch the probes together *(left)*. The needle will sweep from left to right toward ZERO; turn the ohms-adjust control until the needle aligns directly over ZERO.

To test for continuity or resistance, set the selector control to RX1, unless otherwise instructed. Touch the probes to the designated terminals or wire ends. If the circuit has continuity and no resistance, the needle will indicate zero ohms. If the circuit is incomplete, the needle will indicate infinite resistance. If the circuit (as in the case of motor windings) has some resistance but not enough to prevent the flow of electrical current, the needle will move to a point between zero ohms and infinite resistance.

The capacity of the multitester to measure low voltage makes it ideal for testing the charging circuit of a battery charger. Set the multitester to 50 volts on the DCV scale. Touch the negative (black) tester probe to the negative (-) charger terminal and the positive (red) tester probe to the positive (+) charger terminal. The multitester should register the voltage specified on the nameplate of the charger or the tool.

PREVENTING ELECTRICAL HAZARDS

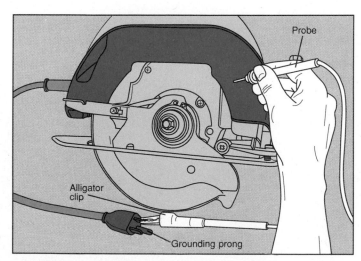

Probe

Alligator clip

Grounding prong

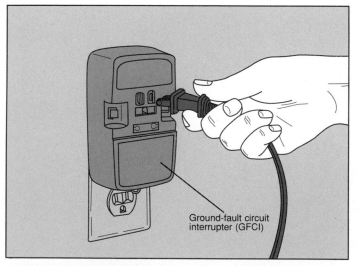

Ground-fault circuit interrupter (GFCI)

Checking for leaking voltage. After reassembling an electrical tool but before plugging it in, check that electrical current cannot leak to the housing. Set a multitester to RX1000 *(step above)* and depress the trigger switch or set the switch ON. Clip one probe in turn to each plug prong and touch the other probe to an exposed metal part; on the circular saw shown, the upper guard *(above)*. The multitester should show no continuity (infinite resistance) in each test—except with any grounding prong, where it should show continuity. Otherwise, disassemble the tool and check for disconnected or damaged wires. If you cannot correct the problem, take the tool for professional service.

Using a ground-fault circuit interrupter (GFCI). A GFCI provides protection against electrical shock by monitoring the flow of electrical current. The moment an irregularity in the electrical current is detected, the GFCI automatically shuts off the circuit. A home built or wired before 1975 is unlikely to have GFCIs permanently installed in the service panel. As an extra safety precaution, buy a portable GFCI at a hardware store or an electrical parts supplier. Plug the GFCI into the outlet, following the manufacturer's instructions, and then plug the tool into the GFCI *(above)*.

TIPS ON DISASSEMLY AND REASSEMBLY

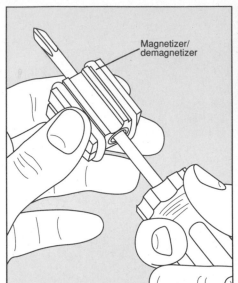
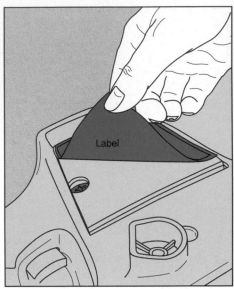

Locating and removing fasteners. Before undertaking a repair, review the owner's manual and check whether the warranty is still valid. Set up for a repair in a clean, well-lit area of the workshop or garage; use a workbench or table for work on electrical tools or components of gas-powered equipment. Magnetize screwdrivers before you start to work by passing their heads through a magnetizer/demagnetizer *(above, left)*. Study the tool or equipment to determine how the housing is put together. On some tools and equipment, the fasteners are recessed or hidden behind labels; use your fingers to feel for fastener heads and recessed areas, then gently peel back a corner *(above, center)*. Check for bolts held in place by a nut on the other side of the housing; use a wrench to hold the nut while removing the bolt. For a stubborn screw, try twisting the screwdriver sharply clockwise a little, then turn counterclockwise to remove it. If you still cannot loosen the screw, apply a few drops of penetrating oil to it *(above, right)*; wait at least 15 minutes for the oil to seep into the screw threads, then try again. A component that can rotate in a counterclockwise direction, such as the chuck of a reversible drill, may be installed with a reverse-threaded fastener; to remove it, unscrew it by turning clockwise.

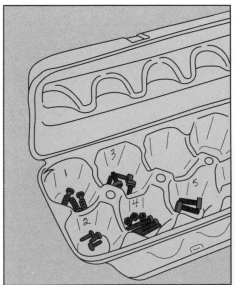
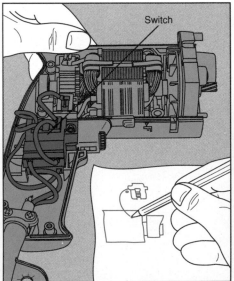
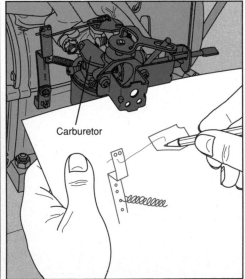

Labeling and sketching parts. Disassemble only what is necessary for access, labeling parts and sketching their connections or linkages. Keep track of your disassembly sequence; usually, the reassembly sequence is its reverse. Store fasteners in the cups of an egg carton *(above, left)* or in small, labeled jars. After removing the housing but before taking out a part, draw a diagram or take an instant-developing photograph of it to ensure its correct placement at reassembly.

If you are servicing the switch, for example, sketch it *(above, center),* than label its wires and their corresponding terminals before disconnecting them; a pinched or incorrectly placed wire can stop the tool or equipment from working at all. Or, before you remove the carburetor, sketch its connections and linkages *(above, right)*, carefully noting, in particular, the opening into which each end of any rod or clip is positioned; a throttle rod incorrectly repositioned, for instance, can negatively affect the engine performance.

SERVICING A POWER CORD

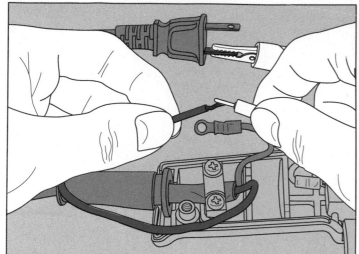

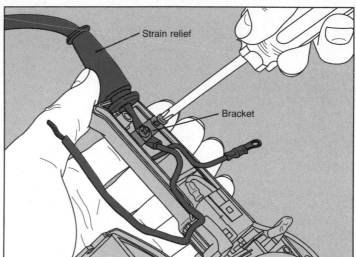

Testing and replacing the power cord. Turn off and unplug the tool. To access the wire terminals of the power cord, consult the chapter on the tool to remove the housing. Label each power cord wire and its terminal, then disconnect it. On the orbital sander shown, there are two wires: one screwed to the switch; one twisted together with a wire to the field coil assembly inside a wire cap. On your tool, there may be a third, grounding wire secured to the housing. If the power cord is damaged, replace it.

To test the power cord, set a multitester to test for continuity *(page 113)* and clip one tester probe to a plug prong. Touch the other tester probe in turn to each wire end *(above, left)*; there

should be continuity once and only once. Clip the tester probe in turn to each other plug prong and repeat the test. If the power cord fails any test, replace it.

To remove the power cord, unscrew any bracket *(above, right)* and free the strain relief. Buy an exact duplicate power cord; if necessary, prepare the wire ends and attach connectors *(page 116)*. Connect each wire to its terminal: on the orbital sander shown, screw one wire to the switch; twist the other wire together with the wire to the field coil assembly and install the wire cap. Position the power cord, fitting the strain relief in place, and put back any bracket removed. Reassemble the tool and check for leaking voltage *(page 113)*.

USING EXTENSION CORDS

NAMEPLATE AMPS	2.0 - 6.0	6.1 - 10.0	10.1 - 12.0	12.1 - 15.0
EXTENSION CORD LENGTH	RECOMMENDED WIRE GAUGE (AWG)			
25 ft.	18	18	16	14
50 ft.	16	16	16	12
100 ft.	16	14	14	Not recommended
150 ft.	14	12	12	Not recommended

Choosing an extension cord. Always use an extension cord of the correct rating and size for the tool. Look for the amperage rating of the tool on its nameplate *(page 112)*, then calculate the length of extension cord you need and use the chart *(above)* to determine the size, or gauge, of extension cord that is appropriate. Never use an extension cord that is undersized, having a gauge number higher than recommended, and avoid working with a series of extension cords; the resulting voltage reduction can cause the motor to overheat and, eventually, to burn out.

For a tool with a 3-prong plug, use only a similar extension cord; do not bend or remove the third, or grounding, prong of a 3-prong plug. If you are working outdoors, make sure the extension cord is rated for outdoor use; check its UL listing. Plug the extension cord into an outlet protected by a ground-fault circuit interrupter (GFCI); use a portable GFCI *(page 113)* or an extension cord with a built-in GFCI. Carefully inspect the extension cord before each use. If the extension cord is damaged, replace it; do not splice it. When the extension cord is not in use, unplug it and store it in a dry, well-ventilated area.

MAKING WIRE CONNECTIONS

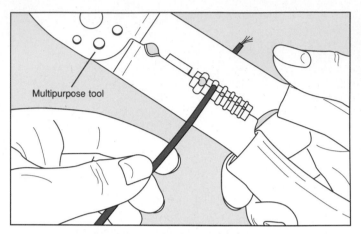

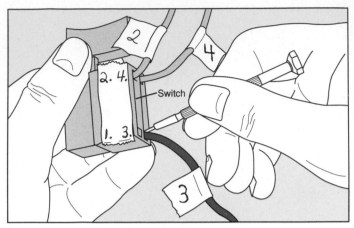

Preparing the wire ends. If the wire ends are frayed or the wire connector is damaged, cut off the end of the wire with wire cutters. Using a multipurpose tool, strip back about 1/4 inch of wire insulation. Fit the wire into the notch for its gauge and squeeze the handles to sever the insulation *(above)*, then pull the insulation off the wire. If the wire is stranded, twist the strands tightly together in a clockwise direction between your thumb and forefinger.

Replacing a wire at a push-in terminal. Power tools and equipment often have a switch with push-in terminals. To release a wire from a push-in terminal, press a small screwdriver or stiff wire into the terminal slot *(above)* and pull out the wire; usually, the wire ends are tinned for easy removal and insertion. To install a wire into a push-in terminal, prepare the wire ends, if necessary *(step left)*, then push the end of the wire into the terminal slot.

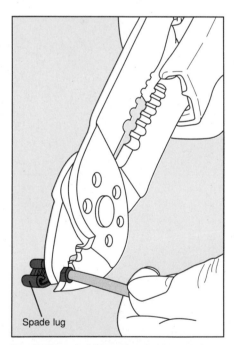

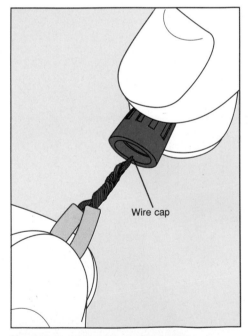

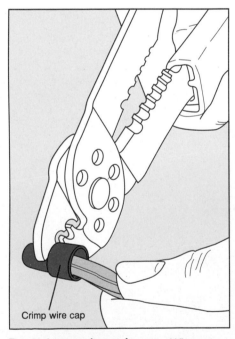

Replacing a crimp connector. A wire can be connected to a terminal with a crimp connector such as a spade lug. If necessary, prepare the wire ends *(step above, left)*. To install a crimp connector, push the end of the wire into the connector sleeve and crimp it with a multipurpose tool. Fit the sleeve into the appropriate notch and squeeze the handles *(above)*. Test the connection by giving the wire a slight tug.

Replacing a wire cap. Wires can be connected and secured with a wire cap. To remove the wires, unscrew the wire cap, then untwist the wires. To connect wires with a wire cap, prepare the ends of each wire, if necessary *(step above, left)*. Twist the ends of the wires together in a clockwise direction. Fit the wire cap onto the ends of the wires *(above)* and screw it until it is snug but not tight. Test the connection by giving each wire a slight tug.

Replacing a crimp wire cap. Wires can be connected and secured with a crimp wire cap. To remove the wires, cut them off using wire cutters; buy a new crimp wire cap for reassembly. To connect wires with a crimp wire cap, prepare them *(step above, left)* and twist them together in a clockwise direction. Push on the wire cap and crimp it using a multipurpose tool, fitting the collar into the appropriate notch and squeezing the handles *(above)*. Test the connection with a slight tug.

SERVICING SWITCHES

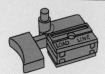
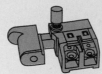

Trigger switch
Four terminals: two pairs of line and load terminals; line terminals may be stamped LINE or C.

Trigger switch
One pair of terminals; when engaged, locking button keeps circuit closed.

Key switch
One pair of terminals.

Toggle switch
One pair of terminals.

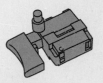

Trigger switch (variation)
Four terminals: only one pair of line and load terminals (next to trigger) controlled by the switch; line terminal may be stamped LINE or C.

Variable-speed reversing switch
Electronic switch with multiple pairs of terminals that cannot be tested; may be stamped TSCR or with symbol.

Testing and replacing a switch. A switch closes a circuit, letting current flow, or opens a circuit, keeping current from passing—a principle applied differently in electrical tools and gas-powered equipment. In an electrical tool, the circuit through the motor is *closed*, letting current flow in it, when the switch is set ON; the circuit through the motor is *opened*, stopping the flow of current in it, when the switch is set OFF. In gas-powered equipment, the grounding circuit is *opened*, letting current flow through the ignition system, when the switch is set ON; the grounding circuit is *closed*, stopping the flow of current through the ignition system, when the switch is set OFF.

Switches common in power tools and equipment are shown at left. To test a switch, label each wire and its terminal, then disconnect it from the switch. Set a multitester to test for continuity *(page 113)*. If there is one pair of terminals, touch a tester probe to each terminal, setting the switch in one, then the other position. There should be continuity only with the switch set in one position: ON in an electrical tool; OFF in gas-powered equipment. If there is more than one pair of terminals, as with the switch in many electrical tools, identify the line and load terminals: a line terminal is for a wire carrying current from the power cord; a load terminal is for a wire carrying current to the motor. Touch one tester probe to a line terminal and touch the other tester probe in turn to each load terminal, setting the switch in one, then the other position; touch the tester probe to the other line terminal and repeat the procedure. There should be continuity between a pair of line and load terminals only with the switch set in one position, otherwise, replace the switch with an exact duplicate. **Note:** There also may be continuity between one pair of terminals with the switch set in both positions, as in the trigger switch variation shown. After reassembling the tool, check for leaking voltage *(page 113)*.

SERVICING BRUSH ASSEMBLIES

Brush assembly (removable parts)
Brush, spring and wire terminal replaced as one unit; plastic housing may be replaced independently.

Externally accessible brush assembly
Reached by removing brush cap on motor housing; brush, spring and wire terminal replaced as one unit.

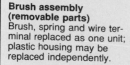

Brush assembly (non-removable parts)
Brush, spring and wire terminal fixed to metal housing; entire brush assembly replaced as one unit.

Bayonet brush assembly
Plastic housing with removable or non-removable brush, spring and bayonet terminal; if parts removable, may be replaced independently.

Inspecting and replacing brush assemblies. In an electrical tool, current from the field coil assembly is conducted through the armature by brushes, spring-loaded carbon rods that press against the motor commutator. Shown at left are typical brush assemblies in electrical tools. Subjected to friction by the commutator as it spins, a brush eventually wears and does not provide adequate contact with it; sparks flying from the motor is usually a sign. To reach the brush assembly on each side of the commutator, refer to the chapter on the tool; there may be a brush cap on the motor housing that can be unscrewed or you may have to remove the motor housing. Carefully lift out each brush assembly—be prepared for the brush or the spring to fly out.

To inspect each brush assembly, gently push the brush to check its spring, then slide it out of its housing, if possible. If the spring is damaged, the housing is cracked, or the brush is pitted, uneven or worn shorter than its width, replace the component in each brush assembly or both entire brush assemblies with exact duplicates; some brushes are marked with a wear line. Fit each brush assembly into position, making sure the brush presses firmly against the commutator and matches its curvature. After reassembling the tool, check for leaking voltage *(page 113)*.

SERVICING MOTOR COMPONENTS

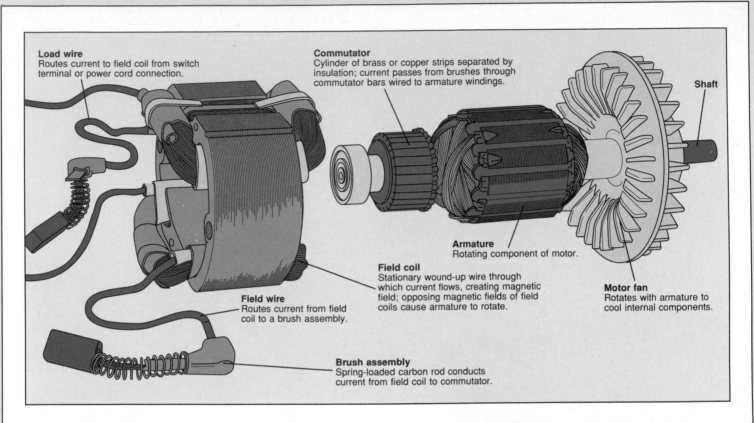

Load wire
Routes current to field coil from switch terminal or power cord connection.

Commutator
Cylinder of brass or copper strips separated by insulation; current passes from brushes through commutator bars wired to armature windings.

Shaft

Armature
Rotating component of motor.

Field coil
Stationary wound-up wire through which current flows, creating magnetic field; opposing magnetic fields of field coils cause armature to rotate.

Motor fan
Rotates with armature to cool internal components.

Field wire
Routes current from field coil to a brush assembly.

Brush assembly
Spring-loaded carbon rod conducts current from field coil to commutator.

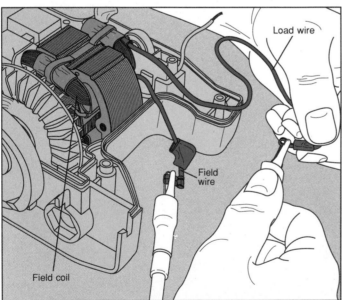

Load wire

Field wire

Field coil

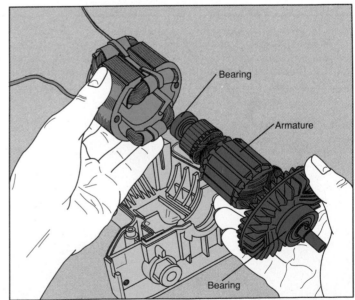

Bearing

Armature

Bearing

1 Testing the field coil assembly. To reach the motor, refer to the chapter on the tool to remove the motor housing. Locate each field coil, then disconnect its field wire from the brush assembly and its load wire from the switch or the power cord, noting the terminals; if necessary, disassemble the motor to reach the wires *(step 2)*. Set a multitester to test for continuity *(page 113)*. To test each field coil, clip one tester probe to its field wire and clip the other tester probe to its load wire *(above)*; there should be continuity. If a field coil is faulty, disassemble the motor and replace the field coil assembly with an exact duplicate.

2 Disassembling the motor. To disassemble the motor, carefully lift it out of the motor housing and slide the armature out of the field coil assembly *(above)*. If the field coil assembly is secured to the motor housing, leave it in place and slide out the armature. To replace the field coil assembly, unscrew it and take it out; if it is riveted in place, take the tool for professional service. Take the bearing off each end of the armature shaft, if possible, and service it *(page 120)*; then, clean the armature *(step 3)*.

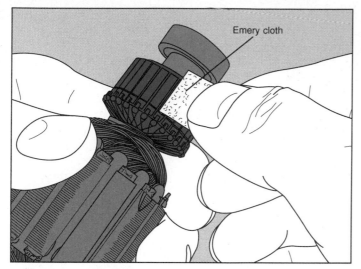

Emery cloth

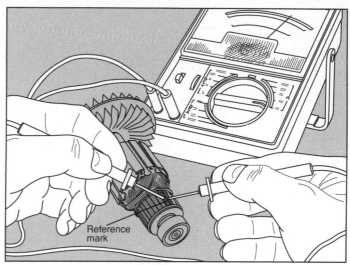

Reference mark

3 **Cleaning the armature.** Carefully inspect the armature, checking the commutator for nicks, scratches and dents, and the windings for darkened areas and damage. To remove dirt, debris and discoloration from the commutator, gently rub each bar with fine emery cloth *(above)*. Use a utility knife to scrape away any mica insulation protruding above a bar until it is slightly below the level of the bar. Clean off the armature and fan with an old toothbrush or wear safety goggles and use compressed air. If the commutator or the windings are damaged, replace the armature with an exact duplicate and test for ground faults *(step 5)*.

4 **Testing the commutator.** Set a multitester to test for resistance *(page 113)*. Mark a bar of the commutator with a felt-tipped pen as a reference point. Touch one tester probe to the marked bar and touch the other tester probe to the bar on one side of it *(above)*. There should be low resistance (between 0 and 50 ohms). Still touching the tester probe to the bar on one side of the marked bar, touch the other tester probe to the bar next to it; there should be low resistance and a deviation of no more than 20 ohms from the first test. Continue the procedure, testing each bar with the bar next to it. If the commutator tests faulty, replace the armature with an exact duplicate.

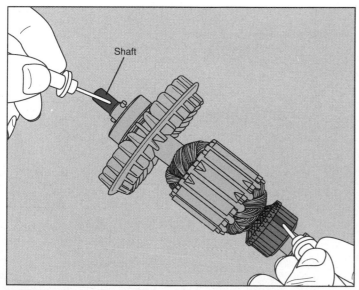

Shaft

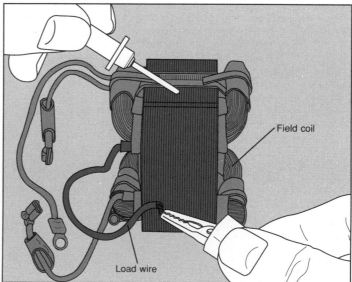

Field coil

Load wire

5 **Testing for ground faults.** A ground fault can be caused by a faulty winding on the armature or the field coil assembly; to test for ground faults, set a multitester to RX100 *(page 113)*. To test the armature, touch one tester probe to the end of the shaft near the fan and touch the other tester probe in turn to each bar of the commutator *(above, left)*. The multitester should show no continuity (infinite resistance) in each test. If the armature tests faulty, replace it with an exact duplicate. To test each field coil, clip one tester probe to its load wire and touch the other probe to a metal part of the field coil *(above, right)*. Again, the multitester should show no continuity (infinite resistance) in each test. If a field coil tests faulty, replace the field coil assembly with an exact duplicate. Reassemble the motor, put back any bearings removed, and connect the field and load wires to their terminals; make sure each brush presses against the commutator and matches its curvature. Then, check for leaking voltage *(page 113)*.

SERVICING BEARINGS

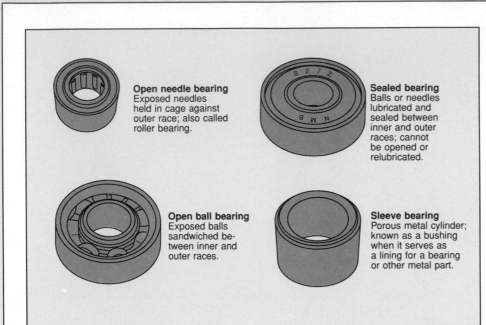

Open needle bearing
Exposed needles held in cage against outer race; also called roller bearing.

Sealed bearing
Balls or needles lubricated and sealed between inner and outer races; cannot be opened or relubricated.

Open ball bearing
Exposed balls sandwiched between inner and outer races.

Sleeve bearing
Porous metal cylinder; known as a bushing when it serves as a lining for a bearing or other metal part.

Identifying and lubricating bearings.
Bearings support drive shafts and other moving components, allowing them to rotate or reciprocate freely and without friction. Bearings rarely wear out, but they must be kept well-lubricated to prevent them and other components from overheating and seizing. Typical bearings found in power tools and equipment are shown at left.

To determine if a bearing needs lubrication, rotate it or move it up and down on its shaft; it should move smoothly without slipping. To lubricate a bearing, consult the owner's manual for any lubricant specified by the manufacturer. Most ball bearings and needle bearings can be lubricated by applying a small dab of white grease to the exposed balls or needles and the races. To lubricate sleeve bearings, apply a few drops of light machine oil.

If a bearing does not move smoothly after lubrication or is loose, replace it with an exact duplicate. If the bearing is machine-pressed to the shaft, take the tool for professional service.

USING MOTOR OILS

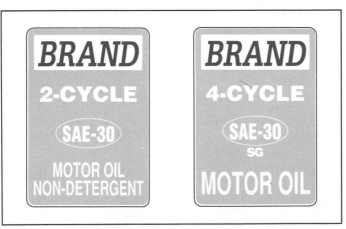

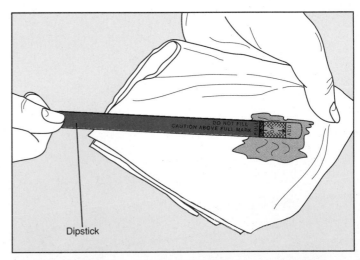

Dipstick

Choosing a motor oil. Motor oils for engines are rated by the Society of Automotive Engineers (SAE) for viscosity, a measure of their weight or thickness. The motor oil you should use depends on the climate; a heavy motor oil compensates for the thinning effects of heat. SAE 30 to SAE 40 motor oil is for use in temperatures above 32 degrees fahrenheit; in winter and temperatures below freezing, use SAE 10W30 motor oil, a light, multiviscosity type.

Check your owner's manual to ensure the motor oil you use meets the specifications of the engine manufacturer. For a two-cycle engine, a non-detergent motor oil *(above, left)* is recommended. For a four-cycle engine, use a motor oil marked SF or SG on the label *(above, right)*, the most recent rating categories of the American Petroleum Institute (API).

Adding motor oil to a four-cycle engine. Turn off the equipment, move it to a level surface and disconnect the spark plug cable. Wait a few minutes for the oil to settle in the crankcase. Unscrew the oil cap and lift it off; the dipstick is usually attached to it. Wipe off the dipstick with a clean cloth, reinsert it and lift it out again, then check the oil level against the markings on it *(above)*. If necessary, add only enough of the appropriate oil *(step left)* to raise the level to FULL, without exceeding it. Reinsert the dipstick and screw back on the oil cap. If the engine does not have a dipstick, consult your owner's manual to locate the filler plug, then remove it and add enough of the appropriate oil to fill the crankcase to the top of the filler opening. After filling the crankcase, reinstall the filler plug.

FUELING UP

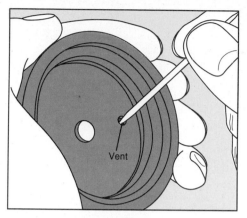

Mixing fuel for a two-cycle engine. Consult the owner's manual for the proportions of motor oil and gasoline required for the fuel mixture; use only the motor oil *(page 120)* and grade of gasoline recommended. Put 1/4 of the gasoline into an approved fuel container, measure the motor oil *(above)* and add it, then screw the cap onto the fuel container and shake it. Remove the cap and add the rest of the gasoline to the fuel container, then screw back on the cap and shake again.

Filling the fuel tank. Turn off the equipment, move it outdoors to a level surface and disconnect the spark plug cable. Unscrew the cap of the fuel tank and carefully pour in the fuel using a funnel *(above)*. Wipe up any spill and dispose of the rags safely *(page 11)*. Clear the cap vents, if necessary *(step right)*, and screw it back onto the fuel tank. Move the equipment at least 10 feet away from the fueling site before reconnecting the spark plug cable and starting the engine.

Clearing the fuel tank cap vents. The cap of the fuel tank is equipped with vents to allow air to enter the fuel tank as it empties; clogged vents can cause a vacuum lock in the fuel tank, stopping the flow of fuel to the carburetor. Check the cap of the fuel tank for clogged vents each time you refuel the equipment. To clear a clogged vent, gently fit a toothpick through it *(above)*, taking care not to enlarge it.

SERVICING IGNITION SYSTEMS

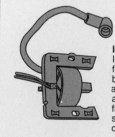

Ignition coil
Ignition coil beside flywheel connected by wires to points-and-condenser assembly under flywheel; an outdated system found on older equipment.

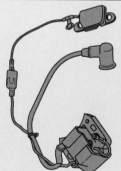

Two-part electronic ignition module (EIM)
Coil module beside flywheel connected by wires to electronic circuitry contained in trigger module; a system typically found in equipment such as string trimmers *(page 46)* where space around flywheel is limited.

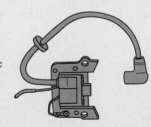

Electronic ignition module (EIM)
Electronic circuitry and condenser components contained in one unit beside flywheel; a modern system typically found in chain saws *(page 56)*, lawn mowers *(page 68)*, garden tillers *(page 84)* and snow throwers *(page 96)*.

Identifying the ignition system. An engine requires an ignition system for the combustion of the air-fuel mixture in the cylinder. Shown above is the identifying component of typical ignition systems found in gas-powered equipment. With an ignition system containing an electronic ignition module (EIM), the magnetic field created by the flywheel as it rotates is transformed into electrical current sent at timed intervals through the spark plug cable to the spark plug; the arcing of the electrical current across its electrodes of the spark plug creates a spark that ignites the air-fuel mixture in the cylinder. With other ignition systems, the same principles are applied.

To identify the type of ignition system used by the engine in your equipment, consult the owner's manual; an EIM may be referred to as a solid state ignition. Look for a black module beside the flywheel and trace each wire connected to it; a wire that runs under the flywheel is likely connected to a points-and-condenser assembly. To confirm the type of ignition system, if necessary, contact the engine manufacturer; make sure you supply the model number and serial number of the engine, along with any letters stamped on the module. If the ignition system contains an ignition coil and points-and-condenser assembly, take the equipment for professional service; an ignition coil and points-and-condenser assembly can usually be replaced with an EIM.

SERVICING CARBURETORS

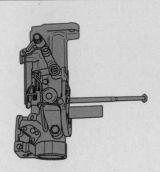

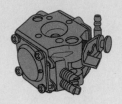

Suction-lift carburetor
Fuel drawn in by suction action of diaphragm assembly. Found in four-cycle engines of equipment such as garden tillers *(page 84)*.

Float carburetor
Fuel drawn in regulated by needle valve and adjusts float level; float in turn controls needle valve. Found in two- and four-cycle engines of equipment usually operated horizontally such as lawn mowers *(page 68)* and snow throwers *(page 96)*.

Diaphragm carburetor
Fuel drawn into pump chamber regulated by diaphragm; flow of fuel into metering chamber regulated by needle valve. Found in two-cycle engines of equipment operated at any angle such as chain saws *(page 56)*.

Identifying the carburetor. A carburetor measures and mixes fuel and air in specific proportions, then feeds it into the cylinder of the engine for ignition by the spark plug. Typical carburetors found in gas-powered equipment are shown above. The amount of air passing from the air filter and mixed with fuel in the carburetor is regulated by the choke plate. The amount of fuel-air mixture fed into the cylinder of the engine by the carburetor is regulated by the throttle plate. Often, the proportions of air and fuel entering and leaving the carburetor can be adjusted *(step below)*.

Because of the many small and delicate parts in a carburetor, disassembly requires patience and attention to detail. Before removing the carburetor, draw a diagram or take an instant-developing photograph showing all its linkages; in particular, note the throttle linkage, with the position of the throttle rod, the throttle lever, the governor bracket and each spring. Buy the basic carburetor rebuilding kit offered by the manufacturer for your model; it contains the replacement parts you are most likely to need and usually an exploded diagram. The carburetor number may be stamped on the carburetor.

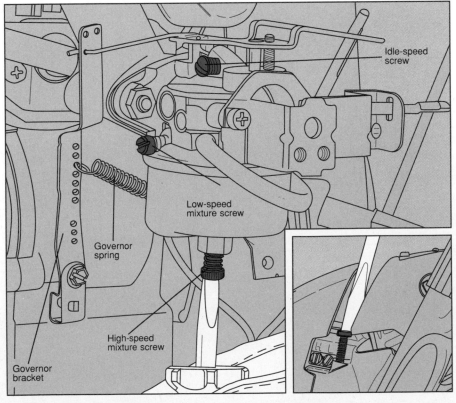

Idle-speed screw

Low-speed mixture screw

Governor spring

Governor bracket

High-speed mixture screw

Identifying adjustment screws. A carburetor seldom needs adjusting unless its operating conditions are changed or it is disassembled for servicing. Consult the owner's manual to identify adjustment screws and reset them. Some carburetors cannot be adjusted; other carburetors may have as many as 4 adjustment screws. A common float-type carburetor, for example, may require the setting of 3 adjustment screws: a high-speed mixture screw *(left)*, a low-speed (or idle) mixture screw and an idle-speed screw. A mixture screw positions the needle at its tip in the carburetor and may be identified by a letter: H for high speed; L for low speed. An idle-speed screw is usually not identifed by a letter, as in a typical diaphragm-type carburetor; it adjusts the throttle plate and is most likely to require adjustment *(inset)* if the engine stalls repeatedly. Do not attempt to adjust the governor bracket or its linkages; if you suspect a problem, take the equipment for professional service.

SERVICING SPARK PLUGS

SPARK PLUG DIAGNOSIS

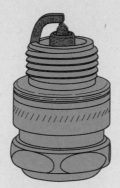
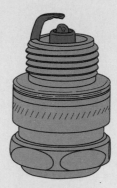

Normal spark plug
Squared or slightly rounded electrodes with a light coat of brown carbon deposits. Indicates carburetor adjusted correctly and engine in good condition.

Fouled spark plug
Dry, black soot or wet, oily film at tip. In a two-cycle engine, indicates too much oil in fuel mixture; drain fuel tank and refill it with correct fuel mixture, adjust carburetor and clean air filter. In a four-cycle engine, indicates worn valves or piston rings; take equipment for professional service.

Bridged spark plug
Hard build-up of carbon deposits between electrodes. Clean or replace spark plug and clean air filter; if build-up recurs, suspect an engine problem and take equipment for professional service.

Eroded spark plug
Whitened or yellowed, thinned electrodes. Indicates engine overheating, possibly due to incorrect fuel mixture or fuel contamination; drain fuel tank and refill it with correct fuel mixture, adjust carburetor, clean cooling fins and muffler, clean two-cycle engine exhaust port and check that spark plug of correct specifications.

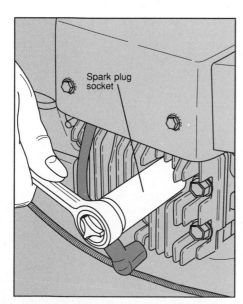
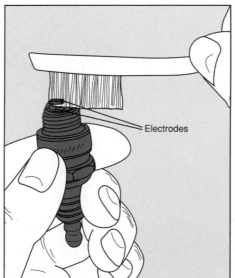
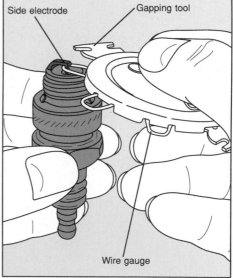

1 Removing the spark plug. Turn off the equipment, move it to a level surface and disconnect the spark plug cable. Wearing safety goggles, clean off any dust and debris around the spark plug with compressed air. Loosen the spark plug using a socket wrench fitted with a spark plug socket *(above)*, then unscrew it by hand. Use the spark plug to diagnose any problems *(chart above)*.

2 Cleaning and gapping the spark plug. If the spark plug is damaged, buy an exact duplicate. To clean carbon deposits off the spark plug, use a small wire brush *(above, left)* or the gapping tool of a spark plug gauge. Wearing safety goggles, blow compressed air onto the electrodes; any dust or deposits left on them can damage the engine. Before installing a new or used spark plug, gap it using a spark plug gauge. Consult the owner's manual for the gap specifications and fit the appropriate wire gauge between the electrodes *(above, right)*. The wire gauge should pass smoothly between and just touch the electrodes. To narrow the gap, gently press the side electrode against a hard surface. To widen the gap, gently pull up the side electrode with the gapping tool of the spark plug gauge. When the spark plug is gapped correctly, screw it into its opening by hand and tighten it with a socket wrench fitted with a spark plug socket.

SEASONAL STORAGE

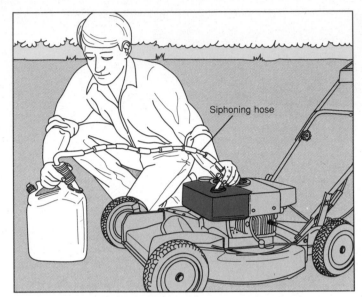

Siphoning hose

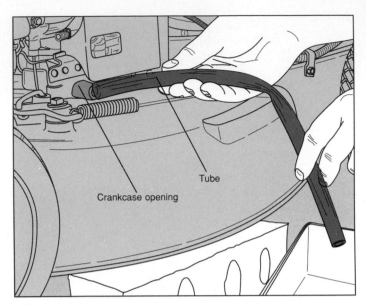

Tube

Crankcase opening

1 **Draining the fuel tank.** Turn off the equipment and disconnect the spark plug cable. The safest way to drain the fuel tank of equipment such as a lawn mower is using a siphoning hose. Unscrew the fuel tank cap, feed one end of the hose onto the bottom of the fuel tank and feed the other end into a fuel container for disposal. Pump the bulb until fuel flows through the hose *(above)*; continue until the fuel is drained. Wipe up any spill and dispose of the fuel safely *(page 11)*; do not reuse the fuel. Screw on the fuel tank cap and move the equipment at least 10 feet away from the draining site. Reconnect the spark plug cable and start the equipment; let it run until any remaining fuel is used up, then disconnect the spark plug cable again.

2 **Servicing the crankcase.** If the engine is two cycle, clean the air filter *(step 3)*. If the engine is four cycle, drain the crankcase while the oil is warm from having run the engine to use up the remaining fuel. Locate the drain plug, set a metal container under the opening and remove the drain plug; on equipment such as a lawn mower with a side drain, prop it up with a brick before removing the drain plug, then run a tube from the opening to the container *(above)* and remove the brick. After draining the oil, put back the drain plug. Remove the oil cap, fill the crankcase with the oil specified by the manufacturer *(page 120)* and put back the oil cap. Wipe up any spill and dispose of the oil safely *(page 11)*; do not reuse the oil.

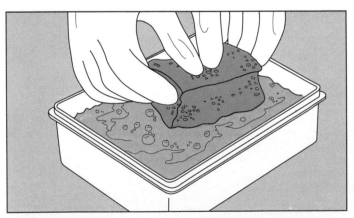

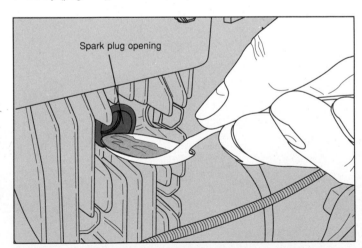

Spark plug opening

3 **Cleaning the air filter.** Consult the chapter on the equipment to access the air filter and for information on servicing it. If the air filter is of sponge, wear rubber gloves and wash it using a solution of mild household detergent and water *(above)*; immerse it in the solution and squeeze it out several times. Rinse off the air filter and dry it thoroughly, wrapping it in a clean cloth and squeezing to remove excess moisture. If the air filter is clogged with embedded dirt or damaged, replace it with an exact duplicate. Apply a little SAE 30 oil to the sponge and squeeze to distribute it; usually no more than 5 teaspoons is recommended. Wipe off the air filter housing with a clean cloth, install the air filter and put back any cover removed.

4 **Oiling the cylinder.** Remove the spark plug and, if necessary, service it *(page 123)*. Then, carefully pour 1 tablespoon of the oil specified by the manufacturer for the engine *(page 120)* into the cylinder through the spark plug opening *(above)*. Slowly pull out and release the starter cord several times to distribute the oil in the cylinder. Screw back in the spark plug by hand and tighten it using a socket wrench fitted with a spark plug socket. Then, slowly pull out the starter cord again until it reaches its maximum resistance; slowly release the starter cord, leaving the piston at its highest position in the cylinder.

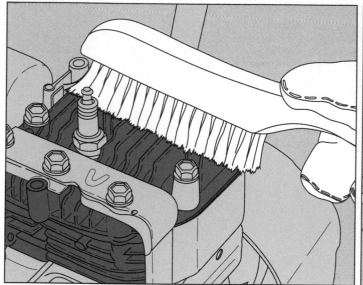

5 **Cleaning the engine and the housing.** Refer to the chapter on the equipment for any specific instructions required on removing housing or turning over the equipment. Using a wire brush, clean off the engine cooling fins *(above, left)* and the muffler; for stubborn carbon deposits, first apply a small amount of decarbonizing spray, then scrub with the brush. Wipe dirt and grime off the engine block and the engine housing using a clean cloth. For equipment such as a lawn mower, use a stick or a flexible putty knife wrapped in a cloth to clean clumps of grass clippings and

dirt off the blade and the bottom of the deck; then, use a garden hose to wash off any remaining dirt and debris *(above, right)*, being careful not to splash water onto the engine. The same procedure can be used on the tines of a garden tiller or the auger assembly of a snow thrower. Wipe the equipment dry with a clean cloth. Touch up scratches on painted surfaces following the instructions of the manufacturer. To help prevent rust, rub the housing and other metal parts using a clean cloth dipped in light machine oil; avoid getting any on the engine. Make sure you reinstall any housing removed.

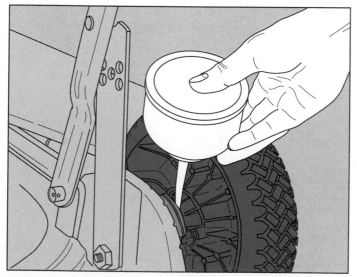

Drop cloth

6 **Lubricating the moving parts.** Consult the owner's manual for lubrication points on the equipment and the lubricant recommended by the manufacturer. The wheels and other moving parts should be lubricated to prevent rusting during storage. Using an oil can, apply a few drops of light machine oil at the base of each wheel *(above)*, then rotate the wheels a few times to ensure the oil is evenly distributed. Use the same procedure at other lubrication points such as gears, shafts, control rods and springs, applying the specified lubricant; lubricate controls and cables as you would for a lawn mower *(page 81)*.

7 **Covering the equipment.** Move the equipment indoors to a clean, dry and level area away from temperature extremes. Make sure the equipment is turned off and the spark plug cable is disconnected. Set the choke control to its fully closed position; on some equipment, marked CHOKE. If possible, collapse or take off the handles to save space. To protect the equipment from dirt and dust, place a canvas or plastic drop cloth over it *(above)*. Secure the drop cloth under the wheels and tuck the edges loosely under the housing, leaving room for air to circulate.

INDEX

Page references in *italics* indicate an illustration of the subject mentioned. Page references in **bold** indicate a Troubleshooting Guide for the subject mentioned.

A

Air filters, *124*
   Chain saws, *59*
   Garden tillers, *87*
   Lawn mowers, *74*
   String trimmers, *52*
Armatures, *118-119*

B

Bearings, *120*
Belt sanders, **19**-*20, 23-25, 27*
Bits (Drills), 12, *14*
Blades:
   Circular saws, *36*
   Hedge trimmers, *43, 45*
   Lawn mowers, *73*
   Saber saws, *30*
Brush assemblies, *117*
   Circular saws, *38*
   Drills, *16*
   Hedge trimmers, *44*
   Saber saws, *31*
   Sanders, *27*
   String trimmers, *50*

C

Carburetors, *122*
   Chain saws, *63-64*
   Garden tillers, *91, 92-93*
   Lawn mowers, *75-76*
   Snow throwers, *104-106*
Chain saws, **57**, *56*
   Air filters, *59*
   Carburetors, *63-64*
   Chains, *59, 60-62*
   Drive sprocket and clutch assemblies, *62*
   Electronic ignition modules, *67*
   Fuel
      draining, *60*
      lines and filters, *64-65*
   Guide bars, 56, *59, 61-62*
   Mufflers, *67*
   Operation, *58*
   Spark plugs, *58*
   Starter assemblies, *66*
   Switches, *65*
Circuit breakers, *112*
Circular saws, **34**-*35*

Blades, *36*
Brush assemblies, *38*
Guards, 34, *38-39*
Motors, *40*
Operation, *35*
Switches, *37*
Cooling fins, *125*
   Garden tillers, *93*
   String trimmers, *55*
Cordless drills, 12, *18*
Crankcases:
   Oil drainage, *124*
      garden tillers, *88*
      lawn mowers, *72*
      snow throwers, *101*

D

Drills, **13**, *12, 14, 16, 17*
   Bits, 12, *14*
   Brush assemblies, *16*
   Chucks, *15*
   Cordless, 12, *18*
   Motors, *17*
   Operation, *14*
   Switches, *17*

E

EIMs. *See* Electronic ignition modules
Electrical emergencies, 8, *9-10*
Electrical tools:
   Preventing hazards, *113*
   Safety precautions, *8*
Electric drills. *See* Drills
Electronic ignition modules, *121*
   Chain saws, *67*
   Garden tillers, *95*
   Lawn mowers, *78-79*
   Snow throwers, *109*
   String trimmers, *54*
Emergency procedures, **9**, 8
   Electricity, 8, *9-10*
   Fire, 8, *10*
   See also Safety precautions
Extension cords, *115*

F

Field coils, *118-119*
Fire, 8, *10*
First aid, *11*
   Electrical shock, 8, *10*
Flywheels:
   Lawn mowers, *79-80*
Fuel filters:
   Chain saws, *64-65*

Lawn mowers, *74*
Snow throwers, *107*
String trimmers, *53*
Fuel, 8
   Drainage, *124*
   Mixing with oil, *121*
   Refueling, 8, *121*
   Spills, *11*
   See also Oil; Subheading Fuel under names of specific equipment
Fuses, *112*

G

Garden tillers, **85**, *84*
   Air filters, *87*
   Carburetors, *91, 92-93*
   Cooling fins, *93*
   Drive belts, *89*
   Electronic ignition modules, *95*
   Fuel
      drainage, *88*
      lines and filters, *91*
   Gear cases, *90*
   Mufflers, *93*
   Oil, *88*
   Operation, *86*
   Spark plugs, *87*
   Starter assemblies, *94*
   Tines, *86, 88*
Gasoline. *See* Fuel
Ground-fault circuit interrupters (GFCIs), *113*
Ground faults, *119*

H-J

Hedge trimmers, **42**, *41*
   Blades, *43, 45*
   Brush assemblies, *44*
   Motors, *44*
   Operation, *42*
   Switches, *43*
Ignition systems, *121*
   See also Electronic ignition modules; Starter assemblies; Spark plugs
Jig saws. *See* Saber saws

L

Lawn mowers, **70**, *68-69*
   Air filters, *74*
   Blades, *73*
   Carburetors, *75-76*
   Controls, *81-82*
   Drive belts, *80*
   Electronic ignition modules, *78-79*

Exhaust ports, *83*
Flywheels, *79-80*
Fuel, 68
    drainage, *72*
    lines and filters, *74*
Mufflers, *82-83*
Oil, *72*
Operation, *71*
Spark plugs, *71*
Starter assemblies, *77-78*
Two-cycle engines, 68, *83*

M

Manuals, 8, 112
Motors, *118-119*
    See also names of specific power tools
Mowers. *See* Lawn mowers
Mufflers:
    Chain saws, *67*
    Garden tillers, *93*
    Lawn mowers, *82-83*
    String trimmers, *55*
Multitesters, *113*

O

Oil, *111, 120*
    Changing, *124*
        garden tillers, *88*
        lawn mowers, *72*
        snow throwers, *101*
    Lubrication
        bearings, *120*
        moving parts, *125*
    Mixing with gasoline, *121*
    Spills, *11*
    See also Fuel
Operator's manuals, 8, 112
Orbital sanders, *20*, **19**-20, *22, 26, 27*

P

Power cords, *115*
Professional repairs, 112
    Carburetors, 122
    Chain saws, 56, *58*
    Cordless drills, 12
    Ignition systems, 121
    Snow throwers, 104
    String trimmers, 50

R

Repair procedures, *114*
    See also names of specific power tools
    and equipment

Replacement parts, *112*
Rotary tillers. *See* Garden tillers

S

Saber saws, **29**, *28-29*
    Blades, *30*
    Blade shaft assemblies, *32*
    Brush assemblies, *31*
    Motors, *33*
    Operation, *30*
    Switches, *31*
Safety clothing, 8
    See also Subheading Operation under
    names of specific tools and equipment
Safety precautions, 8
    Chain saws, 56, *58*
    Electrical power tools, *113*
    See also Emergency procedures
Sanders, **19**-*20*
    Belt, *20, 23-25, 27*
    Brush assemblies, *27*
    Cleaning, 19, *21*
    Motors, *27*
    Operation, *21*
    Orbital, *20, 22, 26, 27*
    Switches, *22*
Sandpaper, *21*
Saws. *See* Chain saws; Circular saws;
    Saber saws
Service panels, *9, 112*
Snow throwers, **98**, *96-97*
    Auger assemblies, *101*
    Carburetors, *104-106*
    Drive belts, *103*
    Electronic ignition modules, *109*
    Fuel, 97
        drainage, *100*
        lines and filters, *107*
    Oil, *101*
    Operation, *99*
    Spark plugs, *100*
    Starter assemblies, *108*
    Switches, *109*
    Wheel drive assemblies, *102*
Solid state ignition systems. *See* Electronic
Ignition modules
Spark arrestors:
    Chain saws, *67*
    Garden tillers, *93*
Spark plugs, *123*
    Chain saws, *58*
    Garden tillers, *87*
    Lawn mowers, *71*
    Snow throwers, *100*
    String trimmers, *48*

Starter assemblies:
    Chain saws, *66*
    Garden tillers, *94*
    Lawn mowers, *77-78*
    Snow throwers, *108*
    String trimmers, *51*
String trimmers, **46**-*47*
    Air filters, *52*
    Brush assemblies, *50*
    Cooling fins, *55*
    Cutting head assemblies, *49*
    Electrical, *48, 50*
    Electronic ignition modules, *54*
    Fuels
        drainage, *48*
        lines and filters, *53*
    Gasoline, *48, 51-55*
    Mufflers, *55*
    Operation, *48*
    Starter assemblies, *51*
    String, *49*
    Switches, *50*
    Throttle assemblies, *53*
    Trigger modules, *54*
Switches, *117*
    Chain saws, *65*
    Circular saws, *37*
    Drills, *17*
    Hedge trimmers, *43*
    Saber saws, *31*
    Sanders, *22*
    Snow throwers, *109*
    String trimmers, *50*

T

Tools, *110-111*
Toxic fumes, *11*
Troubleshooting Guides:
    Chain saws, 57
    Circular saws, 34
    Drills, 13
    Emergency guide, 9
    Garden tillers, 85
    Hedge trimmers, 42
    Lawn mowers, 70
    Saber saws, 29
    Sanders, 19
    Snow throwers, 98
    String trimmers, 46
Two-cycle engines, 68, *83, 121*

V-W

Voltage leaks, *113*
Warranties, 112
Wire connections, *116*

ACKNOWLEDGMENTS

The editors wish to thank the following:
Michael Bertoldi, La Maison Bertoldi Inc., Montreal, Que.; Briggs & Stratton Corporation, Milwaukee, Wisc.; Canada Power Technology, Montreal, Que.; Claude Cloutier, Turfquip Inc., Longeuil, Que.; Jon Eager, Gates Energy Products, Gainesville, Fla.; Emerson Electric Supply, Salisbury, Mass.; Clarence Good, LeRoy's Repair and Rental Inc., Gordonville, Pa.; Bernie Hamilton, Kango International Inc., Montreal, Que.; Location d'Outillage ERA Inc., Montreal, Que.; Milwaukee Electric Tool (Canada) Ltd., Scarborough, Ont.; Ren Molnar, Ren Home Consulation, Ottawa, Ont.; Chris Gade, Mona, Meyer & McGrath, Bloomington, Minn.; John Morlino, The Jacobs Chuck Manufacturing Co., Clemson, S.C.; Ray Robillard, Hull, Que.; Snap-Cut Tools by Seymour Smith and Sons, Inc., a subsidiary of Gilmour Group, Somerset, Pa.; Michel St. Laurent, Distributions TTI Inc., Quebec City, Que.; Stihl, Inc., Virginia Beach, Va.; Tecumseh Products Company, Engine & Transmission Group, Service Division, Grafton, Wisconsin; Linda Colliander, Karl Kaukis, James Peterson, Greg Tonsager, The Toro Company, Minneapolis, Minn.; Walbro Corporation, Cass City, Mich.

The following persons also assisted in the preparation of this book:
Daniel Bazinet, Francine Lemieux, Line Roberge